One Short Life

Jane Ache

Photography by Harvey E. Ache

Cover, graphics and website by Kevin Ache

Editorial assistance by Kelly Bixler and Sean Burns: thewriteproofreader.com

ISBN-13: 978-0692661208
ISBN-10: 0692661204

Scripture quotations are from the King James Version of the Bible.

One Short Life

Published by Red Jet Publishing
RedJet@oneshortlifebook.com

Purchase additional copies at www.oneshortlifebook.com

Printed by Create Space

First Edition

Jane was born Leona Jane Ford on March 13, 1929 to Audrey and William Ford in Rosewood, Ohio, a small rural farming community northeast of Dayton, Ohio. Her mother had taught school in a one room school house and her father ran an auto repair shop, selling Chevrolets on the side. Later in life he was called into the ministry. Jane graduated from Rosewood High School as valedictorian of the class of 1947 and graduated from Fort Wayne Bible Institute in 1950. At Fort Wayne, she met her future husband Harvey E. Ache; they were married on May 24, 1951. In addition to being a missionary, she served alongside her husband as a minister's wife, and retired from the Painesville, Ohio school system after a career as a bookkeeper and secretary. She enjoyed sewing, playing the piano, spending time with her grandchildren and prayed every single day for her family and foreign missionaries.

SIERRA LEONE

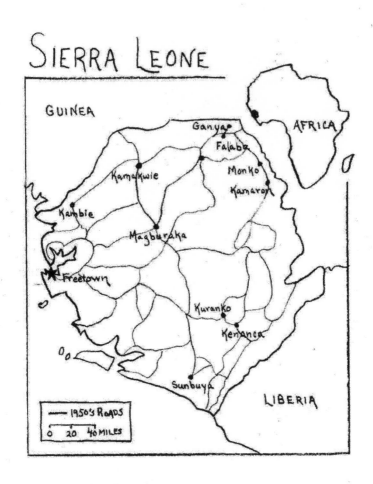

GUINEA

AFRICA

Ganya
Falaba
Monko
Kamakwie
Kamaron
Kambie
Magburaka
Freetown
Kuranko
Kenanga
Sunbuya

LIBERIA

— 1950's ROADS

0   20   40 MILES

Dedication

This book is dedicated to the believers of

the Yalunka tribe in West Africa.

My heartfelt thanks to my family

—Joy, Andy and Nancy—

for preparing the manuscript.

-Jane

Please journey with me on a trek back
over a half century of time. Read about
the faithfulness of our heavenly Father
and His wonderful son,
the Lord Jesus Christ.
Sometimes you may laugh, and at other
places, you may drop some tears. But in
everything, I hope you will experience a
growing sense of
God's faithfulness.

Sometimes, our Lord becomes all the more
precious to us when we travel
the road of suffering.
His strength is made so perfect in our
weakest moments and His grace is always
available to transform weary days and long
nights with His perfect strength and peace.

"The Lord will give strength unto his
people; the Lord will bless his people with
peace."
(Psalm 29:11).

6

Contents

Introduction

Slowly, my eyelids began to open on that unforgettable day in mid-May, 2010. I hoped to be awakening in my own bed at home, but seeing the surrounding bright lights, snow-white bedsheets, and IV lines busily pumping medication into my veins, I had to face the disappointing reality that I still remained as a patient in a hospital bed. Something about my awakening seemed strangely unusual, as though I had been trapped in an extremely exhaustive ordeal. Then, as I became more fully aware, my mind formed a hope—a hope that I had merely experienced a bad dream that would be remembered, laughed away, and forgotten. Actually, the bad dream became my first experience on a ventilator in critical care.

I then began to recall happenings prior to that moment, remembering it all had started a few days before when severe pain had forced me to the emergency room of Marion General Hospital in Marion, Indiana. After a general examination, a quick decision was made by the emergency room physician to admit me and start diagnostic tests. The same symptoms had afflicted me the year before—only this time, my condition worsened as more of my organs became involved. It did not take long to discover internal bleeding. Renal failure had struck again, as had happened the previous summer. But instead of treatment improving my condition as it had before, my blood work reports remained abnormal and my overall condition continued to deteriorate. It seemed providential for an alert, concerned internist to be on duty that week. The internist recognized I needed more specialized help and gave orders to have me transferred to Methodist Hospital, a large hospital in Indianapolis, Indiana, where I would receive the advantage of treatment from a multi-system medical team.

Despite diligent care for my renal failure by the team of Indianapolis physicians, pneumonia developed. As I gasped for breath, Andy, my physician son from Ohio, told my physician, "She's going to wear out breathing like this!" Yet my respirations increased. Even though in my living will I had given instructions that I was not to be put on a ventilator, the intensive care physician persuaded me to permit him to temporarily place me one. "You've made a wise decision," the doctor reassured me as he stood beside my bed.

During intubation, by heart went into a non-viable rhythm, and as a result, a defibrillator was used to correct my heart arrhythmia. Later, cardiac tests revealed I had suffered a heart attack during this procedure. While reviewing my current status, the intensive care attending physician reminded my registered nurse daughter at my bedside, "Joy, your mother is in grave condition because so many organ systems are affected." Five days later, the ventilator was discontinued and I returned to the metabolic floor where the nephrology team from Indiana University continued to pursue the etiology of my unusual renal failure. The rare disease of acute necrotizing glomerulonephritis was the final diagnosis.

But soon, another serious complication occurred. The administration of heparin, a drug to prevent blood clots, caused a large bleed in my abdominal cavity, requiring the infusion of seven units of blood. While still in critical care receiving blood transfusions, a hospital chaplain stood by my bedside and kindly comforted me with God's Word and prayer. He asked, "Why do you think God wanted you to live despite all these complications?"

I replied, "Because I'm writing a book for Him." I continued to be amazed at God's care and the concern of the staff for a woman of my age, but I knew the reason why. I clearly remember the day in 2009; standing in my kitchen, a voice suddenly spoke in my mind: "I know you do not want to do it, but do it for Me." Immediately, I realized the meaning of "it." I had a book to finish.

More than forty years ago, I had written and submitted a manuscript of a book relating our time as missionaries in Sierra Leone, West Africa from August 1954 through July 1957. Although it was not accepted for publishing at that time, it remained on my heart until family experiences in the 1970's inspired me to resume the project.

I found enjoyment whenever writing it, but as I neared the final chapters, I began to realize it would need to be published. Being a person who does not readily relate personal affairs, a portion of my heart wanted to finish, but the other part did not. But from that moment in 2009 forward, I was deter-mined to please my Lord; my desire to finish the book and bring glory to Him remained central.

My missionary zeal has not diminished over time. It is my desire that all proceeds of this book be used to continue to spread the news of the Gospel of salvation until all tongues, tribes, and nations have heard that Jesus saves and forgives all those who do the will of our Father in heaven.

Jane Ache
Marion, IN
August, 2013

Chapter 1: Born To Travel

It was a bone-chilling January morning in 1973, when a white ambulance pulled up to toll gate number eight on the Ohio Turnpike. As the driver reached to take the ticket, the gate attendant queried, "Emergency?" With a silent affirmative nod, the ambulance driver closed the window, released the brake, and steered the vehicle down the emerging lane onto the highway toward the Cleveland Clinic.

Only seven months earlier, the young man at the wheel and the girl on the stretcher in the back of the ambulance had graduated from the same high school in Wellington, Ohio. Somber-faced, the driver glanced at the rearview mirror periodically to check on the patient, as the nurse on the seat beside him made conversation. Frequently, she turned to peer through the glass separating the back of the ambulance from the front, and waited for a signal from the girl's mother that all was well.

I reached to adjust the heater control, trying to keep Jewel as warm and comfortable as possible. The blood smears on glass slides in my purse (microscopically examined to determine causes of abnormal blood count numbers), which the internist had handed back to me as we left the hospital, explained the serious condition of our daughter.

Jewel had not wanted to be moved from Allen Memorial Hospital in Oberlin, Ohio. She had volunteered over five hundred hours of candy striping during her high school years and had bonded with the hospital and staff. Consequently, she considered it to be "her hospital." Nevertheless, as her condition progressively worsened and the doctors arranged for her to be transferred to the Cleveland Clinic, she quietly accepted the move.

For some time after we left the hospital, Jewel peered out the window at the tops of vehicles moving alongside the ambulance. After a while, her eyelids closed, but a little smile played on her lips, indicating she was enjoying the ride. The high fevers her body had been fighting and the strong medications amazingly had not hampered Jewel's alertness. Every now and then, her eyelids slipped open and she inquired where we were.

When the traffic became congested and motorists failed to observe the right-of-way of the ambulance, the driver turned on the siren for a few seconds. Immediately, Jewel roused and wanted a play-by-play description of the cars trying to maneuver out of our way. She found it amusing and giggled softly as her eyelids closed again.

How typical of Jewel—always ready for a ride and loving to travel since her infant days. Many times through the years, it had been an asset. And even on that difficult January morning, it made the going a little easier.

Nineteen years earlier, a neighbor peered down at baby Jewel Kay, smiling and kicking in her basket. Raising her eyebrows, the woman's voice intonated disapproval as she asked, "You mean you are going to take that baby to Africa?"

It was true: from the viewpoint of a registered nurse who stood observing the bright-eyed, cooing baby, our plans did not seem logical. However, my husband, Harv, and I had intentions to do missionary work in Africa before we met, so we held no reservations about taking our baby daughter. We considered Jewel Kay a special little cargo of happiness sent from the heavenly Father to make our way brighter and more cheerful. And that she did, many times.

On the other hand, had I known then what the next three years were to hold, perhaps I would have sipped on an ounce or more of apprehension. Fortunately, we live each day and each experience one moment at a time. Our baby looked to be a perfect specimen of health and appeared in shipshape condition for travel; and travel she would!

Packing for a three-year term of living in the bush country of Africa turned into an extensive undertaking. Shopping lists seemed to never end. Many people became involved with our preparations, donating equipment and money for supplies.

Apparently everyone wanted a part in supplying clothing for the missionary baby. Sewing machines hummed and dresses came tumbling in from many church groups, until the final count mounted to well over the need—or so I thought. Looking at the accumulation of pretty dresses, it seemed as though the little miss would be more prepared for a city social life, than that of the backward, pioneer terrain of West Africa, where we found ourselves assigned to work.

Shoes in progressive sizes joined the stacks of clothing, along with cartons of baby food, cereals, and a large supply of baby care products. A teddy bear, story books, dolls, and other toys snuggled among supplies in metal drums used for shipping. And a church in Cleveland surprised us with a screened baby crib designed for the tropics that proved to be a real godsend.

Finally, with the last drum locked and the final crate nailed shut, time for farewells arrived. Jewel and her little cousins innocently waved bye-bye on the last Sunday my family spent together in Rosewood, a small town in a farming community in west central Ohio. The following week, my brother, Joe, set out for the shipping docks at New York City in a borrowed truck loaded with our possessions. Harv led the way in our new Willys Jeep.

My parents drove Jewel and me to Allentown, Pennsylvania, where we met Harv at his parents' home when he returned from New York. We listened, amused and amazed, as Harv and Joe related their bridge-crossing into New York City experience.

Approaching the bridge, Harv failed to notice the "No Trucks" sign until it was too late. Following close behind in the truck, Joe soon became aware that he had been spotted, as flashing red lights pulled him to a stop. After Harv delivered an explanation of their mission, along with the fact that they were from out of state, the officer let them proceed across the bridge without issuing a ticket.

The patrolman probably either shook his head with impatient dismay or chuckled to himself as he watched the board-slatted truck bed with "Rosewood Feed Mill" painted on the cab progress across the bridge in the flowing city traffic. To Joe, it seemed an extremely long bridge and the other side came none too soon. Despite this, the crossing turned into a laughable story they enjoyed retelling each time they were given a chance. After unloading at the shipping company, Joe and Harv made certain they departed from the city via a truck route.

By our second day in Allentown, away from his previous heavy schedule of working all day and building crates and helping me pack drums in the evenings, the full reality of our departure began to close in on my dad. We had stayed with my parents for a few months before Jewel's birth and until it was time to leave for Africa. During that waiting period, Harv commuted to and from Michigan to fill in as an interim pastor for a church.

Naturally, it is easy to slip into a fond attachment with a baby living in the same house. Thoughts of the empty spots my parents would face when they returned home began to squeeze on my dad's heart. Wisely, he decided to give those last hugs earlier than they had planned and head back to Ohio. Presuming Daddy became anxious to return to his business, I did not realize the true reason for their early departure until years later when Mother explained it to me. She also added, "It was difficult changing Jewel's diaper for the last time the morning we left Allentown. I kept thinking how it would be three years until I would see her again."

For over six months, Mother had helped care for the baby. Many times during those first several weeks, Grandma

Ford's rocking and singing had quieted the colicky baby to sleep. Even though Jewel's tummy cramps were a nightly occurrence, Grandma Ford maintained a high level of loving patience and would not go to bed until she was certain the little one appeared settled for the night.

Mother also related that the morning they left Allentown, after they had driven a few miles, Daddy pulled to the side of the road, reached for a Bible from the dashboard compartment, and turned to Isaiah. He read aloud from the forty-third chapter, second verse: "When thou passest through the waters, I will be with thee; and through the rivers, they shall not overflow thee; when thou walkest through the fire, thou shall not be burned, neither shall the flame kindle upon thee." Claiming those promises, he committed our travel and the coming three years in Africa to the care of Almighty God.

Mother went on to share that a few months later, when Daddy returned from a walk one night, he said to her, "There's a bright moon tonight. I was just thinking that it's the same moon up there that shines on Jane and the family over in Africa." Apparently, thinking of it in that perspective made us seem not as far away. Without a doubt, he had been praying for us as he walked.

Even though Harv was their only child, and of course Jewel was the only grandchild, Harv's parents followed through with the same determination and gave us a brave sendoff at the train station. We counted ourselves fortunate to have parents who stood behind us in support of the mission we were determined to follow. It helped immensely. Knowing their prayers would be faithful brought consolation as we faced different, unknown tomorrows.

Jewel reached seven months old that day in 1954 when we boarded a Dutch ocean liner in Quebec, Canada. As soon as we crossed the gangplank, a ship hostess met us, holding out her arms to take the baby. She cordially told us that she would take care of Jewel in the nursery while we settled our luggage in our cabin. As we started out to find the steps leading down to the deck assigned to us, the cheerful hostess, in limited English, called after us, "Take time to watch ship leave port before you come for baby in nursery!"

Jewel seemed happy as she watched the smiling face of the woman holding her. I felt confident she would be fine. Later, however, when we returned to the nursery, we found a tearful, unhappy baby. We had not reckoned on the screaming blasts of the boat whistle and tugboats frightening the little passenger into a state of panic without Mommy or Daddy around. It introduced an unfortunate beginning to ship life, and a lot of reassurances became necessary on future visits to the nursery.

And to the nursery Jewel had to go, since ship regulations required babies to be there during adult mealtimes. Passengers had assigned tables in the dining area with meals served in proper European style, and the setting did not allow for babies or small children. Therefore, the steward delivered Jewel's food to our cabin before regular mealtimes, allowing us time to feed her and take her to the nursery on our way to the dining room. Until then, Jewel had a healthy appetite and had eaten every food spooned her way. But after the second taste of the strange, new diet, she closed her eyes, wrinkled her nose, shook her head, and out came the food.

Fortunately, an alternative provision came from the baby-supply suitcase stored under our lower bunk. As the baby girl enjoyed her Gerber dinner, I looked at the pureed food from the ship's kitchen and asked Harv, "What are we going to do with this?"

Harv suggested the most polite solution. Afterwards, he agreed with Jewel: the food also failed to pass his taste test. At least the plate was empty by the time the steward came to pick up the tray. And so it continued, with one male passenger being served an unsolicited appetizer before each meal. Meanwhile, the chef probably smiled with satisfaction as he saw the empty dishes returned, assuming his cooking efforts met the satisfaction of the American baby.

On the evening which pureed spinach announced itself as Harv lifted the cover from the plate, things took a different turn. "No way!" Harv proclaimed. When I suggested, "Why don't you hold your nose and quickly swallow it?" Harv's response sounded even more adamantly negative.

In all probability, we extended our consideration beyond required politeness by not sending the food back to the galley. But with the ship's personnel seeming so intent to please, we did not have the heart to risk offending anyone. Hence, down the passageway slipped Harv, sneaking the dish of spinach to the men's bathroom, all the while hoping he would not meet another passenger, least of all a steward. Minutes later, when the courteous steward returned to pick up the tray, he remained unsuspecting as to the true destination of that particular meal, as well as any of the other meals.

As we strolled about the decks, I found myself straining for the sound of English words. Among over twelve hundred passengers, only a small minority spoke English. Thus began our indoctrination into the isolated world of not being able to understand conversations of people around us. We quickly learned to rely on smiles for our mode of communication.

Previously, the *Johan van Oldenbarnevelt* had navigated Mediterranean waters for pleasure cruises. By the second day at sea, passengers realized the ship had not been fortified for a voyage on the cold and breezy North Atlantic. Not only were the cabins a chilly temperature, the water pipes yielded only lukewarm water. Even though the captain constantly promised more comfortable conditions soon, neither heat nor hot water ever arrived. In spite of efforts to keep Jewel warm, after a few days, she developed a heavy cold. To complicate matters more, she was teething. Not many children can say they cut their first two teeth while crossing the Atlantic Ocean, but Jewel did just that.

Jewel seemed as delighted as we felt the day it warmed up enough to take her out on deck to soak in some sunshine. Without a doubt, the feature she enjoyed the most during our ocean crossing was the constant rocking service the great Atlantic provided day and night. Certainly, she was more impressed with it than her parents, especially as we navigated up and down stairs on some of the rougher days. Even though we had suffered no seasickness, we gladly left the ocean behind the day we walked onto firm land in Southampton, England.

Despite all its challenges, the ship had become a friend during those days of roaming her decks and watching the waves from our cabin porthole. I did not realize that fact until several years later when a picture of the same vessel burning at sea caught my attention while I was scanning a news magazine. Feeling saddened at the tragedy, scenes of various areas of the ship flashed back. I tried to imagine what horror must have seized the passengers as they tried to grope their way to safety in the smoke-filled passageways. Unfortunately, many of them did not escape and sank with the ship. Later, another company purchased, raised, and restored the ship to service again.

While waiting in London over a week for our flight to Africa, we planned our itinerary for sightseeing. But as the days passed with damp, chilly weather and a rather upset, teething baby, we spent more time in our room than we counted on. Some days, though, the weather improved for a few hours and we snatched an opportunity to escape our room.

Seeing the impressive Changing of the Guard at Buckingham Palace, catching a glimpse of Number Ten, Downing Street as the taxi driver motioned toward it without slowing down, walking over for a close inspection of the Coronation Chair in Westminster Abbey, viewing the location where King George had laid in state at Westminster Court, gazing at the strikingly beautiful stained-glass windows in St. Margaret's Cathedral—each generated awesome respect for historical grandeur.

For young missionaries en route to Africa, the highlight came when we stood at the tomb of David Livingstone in Westminster Abbey and read the inscription: "BROUGHT BY FAITHFUL HANDS OVER LAND AND SEA HERE RESTS DAVID LIVINGSTONE."

As we lingered, portions from the biography of this great missionary statesman returned to my thoughts. Energized with compassion, the man whose heart had been haunted by the scenes of smoke from a thousand villages, set out to take the good news of Christianity to the people of those villages and beyond. Far from home and family, hampered with tropical diseases, weakness, and dangers, Dr. Livingstone pressed on to pioneer a trail across Africa from coast to coast. A century later, the Dark Continent needed that same devoted love that Livingstone had given. It presented an inspiration and a challenge.

Attending church Sunday morning at Westminster Chapel turned out to be more than we had bargained for. Earlier in the week, when we heard that Dr. Crosley Morgan, son of the famous G. Campbell Morgan, was scheduled to speak, we planned to attend and eagerly looked forward to hearing him.

As we entered the stately sanctuary, I noticed the usher approaching us appeared to have a puzzled expression. Or could that be my imagination? After being seated and settled, in glancing about the congregation while waiting for the service to begin, an alarming fact suddenly dawned on me. There were no children seated beside adults in the straight-backed pews. Not one child to be seen—and there I sat, holding a baby!

The gentleman who stood to read the announcements wore a long tuxedo, complemented by an eighteenth-century, white wig. Between sentences, silence loomed—a breathtaking quietness to me. I had only one prayer on my heart: Lord, please don't let Jewel cry, laugh, or even click her tongue. (She had learned to do this only that week.)

As the service progressed, the little body on my lap relaxed more and more, until she finally fell asleep. Nonetheless, my mind still stood at attention, knowing there remained the possibility of her waking up at any moment. Glancing to my right, I planned a jolly-fast exit should it suddenly become necessary. Thankfully, Jewel must have been sent into a deep, baby dreamland, for she did not open her eyes until we stood to leave and then remained quiet all the way to the door. While slowly moving along with the crowd, I sensed a polite but keen surveillance in our direction. Without doubt, many parishioners were silently thinking, "Oh, I say; they must be Americans!"

Back at the boarding house, someone informed us that in England, children do not attend Sunday worship services. Instead, they are taken to Sunday school classes in the afternoon and babies are kept home—where they belong. To this day, I still wonder if Jewel made history that Sunday morning as being the only baby ever to attend and remain through a service in Westminster Chapel.

After almost two weeks in London, we climbed the steps of a two-engine Air Work Limited prop plane and began the final stage of our journey to Sierra Leone. A small country between Guinea and Liberia along the western coast of Africa, Sierra Leone remained a British colony and protectorate at that time.

The flight turned into a sightseeing tour from the air as the pilot lowered altitude and banked at points of interest. Fascinated, we peered down at the Strait of Gibraltar, Rock of Gibraltar, Casablanca, and other sights as our flight pattern followed the coastline of Africa.

The scenery displayed one stunning picture after another, with deep-blue ocean fading into foaming, white waves dashing against sparkling, snow-white sand. The bleached sand contrasted against the green, lush foliage in some locations, then blended into brown desert in other places. The views below cast a captivating display of creation—the work of a powerful, beauty-loving Creator!

The plane grounded by late afternoon each day, and the first overnight stop introduced us to Tangiers. Before we left the plane, the pilot warned passengers not to wander too far from the hotel after dark and to keep a close watch on personal possessions. It took only a short while for us to realize precautions were indeed necessary. The following morning, as passengers compared notes, we found there had been no serious incidents. But everyone seemed more than happy to be back on the plane and ready to take off.

The second night, a luxuriously modern hotel in Dakar gave us a delightful contrast to the suspicious, dingy hotel of the previous night in Tangiers. With a balcony extending from each room overlooking the ocean front, nothing lacked for comfort, even down to an abundance of brightly-clad bellboys always available to give service (in return for tips, of course). Certainly not what we had expected, the atmosphere made it difficult to believe we had arrived in Africa. But we would see the real Africa a few days later.

The most disturbing event during the flight came during a fuel stop in the Sahara Desert. After the plane rolled to a stop, the pilot announced that the passengers could go out to stretch for a few minutes. As soon as the door opened, an African army official marched in and started spraying the cabin with a strong-smelling disinfectant, aiming the can from side to side as he walked down the aisle.

How incredible! We—all citizens of civilized countries—being fumigated before being allowed to set foot on an isolated fuel station in the desert. It became even more unbelievable when we heard that the post was occupied solely by prisoners and their African guards. Perhaps logical reasons rested behind the act, and they took no chances of civilized germs invading their domain, but we found it slightly difficult to cope with.

With the spraying completed to the satisfaction of the officer, the passengers quickly exited to cough and clear out our lungs in the open air. I had attempted to keep Jewel's head covered, against her protests, and she managed to survive the sterilization procedure along with the rest of us. Maybe our pride had been injured more than our lungs. We noted the absence of a fence or guard stations to enclose the Sahara prison. Should a prisoner attempt an escape, he would face a vast desert defying him from each direction. It provided total security against potential runaway inmates.

Information quickly passed among the passengers that pop was available in the main building. But when we reached for the bottles on the counter, our anticipation of a cold drink fell flat. With no water available, we had our choice to either drink room temperature pop, or nothing. It did not help the temperament of some passengers. Nor did it help their mood for a slight delay coming up.

After Harv returned from the restroom, I left him holding Jewel while he visited with other passengers. By the time I found the ladies' room, everyone had left except the flight attendant, who stood at the mirror combing her hair. I stepped into a stall and closed the door behind me.

Minutes later, the unexpected happened. When I pulled at the rusted bar that locked the door of the stall, it refused to slide open. I gathered all my strength and tried again. Nothing happened. Again and again, I tugged at the bar, but it did not even slightly move. Starting to become alarmed, I called out for the flight attendant. I heard the clicking of her heels echoing as she walked away from the room. But it was too late; she did not hear me.

It just has to open, I thought, frantically trying again and again. I began to realize it seemed hopeless for me to get it open. There I stood, tightly imprisoned in a toilet stall cell in a Sahara Desert penitentiary. I called out for help a few times, but only an echo responded, followed by empty silence.

Apparently, everyone had gone to the plane, and the residents were outside to watch the takeoff. Remembering the looks of some of the inmates, I was not certain I would want any of them to come to my rescue. In fact, the more I thought about it, the more I hoped they were all outside.

Looking down and then up at the high ceiling, I decided the stall was inescapable. The partitions reached from the floor to only a small distance from the ceiling. My thoughts flashed outside to the plane preparing to take off. Surely, they would not leave without me. Or could it happen? Suppose Harv became preoccupied with Jewel and watching final activities for departure from his window seat, and did not realize I had not joined him yet.

Anxiety mounted with each second, especially when I thought of the baby. Even though Harv had helped tackle the Allentown High football team to state championships for two years, he had tackled diaper changing only one time—and fumbled. Time after time during the trip, my decision to continue nursing Jewel until we settled in Africa proved to be a wise choice. Naturally, Harv could not substitute in that capacity either. Everything seemed conclusive: Jewel needed her mother.

Then, for the first time, I suddenly noticed the water tank attached to the wall, high above the stool. My eyes quickly darted from the tank up to the top of the partition. Without thinking, I started to climb. Had I taken time to consider the probability of being able to make it up and over the partition, I am sure I never would have attempted the stunt.

Far from being acrobatic by nature, but with adrenaline gushing, I struggled from the stool to the top of the water tank, all the while wondering if it could hold my weight. Crouching on the narrow tank, the next challenge was to turn around and work to a standing position. Struggling for balance, I pressed hard against the wall and slowly straightened, making certain not to look down. Leaning toward the partition and stretching out my arm, I was able to grasp the top. Clutching tightly, I began pulling myself up. Once up and hanging over the narrow top of the partition, I then had to maneuver around to drop my feet onto the water tank in the adjacent stall.

Guards and prisoners must have blinked with wonder at the speed of the female dashing from the building toward the waiting plane. The hostess smiled without asking questions as I passed her at the door. Too breathless and exhausted to give an explanation, I merely whispered, "Sorry."

It seemed a long trek back to the tail section and our seats. I wondered if I did not sense some impatience mingled with the hot air in the cabin as passengers watched me walk by.

Certainly, everyone had wanted to climb and fly away from the desert heat as quickly as possible, instead of being delayed by a straggling passenger.

Once airborne, Harv and the flight attendant laughed with me as I related the story of my Sahara imprisonment. By then, the story actually did sound amusing. But only the Lord knew how traumatic the ordeal had been at the time—to be locked in a back room of a large building in the Sahara Desert. I still smile whenever reading Psalm 18:29 as I relate to David's words, "By my God have I leaped over a wall." I did not leap over, but my God certainly brought me over that high partition with amazing help.

Chapter 2: The Real Africa

After three days and numerous flights, we finally circled above Freetown, the capitol and main seaport of Sierra Leone. Around and around we continued to fly, due to a tropical storm raging below. The pilot seemed relaxed and matter-of-fact as he explained the situation over the speaker. Apparently such delays became routine during the rainy season.

The passengers took in the activity of the rolling, black clouds below. After a half-hour had passed, watches received glances more frequently. At the start of the delayed landing, conversations had ceased among the passengers. Everyone remained silent—watching and thinking. Jewel napped.

Like myself, everyone was probably wondering if the fuel gauge in the cockpit registered a safe amount, should this delay continue much longer. Only the pilot knew that answer. After some time, the plane lowered altitude and headed into the dark mass of clouds, as though the pilot was checking the possibility of landing despite the storm. But immediately, heavy turbulence struck the aircraft. Engines roared, up went the nose, and we climbed to the safety of the blue sky above. With that, we wondered if the pilot also had some misgivings about the continued delay.

All storms must end sooner or later, and this one eventually subsided. As the clouds parted, we caught our first view of the beautiful Freetown Harbor. The wide, deep body of water had served as an important naval base during

World Wars I and II. In 1787, when the settlement became a haven for freed slaves, the city was renamed Freetown.

What a happy moment to descend the steps of that Airwork Limited and realize we had finally arrived. We soon learned, however, our trip had a grand finale remaining. "Now, city of Freetown be across water," an African informed us as he motioned toward a waiting boat launch.

Clutching the wooden benches we sat on, we tried to brace ourselves as the bay churned viciously from the recent storm. In comparison, it made the wait above the clouds seem like a party. Only one traveler on the boat did not mind the strong, heaving waves. The ship whistle may have frightened Jewel at the start of our trip, but the up and down, roller coaster ride across the bay did not. While adult passengers started turning pale, Jewel laughed and jabbered, completely enjoying the new sport.

After we stumbled onto the dock from the bobbing launch and slowly regained our equilibrium, queasy stomachs and a wild boat ride quickly left our attention as we entered the Customs building.

Ken Rupp, mission field chairman, and Bill Harrigan, the missionary of where we would live, were in the city awaiting our arrival. But due to a discrepancy regarding our landing time, when they had gone to meet us, we had not arrived yet. Therefore, when we did arrive, the men were not at Customs to greet us. The person checking our papers told us about another mission not far away and suggested we go there to wait for Mr. Rupp.

With a soft rain sprinkling against our faces, we started walking down the street—Harv loaded with our luggage and me carrying Jewel and some smaller bags. We must have appeared to observers more like worn immigrants than new missionaries fresh from the States.

Via the Freetown person-to-person news service, word of our location reached Ken and Bill. In no time, we loaded into Ken's truck and rode to an apartment used by mission personnel when in Freetown. Along the way, Ken stopped to buy bread for dinner. As he walked from the small bakery, I could hardly believe my eyes. It is known as culture shock; in an open duffel bag, Ken carried loaves of unwrapped bread. Unwrapped and unprotected bread! Flies! And how clean were the hands of the baker who had handled the sale? Certainly, he had been handling money.

Some people would have thought nothing of it. But for me, accepting that bread as clean enough to eat became a giant hurdle in this new environment. By the time the bread plate reached me at dinner, however, I had convinced myself that I should eat it in order to start a missionary career in a proper manner. And I certainly did not want to expose my bread hang-up to the men. Another incentive was that I was hungry. Before eating it, though, I brushed off the crust under the table—hardly a successful sterilization technique. From then on, I slowly accepted unwrapped bread whenever staying in the city.

Freetown represented a typical African coastal city, filled with drastic contrasts. A few modern store buildings spoke of progress, but not far away sprawled the age-old open street markets. Some residential areas held neat, whitewashed houses, while dreary, dark shanties existed within walking distance. The educated Africans spoke precise English with a British accent, which was quite different from the Creole used by others. Skin tones varied from European white to assorted shades of African black.

Jewel Kay added another contrast of her own. She often surprised the Africans by being more outgoing with her friendly gestures than their children. It had started back in New York City the night we waited for train connections to Quebec. We passed the time that evening at what was then Grand Central Station, taking strolls and people watching.

Later that evening, I noticed a man walking toward us who looked strikingly similar to my dad. Jewel must have noted the resemblance to Grandpa Ford also. As he came closer, she started waving her arms and jabbering at him. Needless to say, she caught the stranger's attention. He smiled and stopped to chat with the smiling baby before walking on.

So commenced a spicy little game with strangers that Jewel continued to play throughout the trip whenever the notion struck. Only one time did she receive a cool reception. That happened at Madame Tussauds Wax Museum in London, when one of the waxed figures Jewel focused her attention on completely ignored her. Baffled at the rejection, the wide eyed baby stared at the figure as though thinking, "What's the matter with this person?"

In Africa, Jewel's game was anything but ignored. Not long after we arrived, she discovered she could easily gain an audience with the Africans. They loved her friendly, spirited greeting, and never could she be accused of showing partiality. Whether a person appeared clean, or in dirty rags of a beggar, Jewel beamed a winning smile, followed with an outburst of jabbers. Children usually present a never-fail means of crossing ethnic barriers. There is something disarming about the smile of a child. Who can resist it? Certainly, the Africans could not.

We learned about the nature of Sierra Leone roads the day we rode inland to the town of Magburaka, the location of the mission headquarters—rough, bumpy, and washboard. They certainly could not be evaluated with a very high rating. Yet once we became acquainted with upcountry travel, we thought better of the road between Freetown and Magburaka.

That evening, the missionaries at Magburaka gave us a welcome that made us relax into an immediate sense of belonging to the mission family. After finishing the meal that Ken's wife, Ruth, had waiting for us, orientation to tropical living began. That night, we entered the world of malaria-carrying mosquitoes, scorpions, centipedes, and snakes. As we listened to interesting, exciting experiences the missionaries had encountered, it seemed more like entertainment than a learning time.

The informal briefing session climaxed with a description of the large tarantulas occasionally found in the bedrooms above the garage where we would be sleeping. And how could a lesson in precaution be better taught than with a physical object? Therefore, Joe Shisler brought a huge, black tarantula from the refrigerator, where it was being kept in cold storage to show to a government official. The size of the creature impressed everyone. And after seeing it, we knew exactly what to look out for, but hoped to never encounter.

Planting fear was not their objective. Yet experienced missionaries knew that newcomers needed to develop precaution habits from the start. In the future, we would also learn the reality of The Forget/Remember Cycle. How easy it became to forget that venomous dangers existed, until the sudden appearance of a crawling creature quickly restored safety measures again—for a while, that is.

As soon as Ken had lit the kerosene lamp in the bedroom above the garage, he gave the floor a thorough search with his torch (British for flashlight.) All seemed clear. He found no tarantulas loitering in the dark corners or under the beds.

When I tucked Jewel into the homemade, screened baby crib and turned the lamp wick lower, I realized that we had actually arrived. From that night on, it would be the real Africa—a continent churning with adventure and never-ending challenges.

The first challenge came that night when we dropped our weary bodies into bed, tucked the mosquito netting under the mattress, and experienced our first smell of the effects the rainy season had on a bed. The scent of a musty mattress and netting was a definite challenge for me! After a time, I pulled the sheet over my face trying to block out the odor. But that proved useless; the sheets and pillows smelled the same as the mattress.

Finally, I concluded that musty smells must be something to expect and learn to live with in the tropics. Later, though, I discovered some places housed more moisture than others. *This is certainly a different world*, I thought, remembering Ken's parting words of caution as he walked out the door: "Be sure to shake out your shoes before putting them on in the morning."

With that, my mind replayed a picture of the huge tarantula we had been shown. But soon, a deep sleep rescued me from further pondering on the crawly side of tropical living. By morning, our new world appeared much brighter. Even the musty mattress seemed bearable as the reality and excitement of at least being in Africa settled in.

Jewel woke up smiling, despite finding herself caged in a screened crib with a closed lid. In the dining room, she became more interested in the Rupp and Shisler children than in her bowl of cereal, grinning back at the smiling faces watching her. When her new friends made funny noises to make Jewel laugh, she mimicked them. That started a happy, laughing dual that lasted several minutes until the other mothers decided the fun should be postponed until after the baby finished breakfast.

Jewel and I remained at Magburaka while the men went to Freetown to pick up our equipment that had arrived from the

States. Then, after hauling everything to Magburaka, they journeyed upcountry to ready the bridges for our move in. Meanwhile, Ruth Rupp filled me in on some household tips for tropical households.

I also met up with another side of tropical living while at Magburaka. Sierra Leone does not happen to be listed among the healthiest places to live in the world. In fact, in the past, it had been classified as the white man's graveyard. Grave markers showed that missionaries also numbered among those who had fallen to diseases and the difficult climate.

The situation had improved over the years with advancements in preventative medications, making it more tolerable for foreigners to live there. Yet blood-thirsty mosquitoes still existed, and my blood must have attracted their taste, for within a few days, I experienced an introduction to the discomforts of malaria. Extra medication quickly took care of it, but in the months ahead, I would learn that like some other missionaries, I needed a stronger dose than average of preventive medication to avoid malaria.

Watching the children at a nearby mission day school became an interesting pastime. It kept Jewel occupied for long periods of time. The school bell clanged rhythmically, as did a beating drum, calling the students to class. During recess periods, children marched back and forth across the schoolyard in groups, singing and clapping their hands. They continued to sing almost constantly while at play. We listened to the cute and eager voices of the children as they repeated their class recitations together in accented English. Throughout their day, rhythm surfaced in a natural manner. I smiled one morning as I heard Little Bo Peep and her lost sheep come forth from the lesson plans.

When the men returned from up-country, they were still laughing as they related the story of Harv falling through a footbridge made of vines while crossing the river at Ganya. He seemed to be doing well with his footing, then about half way across, Harv suddenly dropped into the river below. Apparently, it had been a hilarious scene, judging from the amusing description by Ken with interjections of his version of the story by Harv. I did not find myself laughing as long as the others. It was the first mention that I had heard of a footbridge to cross the river at Ganya.

The more I thought about it and envisioned someone carrying Jewel across the river on a risky bridge of vines, the more uneasy I became. As the saying goes, it is always best not to cross bridges until you get to them. But quite often, I found myself rehearsing the process of edging across that dreaded bridge before we actually reached the Ganya River.

Hovering clouds shaded the rising sun the morning we drove out the palm-lined driveway of the Magburaka station and started for Ganya. Outside of town, we met with a delay at the river. A raft ferry, manually transported from one side to the opposite bank by strong arms pulling on a taut rope, provided the only means of crossing the wide river. For the missionaries who traveled upcountry, a long, hot wait for the ferry became an expected occurrence to take in stride.

Ken accompanied us in the mission truck, making it possible to move everything to Ganya in one trip. Our Jeep and the trailer it pulled were loaded to capacity. Swaying and bouncing on the rutted dirt roads reminded me somewhat of how it must have been to travel in covered wagons during pioneer days in the United States. At times, our speed certainly did not exceed that of a covered wagon.

As usual, Jewel enjoyed the bouncy trip. Not only did she like to ride, but to be held for so many hours was a special treat as well. A cuddly baby from birth, spending the day on my lap certainly placed no hardship on Jewel.

Not only did the roads churn up a pioneer spirit within us, the bridges transported us back to another age even more. The first few along the way came as sturdy spans of cement. Cement was fine; what more could one wish for? Had I been in charge of construction, each bridge certainly would have been at least three feet wider with railings along the sides.

I could remember when country roads in the States often had signs that read, "One Lane Bridge." Should there have been signs posted before the rivers we crossed, they would have warned, "Beware: Half-Lane Bridge." At least that measured how narrow they seemed with the swollen rivers swirling immediately below us at the crossings.

But I hadn't seen anything yet. Progressively, the bridges changed from bad to worse. By afternoon, the previous cement spans seemed deluxe models when we crossed the more crudely-made board bridges. And later, I wished for a board bridge as we drove over a primitive structure of heavy sticks tied together with vines, known to the missionaries as a stick bridge.

The bridge rocked and creaked threateningly under the weight of our load as we ventured over the first stick bridge. Even experienced missionaries never crossed that type of bridge in a loaded vehicle with complete confidence. More than one has collapsed under the weight of a heavy load.

Later, we learned from upcountry missionaries to adopt the policy for passengers to walk across any bridge that seemed more hazardous than normal. Not only did it make it safer for the women and children, but the lightened load lessened the strain on the bridge.

We then held our breath as we watched all our possessions—along with provisions for several weeks—slowly creep from stick to stick across the shaky span. Minutes of tension were exchanged for a surge of relief when the trailer tires rolled over the last stick onto solid ground. At that moment, many spontaneous thank you messages—either verbal or silent—ascended to our heavenly Caretaker.

Leaving the level terrain, our speed dropped from slow to slower, winding up and down the lengthening hills. The possibility of cattle wandering down the road called for alert, defensive driving, especially when approaching curves. Should an animal be struck, the driver would be at fault and held responsible for the cost; this was the unwritten law of the land. After all, cattle had been there many years before motor vehicles made an appearance. No one could argue that fact.

The herdsmen would eventually drive the animals off the road, but their action progressed many times slower than a slow motion replay. We learned that people never rushed. Herds of cattle never rushed. Africa never rushed. Why should anyone hurry? A long time spanned from sunrise to sunset, and tomorrow would be just as long.

As we passed by villages along the way, people came out and waved their greetings to us. Whenever the women caught sight of the white baby, many called out or laughed with delight.

The Jeep did a fine job of announcing our approach to the villagers. In fact, we had not been in Africa long until our four-wheel drive acquired the title of Red Jet. One reason for that term appeared evident with its fire engine red color. And then, listening to the motor labor and roar going up and down the hills reminded us of the decibel level of a jet engine, especially after we found it impossible to maintain a muffler.

The morning we left Magburaka, we had expected to reach our destination by late afternoon. But when the headlights had to be turned on to find our way in the fast-converging darkness, several miles still remained between us and the town of Ganya. Then, unfortunately, as the Jeep bounced over a large bump of the end of one bridge, the sudden jolt snapped the trailer hitch. After looking over the situation, Ken stated, "Well, since it is dark and raining like this, the only thing we can do is go on to the next town and stay overnight in the government rest house."

Ken then attempted to persuade his employed African helper to stay with the trailer and guard it while we went on to Falaba. We would unload the truck and then return for the boxes in the trailer. But the frightened worker, with eyes seemingly almost as large around as the trailer tires, did not want to remain alone in the dark.

Coaxing him with a bright torch, umbrella, knife, and a promise to return as quickly as possible finally brought results. Nonetheless, the worker's eyes still held strong reservations. No doubt, he desperately wished that he were safely back at Magburaka with his family.

At Falaba, Ken explained our predicament to the paramount chief, who obligingly issued keys to the government rest house. Located a short distance from town, the building provided a lodging house for government officials when they traveled through on business.

At the rest house, Ken and Harv carried everything from the truck into the house, then prepared to go back to bring the load from the trailer. I overheard Ken tell Harv, "Jane and Jewel might as well stay here instead of going back out in the rain. It would be a good idea for someone to be here in case anyone came around with the intentions of lifting some of these things while we're gone."

Not yet knowing the difference between the more dangerous, knife-carrying city thieves and the upcountry robbers who likely would not bother anything as long as someone was inside, the idea of playing guard did not sound appealing to me. I suddenly associated with the uncomfortable worker back at the trailer. At least he had the big torch—the only flashlight we had available. To me, the building seemed stranded in the middle of a deep, dark nowhere. So it happened that Jewel and I stuck with the party that drove away from the rest house, even though it did nothing to earn me a badge of courage.

When we reached the trailer, the African looked as relieved to see us as I had felt when Ken had not insisted that I remain at the house. While the men shifted the load from trailer to truck, I warmed food for Jewel by using a bottle warmer plugged into the cigarette adapter on the dash. The rest of us divided a candy bar that Ken had, which proved sufficient since by that time, we were too tired to be hungry.

Back at the rest house, we did not find a Holiday Inn situation for our overnight lodging. The door could not be locked from the inside, so Ken and Harv stacked heavy boxes against it. No food, no water, no electricity, no bathroom, no bed, no furniture of any kind—so described the place in a negative outlook. But a more positive observation would note the existence of four walls, a roof, and a cement floor—quite deluxe accommodations compared to the mud huts we had seen in the villages that day.

With help from the light of the torch, we proceeded to scratch together some comfort with what little we had to work with. Ken spread two blankets on the floor for Jewel and me. Two blankets on a cement floor was not exactly a super-firm orthopedic mattress, but a degree better than straight cement or a dirt floor as the villagers slept on.

A small, foam cushion became Jewel's mattress. How-ever, it turned out undersized and each time she moved during the night, she rolled off. Consequently, I spent the night periodically lifting her back onto the cushion, since the floor

felt too cool for a baby. Ken and Harv bedded down on grass mats, using the pad from Jewel's playpen as a pillow. Needless to say, we needed no alarm to awaken us the next morning. We were more than ready to untwist our still bodies from that cement floor at the first hint of dawn.

When the last of the boiled drinking water drained from Ken's canteen to make Jewel's cereal, the rest of us became conscious that not only were we without food, but also drinking water. Nevertheless, water and food would have to be put on hold. Time had come to be on our way and confront the remaining miles to Ganya.

After taking several drums of supplies to the chief's compound for safe storage, we started on. Outside of Falaba, we parted with the dirt road and turned onto what best could be described as the Jeep Trail. From there, it took over two hours to creep the remaining seven miles. At two places, the winch pulled us through when the four-wheel drive failed.

The last few miles of the bush highway tunneled through tall elephant grass on a narrow, machete-cut path Bill Harrigan had a crew of workmen prepare. Reaching the top of the final hill, Ganya could be seen in the distance—a typical African village nestled in a broad valley at the end of the trial.

Chapter 3: Faraway Home

The men had done an excellent job repairing bridges on the Jeep Trail between Falaba and Ganya. Each stick bridge groaned under the weight of our load, but bravely stood the test. Finally, we drove down the last bumpy hill and—wonder of wonders—an unexpected surprise greeted us at the bottom! Bill Harrigan had managed to speed up African production, and instead of the dreaded foot bridge, a long stick bridge spanned the river. What a welcome sight! And there it was: a perfect illustration of how not to cross your bridges before coming to them.

Next, we braced for the maiden ride across the new bridge. It vented the usual creaking and cracking sounds as tires rolled over stick after stick. It swayed, but the bridge proved able and gave us a safe crossing.

Leaving the river, we drove into a spacious, green valley encircled with rolling hills. To our left, the town of

Ganya presented a picture of primitive Africa, containing many thatched, mud huts with trampled, bare ground yards and dirt paths for streets and walkways. Beyond the town, in the distance, hazy-blue mountain ranges bordered the neighboring country of Guinea.

Near the center of the valley, the mission house with a thatched roof sat perched on top of hill. It certainly would not have been a very impressive piece of real estate in the United States. But given the surroundings, the house appeared more than compatible and very inviting to weary travelers. It did not take long for the bush house on the hill to become known as "home."

Bill Harrigan stood at the edge of the mission hill waving a hearty welcome. Some pensive thoughts must have mingled with his excited happiness as he watched our arrival. Bill and his wife, Ruth, had been the first missionaries permanently stationed at Ganya to work with the Yalunka people. When they arrived, no textbooks greeted them to use for language study. Instead, with a pencil and empty notebook, Bill plunged into reducing the Yalunka language to written form. It would be a tedious job.

Being a trained nurse, Ruth used medical clinics not only to relieve the sick, but to gain friendship with and confidence of the people. That project also required patience in the beginning, since the clinics seemed to intrude into the territory of the medicine man. Throughout Yalunka history, midwives, called grannies, had always delivered the babies. Why did they need the service of the white woman?

Contrary to their apprehension, positive results from pills and shots gradually won respect of more and more people. Likewise, phrases and sentences multiplied in Bill's notebook. Advancement did not come in a trouble-free package, however. Problems or illnesses are usually associated with pioneer mission service. The Harrigans did not find themselves exempted.

From the time Bill and Ruth heard we had been appointed to work with them, each letter to us emphasized how greatly they looked forward to having another couple at Ganya. Disappointment squelched those dreams before they could be reality when Ruth became seriously ill and had to be flown to the States for treatment. Only the Lord knew when, or if she would be able to return to Africa. Bill had remained at Ganya to introduce us to the people and acquaint us with the work. As he watched us approach across the valley, certainly the only factor to lessen the joy of the occasion was the absence of Ruth at his side to share the long-awaited moment. For now, the plan of two couples sharing companionship and mission responsibilities had to remain a hope for the future.

Instead, since Bill would be leaving at some point to join Ruth in the States, he faced the reality of handing over the station management to inexperienced beginners. Fully aware of the struggles and obstacles of pioneer work, he wondered how well the novices moving in would cope with the responsibility. Despite disappointment and uncertainty, Bill let nothing cloud the bright moment as he greeted us that day, nor during the weeks that followed. He constantly maintained an optimistic outlook, even when things went wrong.

From the hill, the view of the valley appeared even more picturesque, abounding in bush country charm.

With cone shaped, thatched roofs peaking skyward, over eighty huts completed the town of Ganya. Footpaths ran here and there across the valley. The most active path stretched between town and the river--the people's only water supply.

That morning, I had no idea how enjoyable watching the scenes in the valley below would become, especially in the early evening. At that time of day, men in ankle-length, flowing robes often moved along the paths, while other men and boys herded animals toward town to shelter them from wild animals for the night. Women with loads of firewood gracefully balanced on their heads walked a more determined gait, knowing they needed to start cooking fires soon to prepare the evening meal. For many, it was the only meal of the day.

The change of seasons would bring about different scenes. During the farming season, many sections of the valley would be studded with the black backs of people bending over to cultivate the ground with crude, short-handled hoes. Rain robed the landscape in shades of green from May to November, as we found it when we arrived in September. Then, following the harvest, brown tones would accent the scene as the dry season set in.

Not a particle of ground belonged to us, yet many times while we lived at Ganya, I would stand on the mission hill looking out over the scene below and think, *How beautiful is my valley?*

It appeared so untainted and serene at sunset—smugly camouflaging that behind the picture of a peaceful village lay nagging fears of evil spirits, binding superstitions, and hopeless misery. We would be reminded of this each time the piercing wails of the mourners sounded across the valley as death snatched another life in town.

Contemplation of the scenery on the day we arrived quickly ended as Bill started introducing the mission crew. First,

 we met the cook. Bala - short and hunchbacked - had worked for missionaries on other stations for many years. A spontaneous, bucktoothed smile announced his pleasant disposition. Being as honest as the midday sun was hot, he displayed a rare virtue in Sierra Leone. In rain or torrid sun, he unfailingly carried a large, black umbrella and an aged, brown hat; he never was seen without them. Both were a part of "Bala Cook."

Being scrupulous in properly boiling drinking water made Bala a treasure to have in the kitchen. Another amazing plus was his ability to serve a soft-boiled egg in perfect condition with no clock or timer to assist him. Somewhere in the past, someone had succeeded well with that lesson, as well as his perfection in boiling water long enough.

But confronted with something new sometimes confused the otherwise dependable cook. The week before we arrived, Bill had given Bala a cake mix with instructions to bake a cake. At the next meal, Bill sat dumbfounded as a couple of pancakes were served, made from the cake mix. While Bill drudged through an explanation of the difference between a cake and pancakes, Bala kept assuring that he understood. Yet

Bill realized that come a month of two later, pancakes could turn up again in place of cake, should Bala be entrusted with another cake mix. Those kinds of things could be expected when an unpredictable chore came along. The white man's ways, including cake mixes, were "plenty strong" (very difficult)—so thought Bala.

Most of the time, Bala's addiction to routine worked as an advantage. For instance, we discovered it not necessary to set our alarm clock. Every morning, at exactly the same time, Bala Cook would be near the outside kitchen splitting wood to start a fire. The sound of his axe at work signaled another day had begun. Regardless of not possessing a clock or watch, Bala had an instinctive sense for time that seemed astonishing. Small, deformed Bala was an interesting person, indeed.

Next, we met Bokari, a bright, clean-cut worker in his early teens that Ruth had trained for household duties. Bokari likewise kept a clear record of honesty and dependability in routine chores. He and Jewel launched an immediate friendship as they exchanged smiles.

The six young men hired for outside maintenance pressed in to see the new missionary family while Bill introduced them one by one. Since the Harrigans had no children yet, the white *pickan* (baby) presented quite a novelty. Their eyes fastened on her every move. What a story the workers had to relate to their families in town that evening when they described the mission people who had moved in with Pa Harrigan. They, no doubt, told about the strong, white baby—more active than any baby they had seen before.

After introductions and greetings, Bill suggested we go inside and get ready to eat. By that time, the calories from Ken's candy bar we had shared the night before had long since burned away. In fact, once we stopped and considered that we had not had a meal since our packed lunch almost twenty-four hours ago, we did not need a second invitation from Bill.

Though far from modern, the two bedroom house held a peaceful, homey atmosphere that impressed me as soon as we entered. I experienced no shock at the lawn chairs that served for living room furniture, a grass roof with no ceiling, white-washed walls, and unpainted cement floors. Everything appeared clean, neat, and well-suited for rustic, bush living. A table and chairs made from heavy mahogany added a special touch to the dining area.

While we ate, Bill did more talking than eating. He chuckled as he told us our Pennsylvania Dutch name, Ache, pronounced similar to hockey without the "h," presented a problem. He explained that Yalunka words begin with conso-nants, making English words starting with vowels difficult, if not impossible for Yalunkas to pronounce. Consequently, they instinctively add a consonant prefix to English words starting with vowels.

To them, "h" seemed the natural prefix for our name, making it sound like Hockey. Ache . . . Hockey . . . what's the difference? Having our last name pronounced in various ways presented nothing new to us. But when Bill defined the Yalunka meaning of hockey, we understood the problem. It happened to be the Yalunka word for sin. So there we sat, the new missionaries: Pa Sin and his family!

Harv tried hard to change that phonetic catastrophe. Over and over, he had the mission staff attempt to pronounce our name accurately. But he found his efforts useless. Pa Hockey it was to be. Fortunately for me, the people addressed the white woman with just Madame— perhaps a term that had drifted over the border from what was then known as French Guinea.

We ran into a complication with Jewel's name also. After hearing it, they repeated, Yewel. Since their alphabet did not contain the "j" sound, "y" substituted for it. Yewel sounded neither American nor African. A solution did come for that issue after a few days, though.

Sometime during her first few weeks on earth, Grandpa Ford had tagged Jewel with the nickname Toosie. Discussing it around the table during a conference after dinner, we decided the name Toosie sounded much better than Yewel. Consequently, from that day on, the little girl became known to the Yalunkas as Toosie, often shortened to Toose by our mission helpers.

Since it would be replaced with an aluminum roof as soon as the rains ended, the grass roof on the mission house had not been repaired the previous dry season. Bill had warned us. Yet the first rain after our arrival splashed a certain amount of shock with it. The steady downpour made us agree that the grass roof indeed needed to be replaced.

Usually the heavier rains followed a pattern. At that time, they were coming during the night. After the first night of being startled awake with water dripping in our bed, we became better organized. The first person to hear the rain starting or feel a drop called out a quiet alarm to the others.

Knowing that the quicker we moved, the drier we spent the rest of the night sent us scurrying to perform our rain duties. Either Bill or Harv grabbed a torch and went outside, making his way around the house closing the wooden shutters over the screened windows, while the other person placed pans at the needed locations to catch the drips.

My foremost concerns sent me dashing to cover the baby bed with a sheet of plastic, and then to the living room to place plastic over the portable pump organ. That left one piece to put across the mosquito net stretched above our bed. But the plastic came short of completely covering the bed, making it necessary to move in search of dry spots during a hard down-pour.

Bill's reminders that the rainy season would soon be over made it easier to tolerate the rain at night. We even learned to laugh at the dripping water and stubbed toes in the middle of the night. After living in Africa through the change of seasons, we found that after a long period of much-anticipated dryness, we looked forward to the rains as well.

Living under a thatched roof also presented more challenges than moisture from the rains. Since we never knew what might be lodging above, it became routine to look up from time to time and scan over the board beams and pole rafters that held the thatch in place. Harmless, long, green lizards happened to be the only living things ever spotted, thankfully. Pieces of straw and dirt sifting down from the roof required frequent inspections of Jewel's playpen. Since she was in the everything-goes-in-mouth stage of life, she seemed to have fewer intestinal problems once a metal roof replaced the thatch.

As Ken had impressed upon us our first night at Magburaka, keeping an eye on the floor when walking about the house became an unconscious practice. Since the house had no screen doors, it left an open invitation for crawling visitors to slip in. The hill had been alive with poisonous centipedes when Bill and Ruth first arrived, but keeping the grass cut and the hillside cleared off had helped to eliminate them. We saw very few centipedes or scorpions. Nevertheless, they could not be erased from the precaution list.

The possibility of snakes visiting the hill always existed—long ones, short ones, brown ones, green ones. They came in many varieties and sizes. Every so often, one would decide to seek refuge in or around the house. Ruth had trained Bokari to sweep the entire house every morning, which not only made a cleaner house, but helped to locate any unwanted visitors that might be lingering in the shadows.

Adjusting to our new way of living was no problem up to that point. But soon, the laundry began to develop into a source of contention. In the Yalunka culture, carrying water or washing clothes was a duty that belonged to the women. But Mesa, our first laundry person, was not a woman. Trouble! Furthermore, if washing clothes had to be included in his job description, Mesa preferred to take the clothes to the river. There, he could pound them clean on the rocks as did the women from town. So Mesa argued. Hence, having to carry water and heat it on the stove caused a disgruntled worker.

Trying to teach Mesa to sort the clothes further complicated matters. Whether he was color blind, an exceptionally slow learner, or very stubborn, I never knew for sure—although I had my suspicions. As soon as I disappeared from sight, dark clothes went into the wash water first. And invariably, white diapers went in last, even though they were prewashed in a disinfectant.

Only for the sake of holding his job would he consent to wash diapers at all. Why couldn't the white Madame just hold the baby over the ground and take care of nature's call the normal way as the African mothers did?

I also insisted that the clothes be washed in hot, soapy water to help eliminate sores and infections. But more often than not, when I checked the water temperature, that rule had been disregarded also. Mesa constantly excused himself, "I done forget."

The workers preferred drying laundry in their accustomed manner of spreading them either on the ground or on a grass roof. So I launched a campaign to train the laundry worker to hang our wash with clothespins on a line that Harv had installed. But I found that aspiration turn into a real battle of wits. I did not think it an unreasonable or impossible request, since the laundry at Magburaka dried in that manner.

Nonetheless, I found the clothes on the line nearest the house hung according to directions, while on the lines beyond, clothes had been flung over the line without being shaken out and with no pins to keep them on the line. Then, after a few times of having the wash rehung, clothespins began to mysteriously disappear.

I could have taken an easier route with that problem and looked the other way, had it not been for the wind. A breeze blew over the hill almost constantly, sometimes quite gustily. And wet clothes blown down onto the red, clay dirt, then tossed back on the line without rinsing, did not meet my standards of running a household—not even in the bush of Africa. So the clothespin controversy continued until we finally found a helper who cooperated perfectly. In fact, he became so persuaded that soon his clothes began appearing on the line with our wash, all nicely hung with clothespins. I made no objection to that. Instead, I smiled to myself, knowing that our clothes (and his) were clean.

Ironing with a huge, charcoal iron afforded another challenge, especially when ironing Jewel's baby dresses. After trying it myself, I realized it to be quite a difficult task. Bokari had mastered the spark-spitting, charcoal monster extremely well, so consequently I placed him in charge of training the other workers. The results often seemed to leave more wrinkles that before the clothes had been ironed, and at times, sparks flying from the iron left small burn holes in the cloth. But in time, improvement could be noted.

Our employees' reward for trying to do their work well came in the privilege of being permitted to use the charcoal iron to press their own shirts—used shirts in good condition we had brought from the States. It amounted to a fringe benefit that came with working for the mission. And how delightedly the workers beamed, not only to have shirts to wear, but ironed shirts as well!

Further adjustments to our new environment expanded beyond climate and mission work crew issues. Only a few days after our arrival at Ganya, I stood by a window listening to the speedy flow of Yalunka words in a conversation between some of the men outside. Overwhelmed, I wondered how we could ever learn to hear individual words in such a jumble of sounds.

We had some linguistic training, but Bill was much more gifted in that area than the rest of us. The black notebook Bill had prepared stored written Yalunka material that would serve as our textbook for beginning language study. Also, tapes of Bokari speaking the preliminary phrases and sentences helped give us a start with accurate pronunciation.

Being gifted conversationalists, the Yalunka people loved to talk. But never would they plunge into either a friendly or business conversation without first tossing back and forth several salutations. And when finished, they not only knew the state of each other, but of all their kin.

Their initial greeting took an opposite flow to our accustomed word order. One did not say in Yalunka, "Good morning, Bala," but rather, "Bala, good morning." It sounds insignificant, but try changing a habit without a great deal of concentration. For the first few weeks, the people reacted with delighted smiles and laughter as we attempted our first greetings in Yalunka.

Bill warned us of one problem we would experience with language learning. The people who worked for us would exert more interest in learning English than in helping us acquire Yalunka. That turned out to be an accurate prediction. Later on, however, when Jewel started talking, they responded quickly to teach her Yalunka words and then laughed, saying, "Toosie done savvy [understand] Yalunka!" But as for us, they wanted to hear our English.

Our first visit to town with Miss Toosie brought excited exclamations from the women. Many gave way to irresistible impulses to touch her soft, baby skin. They also wanted to stroke her fair hair, fascinated with such a contrast to the dark curls of their own babies. In the course of greeting the white baby, some mothers reached for her hands—a natural reflex for mothers around the world. But it is also a normal activity for babies to put their hands to their mouth. Without being obvious, I attempted to position Jewel in a way that made it difficult for them to touch her hands. Being aware that offending the people would mean disaster to our relationship with them made protection impossible at times. I learned to rely on a silent SOS to the heavenly Father to protect from germs, worm eggs and whatever else. Trusting the "whatever else" to cover anything else remaining, I continued to smile my greetings to the curious onlookers.

Not all of the people had unwashed hands, but many found a bar of cheap, lye soap too expensive to indulge in. Soap, salt, and sugar belonged in the luxury category. No doubt, the people fared just as well without sugar and perhaps salt, but the soap would have improved their living conditions. Comparing the Yalunkas to some other tribes, they placed a reasonably high rating on cleanliness (bush style cleanliness), as well as being energetic during farming season, and striving for everyday survival overall.

Chapter 4: Alone on the Hill

Bill held church services in a large *berry*, which is a thatched structure for shelter belonging to the paramount chief. Located in the center of town, the berry served as the center for all government and social activities in the community. Town meetings, court sessions, ceremonial dances, and every type of public gathering assembled under the high, thatched roof.

The chief gave his consent for the berry to be used for mission services also. A dried mud ledge around the outer edge provided a place for people to sit. After the seating space filled beyond capacity, some of the remaining people stood, while others sat on the dirt floor.

The town hall additionally functioned as a barn for cattle and sheep to be driven in and tied to at night to help protect them from wild animals. Therefore, in order to convert the berry from barnyard to church on Sunday mornings, a sweeping ritual had to take place. Bill assigned that honor to one of our mission workers each week. Needless to say, no one fought for the janitorial position.

Waiting for evening meals to be finished, the night services always convened after dark. Babies and small children came secured to the backs of their mothers or older sisters. If either the town chief or one of the other important men in town made an appearance, people quickly moved to give him a prominent place. The dim light from a kerosene lantern Bill hung on a pole illuminated many inquisitive eyes shining from a blend of black faces.

For a while, a young Yalunka named Ali taught from the Scriptures at the services. Originating from another town, Ali had attended a mission school in Guinea, which made him more knowledgeable of the Bible than any other Yalunka in Sierra Leone at that time. Being taller than the average African, Ali towered above the other men as his deep, resonant voice read from the Meneca translation of the scriptures. Some of the Ganya men understood Meneca, a trade language of West Africa. After reading a few verses, Ali stopped and explained the meaning in Yalunka.

Every now and then, children became restless and noisy. Immediately, one or more of the men boomed a loud command at the youngsters to be quiet. During one evening service, Ali paused for a few moments and apparently Jewel thought things should be kept moving. Suddenly, she began chattering in an outburst of baby jabbers. None of the men yelled at the white baby. Instead, everyone started laughing as they turned to look at Toosie. After that, I kept a hand positioned to clamp over small lips whenever they started to open.

Since a municipal power plant did not exist in the bush, candles and kerosene provided the only resources for lighting the darkness. Therefore, Bill had suggested that we include a portable generator when we planned our equipment. As soon as Bill and Harv unpacked the heavy crate, they excitedly started to experiment with the new piece of luxury to discover its capabilities.

Sewing with a portable sewing machine, playing the tape recorder, and burning light bulbs when guests visited the hill modernized pioneer living extensively. Nevertheless, because of hauling expensive petrol (gasoline) from down country, the new bush power plant, affectionately called the "light plant," had to be utilized in moderation.

One evening, Bill and Harv loaded the generator on the Jeep and took it to town to use for a service. Parking as far away from the berry as the long extension cord allowed helped to lower the noise level of the generator. Even then, when the first sound started from the chugging motor, several people—mostly women and children—reacted with a fast-as-lightning exit from the berry. But before long, one by one and two by two, they drifted back in, seeing the brave ones who had remained stood unharmed.

The light bulb that Bill hung in place of the usual kerosene lantern immediately captured the attention of everyone in the berry. How strange that the bright thing made light without a flame! Never had they seen anything like it before. For the first time, the village people of Ganya witnessed what Edison invented many years prior. How large the world still remains in some developing countries.

Following the service, Bill played a tape of drums beating in town that he had recorded previously from the mission hill. Unable to comprehend just what they were hearing, faces registered blank stares as the people listened to the sounds coming from the black box that had two wheels mysteriously spinning around on top.

As the drums beat on, recognition of the sound slowly began to turn somber faces into broad grins. And when they heard their own voices singing, which had been recorded during the service that very night, lips stretched into even broader smiles. The black box performed miracles!

Coming to the end of the tape, Bill started rewinding the spool to play it again. But it so happened that a certain tape recorder possessed the nature of squeaking during rewind. And with the volume still turned high, the noise boomed out like an explosion to their unaccustomed hearing. Smiles quickly vanished—as did some of the congregation. Those who did remain drew back as frightened eyes darted from the tape recorder to the light bulb, wondering what to expect next.

Bill mastered the situation with alert action, however, as he reached over and turned the volume up and down to demonstrate that he controlled the black box. His action proved successful in reassuring everyone. They edged closer to gain a better look at the recorder and from then on, enjoyed the listening experience with delighted expressions and exclamations.

One afternoon, as Bill poured a cup of coffee for Harv, he stated, "Taste it well, boy; this is the last cup of joe you will have for a while, or at least until we make a supply run to Freetown." Both ex-Navy men sat at the dining room table relating some experiences they had encountered while in the service. The last cup of coffee; that certainly struck as a sobering thought for two ardent coffee lovers. Should they enjoy it, or could they only lament over it? After enjoying it to the last drop, they looked at one another and laughed. Bush living demanded grace to laugh at such circumstances. Bill did it automatically. We were learning.

I had encountered a similar situation some days earlier as I handed Bala the last of our flour supply to bake bread. In a letter to my parents, I wrote, "I laughed this morning when I saw the flour was finished. I began to wonder if I was losing my mind—better known out here as being 'bush-happy.' But then we find ourselves laughing at things we would not laugh about in the States. I think it is the Lord's grace in action. So many things go wrong. If we didn't laugh, going bush-happy could be a reality."

Two weeks passed before another missionary brought us flour and mail. Needless to say, mail took priority over flour after living with no contact from the outside world for a month. Sitting at the table, sharing the Aladdin light, we spent the evening poring over twenty letters from the States. Hours later, we found our minds too activated to sleep, as sentences and news from the letters spun through our thoughts. The next morning, Bill assured us to think nothing of it. After three years in Africa, he still experienced the same stimulating effects from mail.

A few weeks later, I listened to the Red Jet roar up the hill on the other side of the river as Bill and Harv left before daylight for a supply trip to Freetown. After preparing their breakfast and seeing them off, I had extinguished the lamp and returned to bed. When the last sound of the Red Jet faded in the distance, a pre-dawn stillness shouted the reality that Jewel and I now camped alone on the mission hill.

Previously, when Harv asked Ken what I would do while he and Bill went for supplies, Ken had answered, "Leave a loaded gun with her. She will just have to stay alone like the other women do." I inwardly cringed when I heard that verdict, and for several days before the men left, I mentally added more and more apprehension to the what-if list. What if Jewel became seriously ill? There was no doctor's office to call and no emergency room to rush to. What if I should get sick? No one was available to care for the baby. What if the house caught on fire? There was no fire department. What if a wild animal came on the hill at night? We had no phone to call for help. What if someone was bitten by a snake? The list grew on. I was determined, however, to not make anyone else miserable with my misgivings. If missionary women were expected to stay alone, I would at least pretend to be brave.

Consequently, we decided that if I were to be provided a gun, artillery lessons were necessary. So while Jewel napped one afternoon, to the side of the hill we walked—a shotgun slung over Harv's shoulder while I carried a tin can to use for a target.

The gun felt as heavy as a cannon when Harv handed it to me. I positioned the long barrel, found the can in the sight, closed my eyes, and pulled the trigger. Bang! The jolt delivered an even stronger punch than I expected, while the can remained smugly safe, as though knowing it had nothing to fear. I put forth an honest effort, but after a few more tries and a sore shoulder developing, I decided the shotgun did not belong in my garrison. Instead, another plan began to shape in my mind.

Bill had acquired a dog, Sparky, that was brought to Sierra Leone from Germany. Even though the pet stayed outside at night, I decided that while the men were away, I would keep Sparky in the house as a watchdog. I reasoned that he would serve the purpose of protection much better than the shotgun. And though not a large dog, surely his barking would frighten away anyone or anything.

However, that very evening, Bill found Sparky hiding behind a chair after the doors had been shut for the night. After dragging the unwilling dog outside, Bill explained it was not safe to leave Sparky in the house at night; a hungry leopard might be tempted to jump through one of the window screens for a meal of dog. Of course, that revelation immediately killed my plan to use Sparky as a watchdog. I also jotted a mental note to lower the shutters over the windows the nights the men were away. And my thoughts of Sparky at least acting as a watchdog outside lasted only a few seconds, as Bill added, "Whenever Sparky senses a leopard in the vicinity, he takes off down the path toward town."

An African reported seeing Sparky being chased by a leopard one night. The dog won the race! Short-legged Sparky proved the power of self-preservation to be swifter than the hunger of a leopard as they sped to town.

Each day, as I planned meals from the rapidly-depleting storeroom, I had become more resigned to staying alone. In fact, surprisingly, I found myself wanting the men to be on their way. We certainly needed supplies; that could not be argued. Our storeroom shelves and the cupboard of Old Mother Hubbard held too much in common.

As we worked on the shopping list, Bill kept warning, "Remember: anything we forget, we will do without!" He stated an all-so-true fact, since scheduling allowed us a supply trip only once every three months. At times, other business matters provided a trip sooner, but that was nothing to rely on. And of course, no convenience stores existed to run to before the next supply trip.

The day had arrived. Almost two hours after the Red Jet had mounted the hill, the sound of Bala's ax splitting wood awoke me. I realized I had drifted to sleep while praying for Bill and Harv to have a safe trip. Not long after I was awoken, jabbering sounds started coming from the other bedroom. The mission hill quickly aroused to another day with no time to ponder the what-if list.

Bala and Bokari proved helpful while the men were away. The yard workers, however, did not score as well in terms of cooperation. One afternoon, they decided to put the Madame to a test, no doubt confident they would win out. In the daily schedule, Bill allowed the workers a two hour break in town after our lunch dishes had been washed. Following a short siesta, the remaining time provided us a quiet period to study without those customary interruptions from the mission workers.

The Yalunkas did not have clocks to depend on to schedule their living, as we do. For the most part, the sun provided a leisurely timepiece. Therefore, the boys needed to be summoned back to work following the afternoon break. That communication reached town by striking a metal rod against a tire rim that hung outside our house. The same method served for a church bell, as prior to our driving to town, the clanging announced a service would commence soon.

That particular afternoon, the outside employees did not return for over an hour after I rang for them. When they finally sauntered up the hill, one of them came to the house to act as spokesman for the crew. In broken English, Bokari and Bala explained that the worker said, "We done sleep. We no hear de bell. We be late. We no go back town for rest of day?" With the

Yalunkas, questions appeared in the negative form. So in this case, they meant, "Shouldn't we go back to town for the rest of the day since we are already late?"

Looking at the non-ambitious workers standing in the background, I remembered Bill's advice: "Keep in command at all times or there will be more problems." I told Bokari to tell them they must stay and work hard to make up for the time they had lost in coming so late. As Bokari turned my words to Yalunka, the eyes of the workers widened in surprise. As for hard work to make up lost time, machetes moved no faster cutting grass the rest of that afternoon—perhaps even slower. But I decided not to challenge it, not wanting to push my authority to the point of making enemies. Remaining in the house, I pretended not to notice.

On another day, after pressing Mesa to find a missing baby sock, a loud brawl suddenly started out beyond the kitchen. Usually, people disagreed with words. But by the time I reached the scene, a physical encounter raged between Mesa and the man he accused of taking the missing sock. Soon, the worker's mother appeared and joined in the racket, shouting at the top of her voice. Not understanding the language, I could not tell if she sided with or against her son.

Finally, Bokari and another worker were able to separate the two, with the aid of Bala's commands to stop fighting. When the missing piece was relinquished, Mesa beamed as the proud victor in the case of the missing sock.

In Sierra Leone culture, a person stealing did not consider himself a thief unless caught in the act or with possession of the goods. Therefore, possession incriminated the young chap as he pulled the sock from his pocket. I wondered what he had planned to do with one baby sock that would cause him to risk being caught thieving from the missionaries.

Other than those minor incidents, the days moved on smoothly. I smiled to myself each time I walked past the loaded gun propped in one corner of the bedroom. Perhaps leaving a firearm for our protection had made Harv feel more comfortable, but I knew the gun would remain in the corner—certainly with its safety on. No loss of sleep derived from worrying about the what-if list. Assurance from our heavenly Protector prompted complete peace as I went to bed each night. In fact, I slept as soundly as the baby in her crib, even with the absence of neighbors or telephone service.

After the boys went to town in the early evenings, I pushed Jewel in the stroller around the top of the hill, watching the close of day scenes in the valley below. People and cattle slowly ambled along the paths toward town, while, one by one, flames from fires started to cook the evening meals.

During the rainy season, cooking fires burned inside the huts as smoke lifted its way up through thatched peaks leaving a residue behind in the windowless dwellings. It may have smarted the inhabitant's eyes, but the smoke did discourage reptiles and unwanted malaria-carrying mosquitoes from lingering within.

Being near the equator, sunsets happened at approximately seven o'clock year round. Jewel waved "nighty-night" to the huge fireball as it dropped behind the hills. As soon as it sank from sight, we moved toward the house since darkness settled in quickly. Inside, after lighting the lamp, our strolling continued. It never seemed safe to have Jewel in the playpen after dark. Light from the kerosene lamp caused too many shadows, making it easier for something to crawl along the floor without being detected. So, back and forth from the living room over to the dining area, around the table and back to the living room, we strolled, while a contented baby enjoyed our pre-bedtime togetherness.

Quite often, I stopped at the table to change a record and rewind Bill's manual phonograph. Pacing through the grooves of a small selection of seventy-eight records, the needle did not exactly provide stereo sounds, but it did furnish us with music. Throughout her life, Jewel treasured music. Perhaps the seed had been planted during those evening rendezvous with the melodies from an outdated record player at the Ganya mission house.

One night, after Jewel had been tucked into bed, I decided to start writing Christmas cards to our families to make certain they would be ready to go with the next mail. But trying to capture the spirit of Christmas greetings in the tropics seemed strange. Instead of carols playing and snow falling for inspiration, only a long, green lizard scampered part way down the whitewashed wall and then back up over the top.

Fingering through the box of cards and reading the verses suddenly prompted symptoms of homesickness—the first I had experienced since we arrived in Africa. At that point, I placed the lid back on the box and returned it to the trunk in the bedroom where it had been stored. Alone in the bush, especially at night, certainly was not the best setting for writing Christmas greetings that first year. I assured myself it would be easier to take care of that after the men returned. And so it was.

The Christmas cards soon vanished from my thoughts as chirping crickets and other night sounds became lost to the noise of beating drums in town. A full moon predicted the drums would continue most of the night. Rhythm would increase, growing more frenzied as the night wore on, along with restless voices of townspeople rising in intensity.

At the age of sixteen, I first heard about those night drumming sessions at a weekend missions retreat—my first main exposure to foreign missions. The speaker, a national from Sierra Leone, told about the custom of beating drums all night to ward off evil spirits following the death of a family member and during nights of a full moon.

In each service, the African speaker lamented the sad plight of women and girls in his country. Not being respected with love and care, their lot fell to almost a slave role in life, existing to work and bear children for their husbands. He explained that each wife became the property of the man who paid the dowry price demanded by her parents. Often, the agreement took place while she was a child. Then, as soon as she matured to childbearing age, the girl went to live with the husband chosen for her. He may be young, but could also be an older man with other wives.

A wife would remain at the mercy of the man who owned her. Should she suffer mistreatment, running home to her family would not help. Her parents certainly would have no intention of returning the dowry price received for her. Instead, they would promptly return the screaming girl to her husband, who might give her another flogging for the trouble she had caused.

If the man owned other wives, they would very possibly abuse the new bride also. Only the love of Jesus Christ coming into hearts and homes could reverse the situation. Such a miracle had taken place in other African groups, and we believed it would with the Yalunkas someday.

The sound of beating drums always served to remind me of the reason for our being on the mission hill. At least five thousand Yalunkas in Sierra Leone needed to know that the Son of God suffered and died on the cross for their eternal salvation. Neither the dominant Muslims nor the strong Animism religions prevalent in the country could offer such a sacrifice of love. Nor could those religions claim the power to change lives to such a degree that peaceful hearts would replace the former nagging fears living inside the people. Only the Gospel of Jesus Christ can deliver such a mighty victory.

Watching moving shadows form on the wall from the burning lamp, I suddenly realized I had just experienced the perfect remedy for loneliness. That unpleasant malady had been cured instantly as I pondered the needs of the Yalunkas down in the village.

The words from the chorus of one of the records I listened to earlier returned to sing through my thoughts: "Follow, I will follow Thee my Lord, Follow every passing day; My tomorrows are all known to Thee, Thou wilt lead me all the way."

After checking on Jewel in her crib, I went to bed with faith for the future as the drumming continued in town. As for the Holy City: "He that keepeth Israel [the followers of Christ Jesus] shall neither slumber nor sleep" (Psalm 121:4). Each night, I sensed an awareness that Jewel and I had the Keeper with us in the blessing of His perfect peace. We were not alone on the hill.

Chapter 5 : Kamaron Playmates

"Yeepyna! Yeepyna bata fa!" (Jeep! Jeep done come!) shouted one of the yard workers late one afternoon.

I picked up Jewel and hurried outside. All work immediately ceased as every ear strained to listen. Someone had called the same tidings the day before. But after listening and waiting for some time with no further developments, we had returned to our activities—laughing but slightly disappointed.

Listening for the Red Jet shifting gears on the steep hills several miles away came to be known in the same category as seeing a mirage in the desert. Waiting for the distant sound caused the imagination to play tricks after a few days. And, of course, each of the young employees wanted to be the first to hear the Yeepyna coming.

Several minutes passed, and we began to dismiss it as just another false call, even though the worker who made the announcement remained absolutely certain he had heard the Yeepyna. More time passed. And then everyone heard it at once—the muffled roar of the Red Jet.

When Bill and Harv finally reached the river, they did not notice anything unusual about the bridge. But when they drove onto it, the Jet took a sudden drop and they quickly discovered the sticks were floating on high water. Immediately, water rose up to the seats. Miraculously, the bridge held the load and the Jeep splashed across without stalling.

Jewel wholeheartedly welcomed the travelers home as

they bounced across the valley. It reminded me of holding a frisky puppy as her lungs, arms, and legs functioned at full capacity. The workers watched her, laughing and repeating, "Ayee, Toosie done savvy [know] Yeepyna!" The days had gone by without one thing happening on my what-if list, thanks to our heavenly Father. Yet I did feel relieved to see the men returning, even though I did not express my feelings as visibly as Jewel.

After Bill and Harv finished greeting everyone, they gave a play-by-play description of their precarious river crossing on the floating bridge. The Jet, trailer, and all our supplies could have been dumped into the high water. So amidst chuckles and laughs, there sounded a hearty appreciation for our Lord's definite assistance at the river.

Bill then told us about seeing a family of large baboons that afternoon. He and Harv decided one of the big animals would make a nice dash (a dash is the African custom of offering a gift in order to receive service or a gift in return) for the

81

mission crew to take home for their cooking pots that evening. But they soon realized it would require a higher powered gun than what they had along. The baboons merely threw them a can't-catch-me look and scampered away. The workers seemed interested in the story even though they did not have baboon meat to take home for their cooking pots.

With the time fast approaching when Bill would leave for the United States, one project he wanted completed involved having rafters ready for changing the roof on the mission house. That turned into a project more complicated than expected.

At times, the *sawyermen* (lumberjacks) who cut the logs had a way of being almost as annoying as the pesky small flies that clung to your skin when walking in town. And at the top of the Pesky List stood Black Douda. Africans vary in skin color, and since Douda happened to be as black as any person we'd seen, the missionaries often referred to him as Black Douda. Gifted with the art of being a natural comedian made the chap easier to tolerate and helped to overlook what a rascal he usually proved to be. A white man could give Black Douda a harsh lecture for not following instructions and within minutes, find himself laughing at his antics.

Black Douda's most prevalent weakness rested in his hands, which so often could not resist acquiring articles that did not belong to them. In time, after becoming chin deep in trouble, Douda left town with "borrowed" tools, and neither Douda nor the tools returned. Supervising the sawyermen required true Christian grace—not one doubt about that.

One morning, Bill gave the lawn workers the assignment to gather stones for the veranda that would be added to the front of the house during the renovation project. About mid-morning, spotting a snake in a tree several yards down the hillside, the workers proceeded to hurl stones at it from the pile they had collected.

As soon as Bill happened to see the stones being thrown back down the hill, he ordered a halt to the firing squad. Then, to calm the workers, he carried a gun from the house, aimed, and killed the snake that had interrupted the work progress. It took the crew over an hour to carry the same stones back up the hill again—just another minor incident that went along with doing construction in Africa.

For a few days after Bill left to join Ruth in the States, we felt very alone on Devil's Hill, as Harv and other missionaries often referred to the mission hill whenever things went wrong. Before the mission moved in, the hill had functioned at times as a place to perform ritual sacrifices to appease Satan and other gods. Telltale blood stains on the top and sides of a huge rock gave affirmation to those reports, so we were told. Some days, we did have to wonder if possibly our presence was being contested by the evil powers that once had claimed the hill.

When we arrived at Ganya, Bala Cook and his wife, Pasi, lived in a small hut at the bottom of the hill. But the women in town kept talking to Pasi about the superstitions connected with the hill, until she finally became so frightened that Bala and Pasi moved to town. Not understanding the power of almighty God, it amazed the Yalunka women that I would stay on the superstitious hill when Harv went for supplies.

With Bill no longer around to generally supervise the workers, we soon felt the jolt of being fully in charge and how time consuming it became. Running the household seemed to compete too heavily with language study on many days. I never knew what to expect from one day to the next. Dull or boring times never existed.

One morning, I gave instructions to one of the helpers to clean the dish cupboard, which stood in a small serving room next to the dining area. Several minutes later, when I checked on the operation, I found the worker standing in a pool of water, scrubbing down the cupboard with a brush and bucket of water. I had presumed he would use a wet cloth. How quickly I learned not to take for granted the function of even minor chores. The sight of the soaking wet serving room did cause me to be glad for cement floors, however.

Sometimes, one of the workers performed a task correctly for several days and I sighed with relief. Now he has it! We have arrived! Then, to my consternation, only a day or two later, regression set in. Old habits returned with the habitual explanation: "I done forget, Madame." And there we dangled— back on step one of training procedures.

Faithful Bala constantly tried to please. He looked upset the time he came to the house carrying a broken oven dish. "Madame, oven done get too hot and break dish," he apologized for the oven. I realized his explanation to be partly correct, yet on the other hand, why did the oven get too hot? Nevertheless, I did learn to sympathize with the plight of the oven incidents.

Located a few feet from the house, the small kitchen held no claims of being modern. The cooking stove could not compare to an up-to-date range. The small firebox—not large enough to store a bed of coals to maintain heat—made baking no easy task.

One Saturday, I happened to think about the angel food cake mixes in a storage drum being reserved for birthdays and special occasions. Neither a birthday nor a special occasion happened to be in our near future, but after a while, my fondness for angel food cake sent me to the berry where the drums were located.

During the baking, I tended the firebox myself, determined not to let the cake be ruined. After baking the proper time, the cake appeared to be raised and nicely browned. Proudly, I carried my achievement to the house and placed it upside down over a bottle on the serving room counter to cool. Later, Harv came to the living room from walking through the serving room and asked, "What happened to the cake? It's all over the floor!"

I hurried out to look and found my beautiful angel food in broken pieces, scattered over the countertop and floor. It took only a glance to realize the problem: the oven had baked the outer layer of the cake but not the center.

"There is no use crying over spilled milk" becomes an active philosophy for most missionaries. So while Harv and I enjoyed the chunks on the counter that seemed eatable, Sparky took care of everything on the floor. Sparky must have approved of American cake the way he continued to lick his jaws long after the cake party ended. At least we had a taste of angel food cake. And I realized, from then on, that Bala did have some strong points concerning the difficulty managing the oven. Madame had learned one more lesson.

We are told that when Mary Slessor, an early pioneer missionary to Africa, was alone in the bush, she frequently confused the days because she had no calendar. Once, she held church services on Monday, thinking it to be Sunday. Another time, she repaired her roof on Sunday, thinking it was Monday, with her services already held the previous day. We did have a calendar, however, and managed to keep the days straight, although not always sure of accurate time. Our calendar reminded us when Thanksgiving arrived that first year at Ganya. Otherwise, we never would have known. A holiday had a way of being just another day unless we chose to do something special to promote a holiday spirit.

We had been without meat for a while, and when someone brought eggs to sell the day before Thanksgiving, excitement bubbled as I looked at the eggs. Nonetheless, I reminded myself not to become too elated until the eggs passed the test for freshness.

Eggs emerged small, just like the scrawny chickens they came from. And they always seemed to be a scarce item. Perhaps the people waited to see if an egg would hatch first before placing it in the market for sale. After all, should the egg be fertile, another chicken would be of more value than just one egg. This may have been the reason for a large percentage of the eggs to fail the test by the time they reached our door.

Placing the eggs in a pan of cold water decided their usefulness very quickly. Sometimes, the whole lot floated like dead fish—what a letdown after hoping for at least one or two good eggs for baking or making a pudding.

That particular day, I was delighted as I watched every one of the eggs sink to the bottom of the pan. So even though we did not have a turkey gracing the table at our first Thanksgiving in Africa, the eggs substituted adequately. In fact, we appreciated them so much, we did not think about turkey as we thanked our Father for supplying the eggs.

Life on the hill improved after Harv purchased a radio in Freetown. What a thrill to hear from the outside world, and what a marvel the airwaves seemed when being so far from modern civilization. But one drawback prevented listening to the radio every day. Since it operated on power from the Jeep battery, each time we wanted to listen, the battery had to be disconnected from the Jeep and carried to the house—not as convenient as simply turning a knob.

Regardless of the awkward maneuvers of setting up, it was a treat to listen to the radio for a short while every few days. Another advancement the radio brought to bush living was that we no longer needed to guess at the correct time. The striking chimes of Big Ben sent it directly to the Ganya hill airwaves from the BBC.

One Saturday evening, as Harv turned the dial, a football game being played in Columbus, Ohio suddenly boomed out as clearly as though we were listening to it from Ohio. What a surprise! We could hardly believe our ears. Even though I knew little about football, I sat spellbound, listening with as much interest as Harv. Only my motive existed not to hear plays or scores, but to listen to the words "Columbus" and "Ohio State." With Columbus less than fifty miles from Rosewood, all at once, the world seemed to shrink.

Having the radio also brought the blessing of being able to occasionally hear a church service in English. And later, when we discovered ELWA, a Christian station in Liberia, every Sunday, we gratefully enjoyed familiar programs taped in the United States.

Receiving our mail once every few weeks even proved difficult at times. Once, Jake Schierling, a missionary stationed sixty miles from us, had made arrangements to meet Harv in Falaba on his return from Magburaka with our mail. But that morning, when Harv tried to cross the river at Ganya, he found the bridge submerged underwater. The Red Jet did not splash through that time. Instead, it stalled. Answering an SOS sent to town, twenty men came to the rescue and pulled the Jet from the water without a chain. It had soaked too long by that time, however, and refused to start.

Determined to have mail, Harv set out walking to Falaba. But when Jake had not appeared after a three hour wait, Harv disappointedly trekked the seven mile return to Ganya without mail. Later, we heard that Jake's trip had to be postponed because of high water. That symbolized Africa in the rainy season—rivers often dictated changes in plans. Never could it be said: "The mail must go through!"

By the time Harv arrived back at the river, the Jet had dried enough to start. He drove to the house, but there seemed to be a problem in the gears. When they met a few days later, Harv described the symptoms to Jake. Jake thought the clutch plate might be rusted and explained how to repair it. But the situation became more complicated when Harv discovered a lifeless battery, probably due to an overuse of our radio.

With little mechanical background, learning how to recharge the battery with the generator brought a new challenge to Harv. After almost two days of many tries and much perspiration, he finally mastered the process and once again, the Red Jet was restored to service.

Rivers had receded back to almost normal levels the day we drove to the Kamaron station where the Schierling family lived. Plans had been made for Jewel and I to stay with Ruth, Jake's wife, while Jake and Harv replaced the roof on the Ganya house. It did not take long for Jewel to establish a friendship with the Schierling children, Gary, Stevie, and little Patsy— only six months older than Jewel. In the days that followed, Jewel found having other children in the house proved much more fun than her stuffed toys back at Ganya.

I likewise found our visit a treat in being able to chat with another woman in English, as Ruth and I became acquainted. But eventually, after the men had gone, life had to settle down to daily routine. In the mornings, the dining area turned into classroom as Ruth tutored Gary and Steve using Calvert homeschooling lessons in elementary education.

The veranda became a study hall where I attempted to work on Yalunka phrases from Bill's black notebook. But I found my concentration being tested between Jewel jabbers in the playpen beside me, Calvert lessons drifting out the open door, Kuranko (tribal language at Kamaron) conversations between the mission helpers close by, and people from town stopping by. Even though I failed to make rapid progress in language study, observing operations of another mission station furnished a beneficial learning experience.

The week before Christmas, Jake and Harv returned to take both families to Freetown for a supply trip. To help break up the tiresome ride to Magburaka, we spent the first night in Ganya. Wanting to start early the next morning but having no alarm clock, Jake became inspired as he sat looking at our cuckoo clock on the wall.

After measuring the length the weight had moved in one hour, then multiplying that distance by the amount of hours we wanted to sleep, Jake thought he had a solution. At the designated spot, he placed a spoon on top of a tin can so that the clock weight would knock the spoon onto the cement floor. Surely, the noise would arouse at least one of us.

Necessity may be the mother of invention in some cases. But the next morning, as we drove up the hill on the other side of the river later than we had planned, we knew Jake's cuckoo alarm would never be patented.

Expected hot temperatures greeted us in Freetown—so hot that Patsy and Jewel soon became peppered with prickly heat. Each day followed the same pattern: shopping for provisions during the day, going from shop to shop trying to locate what we needed, then in the late afternoon, driving to the ocean and staying until dark.

Lumley Beach offered miles of soft, white sand, dashing waves, and fresh ocean air with all the privacy one could wish for. We relaxed in that peaceful setting each evening while the children enjoyed the sand and surf.

Nights at the mission apartment failed to provide deep, restful sleep. Radios blared, dogs barked, and people talked loudly. By early morning, as a rooster crowed and the paper boy made his walk up and down the street shouting, "Daily Mail! Daily Mail!" in Creole, our drowsy minds could project only one thought: Did these people ever sleep? If so, it must have been in the daytime.

One night, a group of Africans roamed the streets attempting to play Christmas carols on wind instruments. The blaring, slurring, off-key notes made us laugh when we first heard them coming. But as they drew nearer, it became obvious the would be band members had an intoxication problem. Reportedly, during World War II, soldiers had introduced Christmas as a holiday for drinking and carousing. The tipsy band represented the many people who knew only that false concept of the Christmas season. How sad! How people needed to find the real celebration of Christmas: the Christ Child.

Typical of a provision trip to Freetown, shopping took longer than we counted on. It never failed: the ship due in the next day or the day after should have on its cargo a needed item that came up listed as out of stock in every shop in town. At last, we finally purchased everything of major importance. Seldom could every item be located.

With the exception of leaving the ocean and its invigorating air, we gladly loaded the Red Jet and trailer. Jake and Ruth packed their yellow Jeep—better known as the Yellow Peril—and we headed for the hills. Jake had a business meeting on the way so Ruth and the children rode with us.

After turning off the main road, seven rivers had to be crossed before reaching the Kamaron station. Jake had constructed stick bridges barely wide enough for his Peril to cross, with the intention of discouraging Syrian traders from sending their lorries (British transport trucks) over the bridges. It made no difference to the drivers when they damaged a bridge, and never would they take any responsibility to repair the havoc they left behind. Keeping the bridges passable during the rainy season consumed enough of a missionary's time without maintaining them for lorries also. But even with that logical explanation in mind, the bridges looked frightfully narrow as the Jet tires crept cautiously across the rows of sticks.

At one crossing, everything seemed to be going fine, and then all at once—crack! The noise of breaking sticks caught our attention and took our breath. Fortunately, the front tires of the Jet had reached solid ground. But the trailer rested on its axle with one wheel hanging over the edge of the bridge, leaving all our provisions balanced in a precarious position in the slanting trailer.

This was a model example of a bush-country predicament, with no available wrecker service and not even a village nearby to find manpower assistance. It seemed only natural to turn to the bright side and be grateful that only the trailer extended over the side of the bridge and not the Jet. And even more, we felt extremely thankful the supplies had not been dumped into the river. Not yet, anyway.

But the problem remained—how to free the trailer from its trapped position without taking a chance of our provisions falling into the water. That particular river coursed at the bottom of a rather steep hill and a narrow dirt road wound up the hill hemmed in on both sides with dense vegetation. We all agreed we had landed in a difficult situation as we stood viewing the dilemma.

Then, someone spotted a small clearing about halfway up the hill. With that in mind, a plan took shape. Not certain whether his weight on the bridge would worsen the situation, Harv slowly maneuvered his way to the back of the Jet and unhitched the trailer. So far, so good. He then drove the Jet up the hill past the clearing.

There would be no siesta for us that afternoon. Instead, a tropical sun radiated its searing blaze as we carried the load from the trailer, box by box, up to the clearing. Then, Harv backed the Jet down to the river, struggled to rejoin the hitch to the trailer and pull it loose from the bridge. The motor sounded powerful enough to do the job as Harv tried over and over. But nothing happened. The trailer would not move an inch.

Ruth and I stood by, helplessly watching and praying. Suddenly, the trailer lunged free and leapt forward onto the bank. What a happy relief as we watched the Jet usher the trailer up the hill to the clearing. After the boxes were reloaded, we set off to face the next bridge, wondering what awaited us there.

The rest of the drive, however, progressed with no major incidents, all the way across the seventh bridge. Never had the Kamaron station looked more inviting to weary, dust-coated travelers as it did that evening. The children received priority attention, getting bathed, fed, and put to bed. Later, even though totally bushed, multiplied thanks for all the care and help received that day filled our prayers to our faithful Father.

Chapter 6: A Bewildered Bat

The morning after we returned from Freetown, Ruth and I entered into a Christmas rush that would equal any frenzied, last-minute preparation anywhere, even in America. Earlier, Dave and Eileen Calcutt—along with Eddie and Phyllis Smith, British professors at Forah Bay College in Freetown—had been invited to spend Christmas week at Kamaron. We had thought we would have sufficient time to prepare, but with our schedule thrown off by the delay in Freetown, three days of work had to be poured into one day. And what a day!

Ruth and I directed ourselves and our African workers all day. Our helpers took it in stride and seemed to enjoy sprucing up the house and grounds as they responded to our excitement in expecting company on the station for Christmas. By evening, the delicious scent of baked goods had trailed into every room of the mission house. Propped in one corner of the living room, a large, decorated tree branch adequately imitated the role of a Christmas tree. Even eleven-month-old Jewel sensed the special holiday spirit bubbling from everyone and fell into the excitement as we prepared to celebrate the first Christmas with our little daughter.

On Christmas Eve, the mission church at Kamaron observed the special event with the youth enacting the story of the birth of Jesus. The play, directed by a young African school teacher, presented a successful reminder of the true Christmas observance.

Christmas morning found the small mission house happily bulging with eight adults and six children. Fortunately, a "home on wheels" that Jake had constructed for Ruth and the children to travel along when he journeyed to other towns to evangelize provided overflow sleeping quarters that week.

With so many patrons sharing one bathroom, however, everyone had to keep in mind the golden rule when utilizing the facilities and not overstay a reasonable amount of time. The worker who carried water managed quadruple duty that week to keep enough water for bucket-flushing the stool and bucket-showering. To make a comfortable water temperature in the hanging spigot bucket, a tea kettle of hot water would be poured in and then the rest would be filled with cold water. The ability to take a shower with one bucket of water presented a challenge when we first arrived in the bush, but we found it could be done.

Following breakfast that morning, everyone gathered in the living room for our devotion time. Afterward, the young-sters provided us with lively entertainment as we watched them open gifts and play with new toys. In one package, Jewel found a stuffed teddy bear that sweetly tinkled the tune "Jesus Loves Me." From that night on, the new teddy remained in Jewel's crib where he took on his duty of bedtime companion.

Canned ham from Holland we had found in Freetown made our dinner seem identical to a stateside Christmas dinner. Delicacies from boxes we had received in the mail provided the finishing touches to the meal. Our group symbol-ized a happy adopted family as we surrounded the dinner table.

Even though enjoying our Christmas day to full measure, the heavy pace we had kept for several days eventually overtook my body. I managed to push it aside all morning, but during the meal, I had to excuse myself and take refuge in the bedroom. Nevertheless, listening to the lively conversation of the adults and the happy, excited children made it easier to forget my miserableness as I looked at the beams and dried grass above. A few hours of bed rest restored me back to the active list the next day.

During the week, reports reached Kamaron that elephants were damaging crops in a nearby region. It did not take long for the men to jump at the chance for a big game hunt. The British district commissioner had issued a high-powered rifle to Jake for such times when the Africans needed help to protect their crops. On the trail, the hunters spotted elephant tracks at different places, and after several miles of following, they finally sighted the originator of the tracks. But that elephant declined being killed by white hunters, and after catching their scent, he skillfully made an escape.

So it happened that every evening, the wives listened to the big game hunting tales of that day, along with anticipated optimism that tomorrow would be the day to shoot an elephant, for sure. That sort of tomorrow never materialized, however. Not that week, at least.

On New Year's Day, Jake directed games in town with the village children. Sack races seemed to be the favorite activity for the participants as well as the observers. Creativity controlled whatever entertainment the African children had. Probably the most well-known sport for the boys was to roll a large, homemade hoop by striking it with a stick. The ones who had mastered the act could keep the hoop rotating for quite a distance before it finally fell to the ground.

Some of the village children possessed surprising talent. Once, a boy at Ganya showed us a model lorry he had made with sticks. During the farming season, however, the children had assigned work along with the adults, leaving no time for play. Consequently, the games played on New Year's Day brought something special to a group of children who never had experienced the thrill of receiving gifts and toys for Christmas or birthdays.

In fact, celebrating birthdays never happened, since actual dates of birth were not known. The approximate age of a person had to be calculated. But we did know Jewel's date of birth, and on the morning of the third of January, Dave Calcutt demonstrated his cake decorating talent to celebrate her first birthday.

Unfortunately, Jewel could not enjoy her first birthday completely. On our way back from Freetown, we had a government doctor vaccinate her for smallpox, and in a few days, a strong reaction started. The spot on the front of her upper leg where the injection had been placed became as large as a silver dollar. Other sores developed on her body, and she ran a fever for several days.

Later, we heard that other doctors in Sierra Leone had reported reactions and an investigation revealed the serum—which came from Nigeria— had mistakenly been made ten times stronger than normal. Consequently, Jewel suffered through a few weeks of misery. And to add more discomfort, she cut four more teeth during that time. Even worse, because of the seeping sores, her fun times in the pink, plastic bathtub had to be substituted with less fun sponge baths.

So toddler life suddenly became difficult for the little one-year-old. Nevertheless, an inbred spunkiness surfaced, causing her to come through with some smiles and laughs, even when the sores started to dry and itch. Happy shouts of glee from Miss Toosie celebrated the day she splashed in her pink tub once again.

After our friends returned to Freetown, Jake and Harv went back to Ganya to finish the work on the house, and a disappointing, post-holiday sentiment invaded the Kamaron house after everyone had gone. Going back to kerosene lamps seemed a bit dull the first night. Also, the living room took on an emptiness after the Christmas decorations had been removed. With the holidays over, Ruth and I found ourselves again in the daily routine of Calvert lessons and Yalunka phrases.

But life would not remain without stimulation for long. First, an uninvited guest moved in to share the mission house with us. The intruder happened to be a bat, and needless to say, he did liven up our evenings. Apparently, the bat had entered under the low-hanging grass roof, then up over the wall into the house. Certainly, the bat found no more delight about his state of captivity than we did. During the daytime, he bedded down and slept somewhere in the grass roof. By evening, Mr. Bat came to life and began his nightly flight.

Many nights during her bout of battling the smallpox vaccination, Jewel remained restless and upset with a hurting tummy, and every so often, she woke up crying. Since we had no rocking chair, if she did not settle back to sleep with gentle patting, I walked her about the bedroom until she relaxed into sleep again.

Meanwhile, the bat darted back and forth across the top of the room partitions from one side of the house to the other. Watching his moving shadow against the grass roof, I hoped his sonar operated properly to keep him in a high flight pattern. I was certainly not interested in having my head become a landing pad. More than once, at about the time Jewel fell asleep and I started to slip her back into her crib, Mr. Bat took a low swoop, causing my reflexes to startle her awake again. This, in turn, called for more walking while I mentally dispatched to the bewildered bat what I thought of him for complicating our nights even more.

When the workers finally succeeded in chasing the bat from the house, I don't know who rejoiced more, the freed bat or the people he left behind. We certainly had no lonely spot for him the first evening after he had been evicted, nor ever after.

While staying at Kamaron, I became better informed on African tribal customs. On certain nights, we could hear the "men's devil" (so called by the people) chanting and blowing on reeds in town. Ruth explained that when this "devil" came out each month, all the women and children ran to hide. Terrible things would happen to them should they be seen by the devil-man—so they were taught.

One night, the eerie sounds drew closer as the devil must have been roaming near the edge of town. It prompted me to be more grateful for having been born in a country free from such intimidation as the devil-man imposed on helpless women and children.

Once, at Magburaka, I experienced a closer encounter with one such devil-man while taking a walk with Ester Grody, a mission nurse. Our mission held the policy to avoid the devils whenever possible. But that day, when one unexpectedly came around a corner, we either had to meet or deliberately turn around and go back the way we had come from, making it appear to the man behind the hideous mask that we feared him. Esther, previously a nurse in the Navy, did not care to grant him that satisfaction, and she quietly suggested, "Keep walking and look straight ahead."

As we passed within a few feet, I could feel the penetrating glares of the devil-man and his associates. We were sure that their egos gained no pleasure that the two white women showed no fear of the devil-man and his fierce appearance as we continued down the street looking straight ahead.

None of our mission staff ever met with harm from the devil-men, with the exception of the time when a new arrival to the country snapped a picture of one, not having been instructed yet that it was not a wise thing to do. Immediately, he found himself tousled by the angered devil-man as he lunged for the camera. Most Africans readily cooperated to pose for pictures, some requesting coins to compensate their "services." But not the devils! They vehemently refused to be photographed.

The Kuranko people seemed not to be as deeply involved in witchcraft as some other tribal groups. Information leaked out from time to time, however, that the practice of sacrificing humans still existed on occasions. The government did not hear directly of those inside stories because the people feared being informers. Also, the Kuranko people did not always execute punishment publicly. Instead, many times, someone under suspicion or known to have committed a crime such as human sacrifice suddenly took sick and died. Poison quietly revenged without a trial or defense attorney. Many incidents proved how evil powers continued to weave a spell around the people, keeping them as trapped as a man wrapped in the death grip of a cobra.

Important cultural rituals took place annually at separate times when the boys and girls became of age (around twelve years old) and underwent circumcision rites at a secret location somewhere in the bush. They remained in seclusion a number of days, undergoing instruction and enduring the painful rituals of the tribal customs. Following this circumcision bush experience, the boys and girls of only a few days before, returned to their villages from then on regarded as men and women in the eyes of the community.

Prior to the bush rites, workers who were candidates dressed in female clothing for a certain number of days. The feminine garb created an amusing appearance, causing embarrassment to some. A motive existed for the custom in that being dressed like a woman represented the males as weak—like women—before they entered the circumcision bush. But following the rituals, they returned as men, dressed as men.

Walking through town on the dirt path to church one Sunday morning, Ruth and I came upon a group of women involved in prepping some girls for their scheduled time at the secret bush rituals. Continuous beating of drums all night had preceded the occasion. Then, at dawn, the women started a monotonous singsong chant in the customary minor key.

By the time we walked by, their emotions had become elevated to near a frenzied state. The leaders of the party stood out, easily recognized from the others. With faces painted white, each held in her mouth a stem with the flower dangling below her chin. I do not know what the flowers signified, but they looked too pretty and innocent to be used in such a setting. The eyes of the women caught my attention—glazed, satanic eyes widening with hostility as we walked by. Obviously, the performance was not under the direction of good angels on a mission from heaven.

Fortunately, the Kamaron Christians loved to sing with enthusiasm. And sing they did, that Sunday morning as they sat on backless benches made of boards resting on cement blocks in their open, grass-roofed church. The joyful songs of the redeemed prevailed over the noise from the celebration in town. During the message, however, the wild chanting and cries could be heard again, reminding us of the sharp variance between heathen and Christian, darkness and Light.

As we neared the group again, on our way home, the head women stepped into the path ahead of us, waving sticks and shouting at us. Even though I did not understand the conversation as Ruth attempted to reason with them, it was easily detected that the leaders were not in a friendly state of mind. Ruth explained that the women were demanding a dash of money before they would let us pass. But the only money she had with her was the scant offering from the service—money the Christians sacrificially gave for repairs on their primitive church structure.

"I'm certainly not going to give it to them," Ruth declared. "Keep moving. We're going to hold our own with them!"

And so we continued to edge forward on the dirt path, Ruth carrying Patsy and me pushing Jewel in her stroller. We had to admit, the women did render a sensational performance and we were not certain for a while if they would withdraw their position. Finally, although still shouting at us, they backed off to the side as they realized we would not relent to their threats.

Back at the mission house, Ruth triumphantly deposited the coins in a box where the church offerings were being saved. We felt thankful to be home. But the picture of the scene we witnessed that morning remained in my mind. And as Ruth told more information about the circumcision bush, I felt sorrier for the young girls we had seen standing near the women.

Because of infections from unsterile methods and even some cases of bleeding to death, missionaries tried to discourage the circumcision rituals. They attempted to convince the people that it would be safer to have a government or mission doctor take care of what, in a way, amounted to minor surgery. But the people presented their rebuttal that it had always been the way of the black man for boys and girls to go through the bush experience to step into adulthood. So it would remain.

I had no idea that a year later we were to experience, firsthand, the danger of the custom. When guns periodically fired in Ganya that day, we listened to the explanation from one of the workers. The bush ritual for girls had been performed, and some girls were hemorrhaging at the bush site. When native methods failed to help, the gunfire signaled that nothing more remained to be done—death would certainly follow. Out of desperation only, the women in charge accepted Harv's offer of medical assistance. Even though the help was crude compared to hospital emergency treatment, Harv had some experience from having been in the Medical Corps during his service time in the Navy.

With what Harv could suggest and with prayer, the girls did recover, and the gunshots ceased. Yet, talking the people out of performing the same ceremonies in the same manner the next time would be as impossible as talking them out of breathing.

At one longer-established station, a retreat held for the Christian women and girls during the same time as the circumcision bush initiated a new experience of enriching Christian fellowship—so different from the bush ordeal. We hopefully waited for the time when the Kuranko and Yalunka women would be ready to take such a step.

At Kamaron one day, our early afternoon siesta suddenly became interrupted by the sound of unearthly laughter and singing. Coming from our bedrooms at opposite ends of the house to see what the commotion was about, Ruth and I landed at the living room door at the same time.

Only a few feet from the house, a bizarre scene caught our attention. A grown man, doubled over, rolled across the lawn like a large beach ball. As he rotated back and forth, he repeatedly chanted a weird melody. At first, we attributed too much palm wine as the probable cause for his activity. But the longer we watched, we decided his problem might go deeper than palm wine intoxication.

Fortunately, we were not alone, even though the mission workers happened to be in town taking their siesta break. Being in the area on business, the D.C. (British district commissioner) had left his loads stored on the mission veranda with an African guard to protect them. Occasionally, the newcomer paused, stopped rolling and singing, threw back his head, and let out a laugh that made the eyes of the poor guard almost bounce from their sockets! We did not know if the performer realized he had an audience or not, but Ruth and I aimed to stay out of sight. The uniformed guard shifted uneasily from one foot to the other, keeping his eyes riveted to the psychotic actions out on the lawn.

After a time, the man stopped rolling and quietly sat on the ground looking around. He watched the workers as they walked single file on the path from town. They, in turn, cautiously eyed him as they approached the house. Sihom, Ruth's cook, motioned her to the back of the house where he gave a quick news brief regarding the stories that circulated through town concerning the stranger on the front lawn. During the full moon, he supposedly became so violent that he had to be bound with chains in the town where he lived. Sihom emphasized the fact that at times, he had been known to break loose from the chains.

Since the visitor hailed from another town, Ruth did not know if the reports presented factual or exaggerated data after being passed on from person to person. Having witnessed his earlier behavior in the lawn, it seemed possible the information could be at least partly accurate, even though at that moment, he remained as quiet as a tamed lion, still sitting on the ground eyeing the activity on the compound.

Later, when the D.C. returned for his belongings and heard the report from his guard, he instructed the soldiers with him to order the stranger to leave. Reluctantly, the man started walking down the lane muttering to himself and turning to look back every few steps.

Before the D.C. started off with his men and belongings, Ruth and I received a sound lecture about the risk American missionary women took by staying alone on their stations. After he had gone, we could only shrug our shoulders and use the well-worn Creole phrase, "How fer do?" (What can I say or do?) Inevitably, there would always be times when we would remain alone—an inescapable, unwritten job description for the women missionaries. Of course, we knew our courage came from the Great Shepard and His presence.

Sometime during that night, a noise outside the window startled me to a sitting position. What could it be? It stopped, and everything was quiet. Then, I heard it again! I slipped out from under the mosquito netting and felt my way across the living room, aided by the dim light from the low-burning lantern in the other bedroom where Ruth and her children slept.

By the time I awakened Ruth, everything was quiet again. When she asked what it sounded like, the best description I could offer was something like a chain being dragged over the cement floor of the veranda. We listened in silence for several minutes—not a sound. Even the townspeople remained quiet that dark night with no moon showing.

But while we waited, listening for the noise on the veranda, suddenly something crashed to the floor in the store-room, located adjacent to the living room. Both our minds sped on the same course—the stranger! He had not been pleased when ordered away by the D.C. Perhaps he had come back and climbed up through the space between the overhanging thatched roof to the top of the wall and dropped down into the storeroom.

Huddled together in the dimly-lit living room, whispering, we tried to plan how we could summon help from town. We were too far away for screams to be heard. Besides, neither of us thought we could manage a scream at that point away. Someone suggested blowing Harv's trumpet. If any of the workers heard it, they might surmise that something could be wrong at the mission. We even removed the trumpet from the case. But since neither of us knew how to play, we could not rouse even a peep from the horn. Another sound from the storeroom made us decide we needed to find the source of the noise on the other side of the wall. If the man had returned, we should know before he managed to climb over the wall into the living room. We could take the children out the front door and run to town, if necessary. Ruth went to waken her son Gary. When they returned, I helped boost Gary up on Ruth's shoulders for him to look over the top of the wall. We worked as silently as professional secret agents. Gary held a torch in one hand with instructions to turn it on as soon as he reached the top. On went the light—a pause—then Gary exclaimed, "The only thing I see are two rats running!"

Overwhelmed with relief, we sat down and laughed to the point of tears at what had seemed a potentially serious situation instantly turning into a comical conclusion. Probably never in history had two women been so grateful to be told they had two rats in the house. I had to wonder if our heavenly Keeper smiled while watching that scenario unfold for us.

The storeroom episode had been solved, but the noise on the veranda remained a mystery. No chain or any other clue could be seen when I looked around the next morning. Ruth and I decided the D.C. would never hear the story about the events of that night at the Kamaron mission house. Never!

Chapter 7: Grandaddy Elephant

Replacing the roof on the Ganya house moved as slowly as any building project in Africa ever moved—perhaps a little slower. And it seemed the pace of progress decelerated even more as the work neared completion. In American society, it is possible to suffer hypertension from fast-paced living. In African society, Americans found it possible to suffer the same ailment because of slow-paced advancement.

Delays and more delays had to be accepted with some degree of cheerfulness to avoid becoming overly frustrated, while total perfection had to be tossed aside at times to maintain sanity. Why did it matter if a newly-built wall did not measure straight to the line of the white man? To the African inexperienced at building rectangular structures, it looked "fine-fine."

Furthermore, if the wall were torn down and reconstructed, the second attempt might lean just as much, only in another direction. Hence, the standby expression "how-for-do" might pass through the white man's mind, followed with a verbal "lef-em." In other words, it's hopeless; leave it as it is. Some attempts at proper building had to be maintained, however, and somehow, the completed building always looked surprisingly fine in bush country Africa.

The day Jake and Harv arrived with the news that the aluminum roofing finally covered the Ganya house called for celebration, or so Ruth and I thought. But following the good news about the house, bad news instantly wiped away thoughts of celebrating. Before Jake and Harv returned to Kamaron, they went to Kabala to pick up mail and found only three letters waiting for them. It had been a month since the last mail run, and to see such a small amount of letters for two families created a strong sense of frustration. To live in a country where mail is delivered six days out of seven makes it difficult to appreciate the value of the expected service. But in developing countries of the world, mail is never taken for granted.

Though we all felt disappointed with the scant amount of mail, the reason for the mail not coming through created a sobering atmosphere. Reports of strikes and rioting in Freetown had reached Kabala, with accounts that over twenty people had been killed in the chaos. How fast or how far into the interior the trouble might spread, no one could predict at that point.

Even though we did not find ourselves in any prospective danger, our minds began to speculate how we would react should the trouble spread throughout the country. Starting back with the first-century church, many missionaries have faced the dilemma of whether to evacuate and then return when peace is restored, or remain with the people no matter what happens.

Another aspect to consider, should weapons ever be used as threatening measures to protect missionary families in the event of a surprise attack? We agreed unanimously that our answer to the latter would be negative, since a missionary leveling a gun at nationals would hardly portray the scriptural image of a messenger of the Gospel.

Looking down at Jewel Kay, so small and helpless, I knew what my maternal instinct would suggest regarding staying or leaving should that decision even need to be made. But for then, we realized the only course of action would be to make it a matter of prayer and trust our Lord Jesus to guard and guide.

Fortunately, the outbreak in Freetown soon quieted. We rejoiced when reports trekked upcountry, via verbal express, that the city had returned to normal. We were especially glad to know the Calcutt and Smith families were free to leave their homes to buy food supplies. Just as seeing a rainbow after the storm, so we returned to the work at hand with lighter hearts.

Unlike some African countries, Sierra Leone had progressed with a relatively smooth stride as twentieth-century changes occurred. Even a few years later, the turn to independence took place without full-blown strife. Isolated trouble spots brought concern at times, but never an all-out problem throughout the country, until many years later. Illiteracy among the tribal people represented a barrier to both government and mission workers. Not only did it hold back the development of the country, but also the progress of mission work.

With the nationals needing the Bible, Christian literature, and songs in their vernacular, it necessitated that they learn to read those strange marks on paper that eventually they would recognize as words. Translating the language, transcribing primers, and then teaching the people to read, presented a toilsome job that required perseverance.

The British government officials recognized the importance of establishing schools for the children, even in some villages located off the beaten paths. Being limited with trained

African personnel, the government could only oversee schools in larger towns.

Finally, an agreement resolved the problem in that the government would fund building and operating expenses of schools in a few smaller towns, with the mission authorized to supervise construction and management of the schools. This method made it possible for the mission to hire Christian teachers, when available, and to include religion education instruction in the curriculum—a golden opportunity.

When Jake received as assignment to supervise building a primary school in Kuranko village, located fifteen miles from Kamaron, Harv was asked to help with the main structure before we returned to Ganya. With the village not accessible by vehicle, planning became more involved. The Red Jet and trailer transported supplies to Kamaron, but from there, the Jet stood as useless as a freighter stuck on a sandbar. Cement, other building materials, and equipment had to be carried the rest of the way via human head-loads. Muscles tightened firmly that morning as each carrier lifted his fifty-pound load from the ground and adjusted the weight on top his head.

Then, one by one, African bodies moved off in single file, the only noise being the thud of bare feet hitting the beaten, dirt path. As I watched the long line of carriers move out of sight, I reminded myself to be grateful for our Red Jet and trailer, even though they did create problems at times.

For missionaries located at stations where roads did not exist yet, trekking with carriers still served as their only means

114

of transportation. Riding in rope or cloth made hammocks attached to poles that rested on shoulders of hired carriers served as their mode of travel, especially for the women and children.

Going out to the veranda one afternoon to check the whereabouts of Jewel, I observed an enactment of that means of transportation taking place on the front lawn. Gary and Steve had dragged out an old hammock from past years and brought together a trekking party with Patsy and Jewel happily riding as passengers in the hammock. I smiled at the cute scene until the expedition drew closer. Then I realized the condition of the dirty, worn hammock as well as the unwashed bodies of the boy carriers from town helping with the travel.

With the children enjoying such a great time playing together, how could a concerned mother become a killjoy by

stepping in and halting the fun? Instead, I returned the smiles and waves of the happy trekking party and went back into the

nce again trusting the heavenly Father to protect my
ughter amidst the unhealthy sides of Africa.

The playful, fun times of the children before bedtime
often enlivened what otherwise would have been uneventful
evenings. One night, as the hanging oil lantern threw light over
the living room, Ruth and I sat knitting, while the youngsters
created their own entertainment. Suddenly, Patsy found a new
game to play with Jewel. Jumping out from under a chair or
from behind a door yelling, "Boo!" flung Jewel into hysterics.
Once, she became so tickled at Patsy, Jewel tumbled over onto
the floor, shaking with laughter. That, in turn, caused all of us to
join the giggle party. It became hilarious! The laughter of the
children acted like medicine to Ruth and me, helping us forget
the troubles we had been experiencing of upset stomachs, fevers,
and an infectious eye disorder running its course among us at
the time.

Reports kept coming to Kamaron that an elephant
continued to destroy crops in nearby villages. Since the villagers
never had a greater harvest than what was needed for survival,
to have their food supply depleted by the elephant would im-
pose a major hardship of hunger and possible starvation for
some. In desperation, the villagers sent for Pa Schierling to
come and kill the monster that persisted in harassing them. Jake
and Harv did not require a large amount of persuasion to answer
the call for help.

So it happened that Jake, Harv, and their guide, known
as Hunter Bala, went in search of the bull elephant described as

116

being "huge." Hunter Bala handled a gun well, considering he had only one hand to work with. African hunters used muskets for guns, loading the gun powder by hand. For bullets, they might use nuts, bolts, ball bearings—anything that would fit into the gun barrel. That, among other reasons, explained why a wrecked or broken-down truck left along the roadside soon became stripped of everything removable.

Now and then, a hunter became overly enthused with the amount of gun powder employed, resulting in a hand or even an arm being blown off. That explained how Hunter Bala had lost part of one arm. Hence, amongst themselves, the mission personnel often referred to him as One Arm Bala.

Before starting out in pursuit of wild game, pagan hunters performed a dance ritual around an idol to bring them protection and good fortune on their hunt—so they thought. Usually, a smaller animal would be sacrificed and the blood poured over the idol. Our three hunters declined this ritual and prepared with prayers to our heavenly Father.

While trudging cautiously through thick swamp, brushing off ants and swatting at mosquitoes, the men's excitement increased as Bala quietly informed them that the elephant tracks they followed seemed larger than any he had ever trailed before. Wandering alone, an old bull evidently had been forsaken by his herd, as is the custom of elephants.

A breeze blew against their faces, helping only a little to cool the hunters in the muggy hotness of the swampy region. Then, suddenly, they spotted him about twenty-five feet away— a huge, granddaddy elephant, every bit as large as reported!

Hardly daring to breathe, Jake and Harv cocked their guns and aimed below the ears, for his lungs. Eight shots thundered. The elephant screamed and trampled through the tall bush in a frightened raged, tearing down small trees and bushes as he went. Warily, the men followed his bloody path.

About an hour later, Jake and Harv caught sight of their wounded prey, still standing, but breathing heavily. Twelve more shots torpedoed through the thick hide before the monster finally fell to the ground, dead. Eight miles away at the Kamaron mission house, the yard workers heard the reports from the .404 and .375 caliber rifles.

Cooking fires flickered in the darkness by the time the men drove into Kamaron that evening. The people became ecstatic! In the distance, we could hear the excited welcome as the villagers greeted the hunters. It had to mean one thing: the men returned from the hunt as victors.

Driving down the lane to the mission a few minutes later, Jake and Harv shouted like school boys after just winning a championship game. Running behind the Yellow Peril, many children and adults cheered the white men who had not only rescued farm crops from the giant elephant but also provided the villagers with more meat than they had ever seen before and probably would ever see again.

Bright and early the following morning, Jake and Harv returned to the scene of the kill to officially start the butchering. The enormous elephant reached eight feet high from the ground where he lay to the top of his stomach. After Jake and Harv had taken pictures and obtained the portions they wanted, they turned the rest over to the mob of people gathered from several villages for their share of the prized meat. When the men walked away, knives were slashing into the animal at every angle as voices grew louder with excitement. A few squabbles began to develop when some claimed more than their allotment. Not one scrap of the animal would be considered waste. Following customary procedure, since the trunk represented the best part of the elephant meat, Jake sent a dash of the trunk to the town chief. Another part of the trunk landed in Ruth's pressure cooker for a long, extensive cooking.

The British District Commissioner judged the age of the elephant to be over one hundred years. Today, however, some people believe elephants cannot live past sixty to eighty years. Whether this Granddaddy had reached sixty, eighty, or more, to me, the meat seemed well over a century in age as I attempted to chew it.

Jake stopped gnawing on the meat in his mouth long enough to state, "It doesn't taste bad!" Harv agreed as he took another bite, smothered with ketchup. After all, hunters should enjoy their game. Ruth and I honestly admitted that we preferred the meat from the deer the men had killed some days earlier.

African elephants have very large feet. At Jake's suggestion, after the feet had been cleaned, Harv dried them to be used as souvenir wastebaskets. No arguments developed over who would own the finished product. Be they human or elephant, feet are still feet.

The tusks, however, presented a more interesting keepsake. One tusk weighed seventy-four pounds and measured six feet long. But something had happened to the other one, as part of  it was missing. At that time, a professional hunter held the record in Sierra Leone with an eighty-pound tusk. Nevertheless, Jake and Harv reveled in the size of their spoil.

Several days later, the Red Jet labored with a heavy load as Harv and I drove to Ganya. When we arrived home, the house looked so different. Two rows of mud blocks added to the top of the walls and shining aluminum roofing replacing the thatch resulted in a striking transformation. The change made the interior much brighter and also drier with the extra ventilation. Eliminating musty smells became easier and almost complete, except during the height of the rainy season. Even then, we enjoyed a vast improvement over the former way of living.

Plastering and whitewashing both inside and outside walls brought additional improvement later on. Two coats of paint on the living room and dining area not only added to the appearance, it also helped buffer the results of scratches and bruises Jewel received from tumbles. Cement floors made life a little more difficult for a toddler and required many hugs and kisses to soothe the injuries.

Adjusting to life without her Kamaron playmates brought about a new pastime for little Miss Toosie. Whenever she heard people calling or talking in the valley, she rushed to the doorway and yelled jabber-talk to them. Her soft voice did not carry that far, naturally, but she made strong attempts to communicate from the hilltop.

The people reacted with astonishment to see Jewel walking when we returned from Kamaron. Their children seldom walked before two years—some not that soon. The youngsters continued to be nursed by their mothers until they did start to walk. Bala Cook's wife, Pasi, had a son a little older than Jewel who had made no attempt to walk yet. When Pasi watched Jewel toddling about, she clicked her tongue and followed with, "Ayeee," to show her amazement.

Bokari often reasoned, "Toosie be strong because you give *seena* [medicine] to her every day." No doubt it helped, but try to explain the difference between vitamins and medicine to someone who had never heard of vitamins before. They did come from a bottle, and to him, that spelled seena.

Grandpa and Grandma Ford kept Jewel supplied with vitamins from the States via airmail, or when possible, sent them with missionaries coming to Sierra Leone. Unfortunately, the usefulness of a vitamin-mineral supplement for ourselves never occurred to us. I am sure it could have helped to combat diseases and pressures of tropical living.

Jewel's advancement to the walking stage created other problems, as most parents discover the case to be. Since we did not have screen doors, we barricaded the doorways during the day to keep Jewel inside. At first, stepping over the obstructions became a slight irritation to Bala and Bokari—or so it seemed to register on their faces. Nevertheless, because of their fondness for the little girl, they did the annoying exercise without voicing complaints.

Then came the day when a blockade appeared at the kitchen door also. Bala and Bokari found it easier to keep Miss Curious out of the kitchen than to worry about her being burned by hot coals at the open firebox of the stove.

Somewhere in the past, through the years of being around missionaries, Bala had picked up the word "humbug," and everything that presented a nuisance to him became a humbug. Accurate usage or not, the word remained a regular standby for Bala. "Toosie be too much humbug!" he would say at times, as he guided her back to the house from the kitchen area.

The new veranda Jake had engineered along the front of the house added an ideal place for Jewel to play while I studied language. Eventually, she learned to pull herself to the top and walk along the ledge of mud blocks that skirted the edge of the veranda. She seldom fell, but that favorite stunt explained the origin of a permanent scar on Jewel's upper lip. Trying to keep her from climbing stood equivalent to preventing a monkey from mounting higher.

Likewise came the water fad, which ran a close second to the climbing craze. Since the bathroom stool had been constructed of cement and flushed by pouring in water, we kept two buckets filled with water ready for use. Once, I went to the bathroom where Harv stood shaving and asked, "Have you seen Jewel?"

"She's right here with me-e-e," he replied as he turned and our eyes fell on Jewel, standing on the other side of her Daddy—in one of the buckets of water. Not only was Jewel in the water, but her little white Jumping Jack shoes had gone in with her.

They happened to be the shoes I so diligently polished every day to help preserve them, since we had taken only one pair of shoes for each size. After that dunking, the shoes lacked the soft flexibility they had before, and I eagerly waited for Jewel to grow into the next size.

During the dry season, our noses and throats felt the results of the fine dust in the air blown by the harmattan winds from the Sahara Desert. The nights became comfortably cool, however, even requiring blankets. By the end of February, days became warmer and during March, temperatures rose dramatically, with prickly heat frequently part of the package. Also during March, the first rains of the changing season began to arrive, often bringing forceful tropical storms.

Since they plywood ceilings had not been installed yet, the deafening noise from a heavy rain on the aluminum roofing made conversation impossible without almost shouting. It created a new experience for a toddler, and during those first downpours, she sought the refuge of Daddy or Mommy's arms until the storm passed.

The fifty-five-gallon metal drums we had packed with supplies conveniently caught water rushing from the sloping veranda roof during the rains. One tropical downpour would fill three drums. Rain water looked so refreshingly clean after using discolored river water during the last weeks of the dry season.

To keep the water clean, the workers had instructions to place lids on the water drums. But like most other rules, the observance of that one fell into a hit-or-miss fashion. And the chronic explanation from the workers remained the same: "I done forget!"

A drum full of water seemed to be an open invitation for one small person standing on the veranda ledge to toss things into. The distance to the drum made it impossible for Jewel to fall in, but not too far to throw objects. Usually, it was a toy that went in, but when a Bible sank to its death one day, corporal punishment appeared necessary. Following a spanking, the helpers discreetly held off immediate sympathy. But as soon as tears dried, they showered the little Toosie with noticeable attention. Even Sparky the dog, showed restlessness during such discipline sessions. For certain, Jewel did possess a loyal backing from all the crew on the mission hill.

Chapter 8: A Supply of Joy

In March, we started to prepare for the annual confer-ence of our mission staff at Magburaka. Searching through the storage drums to find new clothing for Jewel turned out to be more exciting than shopping in a store. While rummaging, I also found things I had forgotten about packing that added a homier atmosphere to the house—curtains, dollies, throw rugs, pictures, and other knickknacks. Uncovering a pair of red sandals, I could hardly wait to try them on Jewel when she awoke from her nap. They turned out to be a snug fit, but at least she would be able to use them for dressier occasions at the conference.

After having worn only supportive baby shoes, the low-cut sandals felt so strange to Jewel that when she first attempted to walk, she lifted each foot high in the air before stepping down, like a prancing majorette. Miss Toosie became so engrossed with a "what's-this-all-about" expression, she did not even notice us laughing at her performance.

After all mission personnel gathered at Magburaka, judging who enjoyed being together the more—the children or the adults—made a difficult assignment. What a time of fellow-ship we launched into, from catching up on news of each family and station, to enjoying devotional services conducted in Eng-lish. People did not always agree about policies and business matters during the conference sessions, but after meetings adjourned, differences faded into the background and a healthy, family atmosphere prevailed.

One day, we assembled a special dinner for that evening, complete with candles and decorations. After bush living, the festive affair—with everybody dressed in their best wash-and-wear—seemed to zone in on something slightly similar to a Stateside banquet. When one man saw Jewel in her blue, ruffled party dress, he said, "You look just like a bridesmaid." But the fourteen-month-old walked on past, completely oblivious to any flattery amidst the excitement of being around so many people.

Two realities to expect at the Magburaka station were humid heat and army ants. At times, usually following a rain, a thick line of ants marched across the lawn kept in formation by the larger soldier ants. The older children knew to watch for the invaders and avoid them. Now and then, however, a smaller child wandered into an army of ants and immediate outcries could be heard summoning for help. Whoever reached the victim first lifted the child away from the enemy line, stripped off clothing as quickly as possible, and removed the biting insects.

Such became Jewel's misfortune one afternoon when she stepped into the midst of an ant army out on maneuvers. Gratefully, I happened to be nearby and rushed to her rescue as soon as she started to cry. It was a traumatic introduction to the painful bites of driver ants, but Jewel quickly recovered after a heavy dosage of hugs and kisses.

The experiences at Magburaka helped prepare us for an invasion of marching ants some time later at Ganya. Late one evening, when I noticed a dark line moving in under the door, both Harv and I flew into action. I swept the ant troops out the door as fast as they entered while Harv hurried to the storage shed to get a can of kerosene. Starting a small fire drove the ants into a huddle at one end of the veranda, where Harv sprinkled kerosene on them and tossed a burning match onto the pile. So ended the march of one army of ants! It seemed a radical extinction, but fire was the only available weapon to keep the army from raiding through the house. The men at Magburaka used a blowtorch for a weapon, but Harv did not own one.

The next morning, our workers "Ay-ee-ed" at the huge pile of charred, lifeless ants on the veranda. Had they been flying ants—a different species that appeared for a few nights at the beginning of rainy season—the workers would not have appreciated the waste. What candy bars are to chocolate lovers, so flying ants are to Africans in the bush.

Those delicacies became an easy catch since after dark, flying ants can be attracted with a light, and for some reason, their wings drop off when touched. So during the season of flying ants, our workers borrowed a lantern from us and enjoyed a "fine-fine chop" (delicious meal. Some of the ants never made it to the evening cooking fires because munching on them raw also provided a special treat that could not be resisted.

The days at the conference had challenged and inspired us, and we found ourselves ready to return to our stations, even though it was difficult to drive away from the hearty fellowship we relished so much. Leaving the suffocating heat at Magburaka, however, posed no difficulty to us.

The two workers that had accompanied us to help with kitchen duties, laundry, and to watch Jewel at times had been ready to return to Ganya since the day we arrived at Magburaka. They didn't like the heat or having a different schedule, but primarily, being away from home in another tribal setting made the Yalunka helpers unhappy campers.

Harv had pampered them with dashes (gifts) and even bought canned fish for their rice, which provided luxury eating by their standards. But nothing helped. Long faces extended longer each day until the final day when they knew they would be traveling back to Yalunka country the next morning. Only then did smiles begin to appear.

Since Ken planned a business trip upcountry in a few days, we invited Pauline Wanner, a mission nurse, to travel to Ganya with us for a short visit. Ken would stop for her on his way back to Magburaka.

The trip had gone smoothly when we reached Falaba that day—not even one flat tire. We felt so grateful, for seldom did one travel African roads for several hours without encountering some sort of mishap. Unfortunately, even though it seemed we had it made, that trip would be no exception.

On the other side of Falaba, we found the first bridge on the Jeep Trail washed out with no way to cross the river. The water had risen too high to consider an attempt. What a frustrating situation—so near home, and yet so far.

After a fruitless discussion of what to do next, one of the helpers suddenly remembered that the original road had crossed the river at another point downstream. Heading in that direction, Harv and our two helpers scouted along the bank until they located the place. Crossing the river at that location did seem more possible, but to reach it, the Jet had to worm through tall, stiff elephant grass and prickly bushes.

Arriving at the spot, the Jet navigated through the water gallantly, but faltered when trying to climb the steep, muddy bank on the other side. With each try, the tires sank deeper into the mud. If we had not had the winch to rely upon, we realized we would have been in a hopeless situation.

After unwinding the cable, Harv fastened the end around a tree trunk that stood a few feet beyond the top of the bank. While the motor struggled, the cable slowly rewound. Up, up, and over the top of the bank the Jet crept until it rolled to a stop.

We soon discovered that we had rejoiced over the victory all too quickly, though. The cable of the winch had become so tight around the tree that, try as they would, neither

Harv nor the workers could loosen it. Obviously, the tree would have to be cut down to free the cable. The tree was not large, but the small hatchet Harv carried in the Jet was the only tool we had to work with.

Meanwhile, we faced another dilemma. Not much time remained before darkness would settle in, and if we did not get back to the Jeep Trail before then, it would be difficult, if not impossible, to find our way. And nobody wanted to spend the night where we were—certainly not our helpers. That fact motivated them to work like frantic beavers as they took turns chopping away at the tree trunk. Finally, it fell with a thud, releasing the winch cable.

As the Jet drove back onto the dirt road, with only shadows standing between light and darkness, prayers of gratitude welled up in our minds. We found ourselves struck with the silence of fatigue—even little Jewel, nestled on Pauline's lap.

As planned, Ken came our way a few days later, intending to reach Ganya in time to speak at an evening service. But the gathering had been over for some time when Ken's African assistant arrived at our door with the announcement that Pa Ken's truck was stuck in the river.

And so the Red Jet—with its priceless winch—roared across the valley to the rescue. After living in the bush for almost a year, we were ready to decorate the winch with a gold medal and title the bridges as our number one nuisance.

At about that time, another annoyance began to emerge in the form of the paramount chief at Falaba, Monga Fode. Being a typical African chief, he sported a harem of many wives— reportedly over forty—with flocks of children. One seldom saw a heavily-built African in that area, but Monga Fode was one of the few, and his appearance seemed to demand awesome respect from the Yalunka subjects.

The big chief seemed to play politics from time to time with the important Muslims who sat on his veranda day after day and the missionary family living in his chieftain. Without doubt, his real allegiance aligned with the Muslims, although one factor changed the picture somewhat. The Muslims did not own a vehicle that could transport Monga Fode about. Hence, the Red Jet gave us some advantage at times.

Since Ganya, the chief's hometown, was one of the larger towns in his chieftain, he often paid a visit there. In fact, he conveniently had one wife live in Ganya so that when he visited, it would not be necessary to carry along wife baggage. As the only means of transportation between Ganya and Falaba, the Red Jet became drafted for Royal Service. Whenever a messenger came from the chief with the request that he needed a ride to Ganya, Pa Ache had to drop whatever he might be involved in and travel to Falaba. However, we could not sense a genuine friendship developing with Monga Fode and influence him with the Gospel of Christ. Instead, it seemed apparent he merely used Harv for transportation.

African Bush courtesy required a periodic dash to the town chief and the paramount chief. One day, I impulsively felt motivated to drop the stick-to-culture routine and go Western.

The result produced a two-layer chocolate cake with piles of frosting. Should our anthropologist professor have witnessed my activity, I am certain it would have thrown him into cardiac arrest. When Harv delivered the surprise dash to the chief, I regretted that I could not secretly observe Monga Fode eat his first bite of chocolate cake.

Evidently, the way to a man's heart is via his stomach, even in bush country. From then on, the previously somber chief smiled his gratitude every time he saw us. Whether the broad, flashing grin signified friendship or merely a proposition for another cake, it seemed our relationship with the big chief took a turn for the better after that. One time, later on, he even demanded an apology from a Muslim school teacher when he became rude with us in the presence of the chief.

In the latter part of April, we once again loaded the Jet

and trailer and traveled to Freetown. The reason for that journey would deliver us a new family member—a future playmate for Jewel. Many times during the previous eight months, I had wondered how I could manage another baby so soon. But

as we bounced along on our way to the coast, anticipation to pick up "Jewel's baby" mounted with each mile.

Incidents of flat tires also mounted. In fact, there were so many, Harv ran out of tire patches and could obtain only bicycle patches from a trader in one small town. Through necessity, he proved that trailer tires could be repaired with bicycle tire patches if enough were used. Meanwhile, however, Harv's sense of humor threatened to go as flat as the tires he worked on.

Joe and Fran Shisler, with their children Paul and Elaine, were vacationing in Freetown and asked us to join them at the rented beach house where they stayed. Luxurious would not be used to describe the long, wood frame building that appeared aged and tired from years of standing unprotected against the salty ocean air. But regardless of appearance, it provided an ideal camp setting to relax in.

Since our lodge had no kitchen, we cooked on a two-burner kerosene stove in one of the bedrooms. A cement patio served as a dining/living area, with lawn chairs and two hammocks to lounge in. Old, rusty cots with straw mattresses substituted for beds. But we found going to sleep at night while listening to the splashing roar of the breaking surf granted the summit of tranquility in spite of the peaks and valleys so characteristic to straw mattresses.

The fresh barracuda fish we dined on almost every evening tasted like food from the table of a king after being without meat for some time before we left Ganya. And apparently Jewel thought the same. I could barely inspect the fish for bones fast enough to keep up with her appetite.

Some mornings, we watched tight-muscled African fishermen troll fishing nets to shore between two boats within sight of the beach house. Once, they brought in a man-sized tarpon—that produced many pounds of fish!

At that time, Sierra Leone did not have a residing American ambassador, and to cover special business details, the ambassador to Liberia occasionally visited Freetown. One morning, close to noon, Joe returned from shopping in town and sprang on us the announcement that he had met the American ambassador and his wife.

No one in our group, which also included Esther Grody who had joined us, gave much heed to Joe's news release.

Mildly sedated with relaxing, balmy sea breezes, his listeners did not respond to this newfound social status as Joe had expected. We did not respond, that is, until Joe's following statement: "I invited them to dinner tonight."

That brought each of us to life—like a reaction to the explosion of a bomb one hundred feet away! Entertain an ambassador at the beach house? One look around our seaside villa revealed that the clock had already struck midnight and the carriage had become the pumpkin again. A magic wand did not exist to set the place in order for entertaining dignitaries that very evening. *Joe, how could you?* Esther and I silently thought as our eyes met.

After the initial shock simmered down, we tried to assemble plans for the state dinner we suddenly found ourselves hosting. As we worked, Esther, Fran, and I joked that perhaps we could provide the explanation that our china, silver, and crystal had been misplaced—or lost at sea! Making light of the situation did help, as we prepared a two-course dinner on the two-burner kerosene stove, cleaned the plastic dishes, and polished the stainless utensils to look their best.

Then, about mid-afternoon, Joe and Fran came up with a fantastic idea. Missionaries they knew at another mission in Freetown owned a manually-turned ice cream maker, and perhaps we could borrow it for the evening. That idea saved the day—and the dinner party.

Our guests had not tasted homemade ice cream in years and obviously enjoyed the dessert more than enough to make the preparation well worth our efforts. Harv's knowledgeable discourse with the ambassador on the subject of sports provided a life jacket when our getting acquainted conversation began to run dry.

We had no idea how our distinguished visitors evaluated us as they drove the seven miles back to Freetown that night. At best, we still held the typical reputation as poor, but friendly, American missionaries. And at least they possessed a better understanding of our mission work after the visit.

The dinner did not impress Jewel any more than any other meal. To her, the guests were merely two faces to smile at—no more special than anyone else. What impressed her much more came on the day when we went shopping to replace the outgrown, red sandals.

In a British-owned department store restroom, Jewel observed the eighth wonder of the world as she watched a toilet flush. Little bush-girl stood fascinated watching the water spurt from the side and disappear down the hole with a gurgle. Totally captivated, she had to be gently pulled away from the scene after we already had flushed too many times.

When Nurse Esther, also trained and experienced in midwifery, found out Jewel had been a breech baby, she examined the position of the coming baby. As she expressed her concern that this baby could very possibly be situated for a breech birth also, I did not find the news too upsetting. After living beyond civilization and medical help for the past eight months, I felt certain the Lord would see me and the baby through the rest of the way.

During our stay at the beach, my favorite place for language study was swaying back and forth in one of the hammocks, occasionally scanning the far horizon for ships. Thus, stretched out in the hammock one afternoon trying to memorize another Yalunka phrase, suddenly the baby took a sharp lunge. *This little one is certainly becoming active*, I thought.

A few days later, during an appointment with the British doctor who would deliver the baby, I heard the welcome news that, in her opinion, we could expect a normal birth. That evening, I remembered the incident in the hammock, and the more I wondered about it, the more convinced I became that my gracious Father had flipped the position of the baby to spare the added ordeal and danger of a complicated birth. And it became even more appreciated when a European friend related to us the frightening outcome of a breech baby at the city hospital only a few weeks earlier.

While we camped at the beach, a house became available to replace the apartment used by our missionaries when staying in Freetown. Therefore, Joe, Fran, Harv, and I found ourselves cleaning the new house and moving everything from the old apartment. The new location rested on a picturesque hillside overlooking the Freetown Harbor. Otherwise, I am sure we would have left our ocean retreat rather reluctantly.

For me, being away from the oceanfront brought relief in one area. Jewel sensed no fear of water and delighted in playing close to the surging waves. Even when the force of the surf threw her down on the sand, she squealed with delight. Consequently, her daring caused me to be on alert constantly. Only when Jewel rested safely in her crib could I completely relax.

I even experienced a nightmare one night about Jewel and her daddy playing in the waves, as they often did. Suddenly, the undertow swept Jewel away before Harv could grab her, and she was lost to the ocean. It took some time after I awoke for my clammy skin and pounding heart to settle back to normal. And from that night on, I could not enjoy the ocean as totally as before.

Not long after we moved to the house in Freetown, I spent one night monitoring a small clock by the bed. Watching the glimmering lights on the water being reflected from ships anchored in the harbor helped to pass the hours of waiting. Eying one American tanker we had noticed that afternoon, I found myself wistfully thinking how nice it would be to take a quick trip to the States—just long enough to have the baby. But that thought soon breezed away as I remembered the assurance of Father God's presence to be with me.

Soon after daylight, Harv and I left Jewel in Fran and Joe's care and drove to the hospital. As we climbed the wide flight of wooden steps to the second floor, we instantly became aware that we had entered the obstetrics department. African mothers with nursing babies rested everywhere. Some sat on the steps and in the corridor, while many relaxed in a large room filled with cots. A number of babies slept contentedly, undisturbed by the crying babies as proud mothers enjoyed a great time laughing and visiting.

After we found the nurse in charge, we stood waiting while two African nurses unhurriedly searched through the many drawers of two large, wooden desks looking for the phone number of the doctor. When the number could not be located, one nurse said, "Come, I'll take you to your room. The doctor will be coming in a few hours for rounds."

In a few hours? I thought. Then, reminding myself to keep calm, I followed the nurse down the corridor. The day that followed would be impossible to ever forget. From the time I entered the narrow, stuffy room until the baby came that night, a stream of curious, African nurses flowed in and out, using any excuse possible to see the white woman come to give birth in their hospital. Obviously, it was not an everyday occasion. And when the shifts changed in the afternoon, the parade started all over again. The private room the doctor had arranged for me seemingly became the location for "Exhibit A."

It did not take long for the news to spread through the hospital that a white baby girl had been added to their number. Naturally, that brought each nurse, one by one, to see the baby. That I could understand. Joy Etta weighed in at nine pounds, although the next day, one nurse remembered that possibly an instrument had been weighed with the baby. We could not be sure of her exact weight, but Joy came into our lives a bouncing, healthy baby. We were grateful.

A while after she was born, a nurse brought baby Joy back to the room. "There now, baby had first bath," she said, as she proudly deposited the sleeping baby into the basket by my bed. Then, not believing my eyes, I watched as the nurse reached over to hang the towel and washcloth on a rack—the same towel and washcloth I had used that afternoon.

Could she have? I blinked and looked again. She certainly had! And that was not all. She had also used the bar of soap that the hospital had supplied for me: Life Buoy—the original, strong-smelling Life Buoy soap. It seemed unbelievable to use such a potent soap on the tender skin of a newborn.

Since the Life Buoy provided the only sterilization that either the baby or I received, it no doubt acted as a beneficial service in disguise. Many times during my hospital experience, I reminded myself that silence speaks the best reaction to cultural surprises. The next morning, however, when Harv arrived, I sent him back to the house for baby soap, lotion, and linens.

Attention was never lacking when it came to baby Joy. The slightest whimper, and within seconds, a nurse took her to another room to change her diaper. When the night shift returned the baby after caring for her, Joy smelled strongly of cigarette smoke, but I noticed it never happened during the day shift with the doctor present.

On the morning the doctor released us, a nurse came and took Joy, saying, "I will come right back with your baby." Seconds later, I heard Joy crying. When she returned, the African nurse presented me with a neatly tied package that contained the baby's cord stub that had been pulled from her navel. Apparently, African customs surfaced even among the educated nurses.

When Jewel met her little sister, she loved her, kissed her, and called her "Baby Joy-Joy." Bokari took off from that with the inevitable "J" replaced, and she was Yoy-Yoy. Back at Ganya, some called the new arrival Yoy-Yoy, while other Yalunkas referred to her as Toosie-Fidadina, meaning Toosie second-child. One thing seemed certain: the proper name had been selected. Our baby characterized her name perfectly as a pleasant, happy, Joy-Joy.

Chapter 9: In Case Of Emergency

Nestled in a padded, wicker basket behind the seats of the Red Jet, baby Joy was two weeks old the day we traveled upcountry from Magburaka. The few weeks we had been away seemed more like months, making me realize how much Ganya had become rooted in my heart during the short time we had lived there.

With both children uncomfortable from prickly heat and not in their brightest spirits, the trip went from trying to hectic by late afternoon. For consolation, I presumed that once we reached the Ganya hill and cooler nights, both Jewel and Joy would be more comfortable and life would settle back to a normal state. Little did we know that the next few weeks would be anything but normal.

About two miles from Ganya, we noticed that problems had developed with the trailer. Apparently, becoming wearied with the beatings it had suffered from heavy loads and rough roads, the poor trailer simply started to fall apart. Harv stopped and tied it together with a chain, and we continued on, dragging the trailer the rest of the way. Creeping along no faster than five miles per hour, with the accompaniment of a crying duet by two tired, hungry, little girls, the remaining distance stretched into a long ride home.

Everything in the trailer remained in place until we drove up the mission hill. Then, boxes started falling out the back. But since we had arrived within carrying distance of the house, it made no great problem. With grateful acceptance, we were happy that it had not happened earlier, especially while crossing the river.

When I stepped down from the Jet and had difficulty walking to the house, I attributed it to a chronic back problem that probably had been aggravated from the bumpy ride. Struggling to the bedroom, I laid the baby on our bed and dropped down beside her, feeling as exhausted as though I had walked from Magburaka. Then, I realized I had the beginning of a fever, as a case of malaria set in and lasted for a few days.

Leaving the yard workers with the assignment to paint the cement floors while we were away resulted in returning to a disheveled house. Therefore, that night and the days that followed demanded a surplus amount of patience, waiting for my strength to bounce back so we could restore order to all the chaos.

For a day or two, Jewel remained irritable. Then she, too, came down with malaria. Or at least we assumed that to be the cause of her fever and sore body. She also gave a slight moan each time she exhaled. I felt apprehensive until Jewel's appetite started to return and it became evident she was recovering.

In the midst of it all, Harv also joined our malaria party. So many times after a trip, we seemed to return infested with malaria, though much of the cause could probably be blamed on the exhaustive travel conditions. This particular time, it took several days, many pills, and prayer to pull out of it and feel human once again.

To add to an already difficult situation, Bokari's family insisted that he help with their farm work. Regardless of our attempted persuasions otherwise, Bokari took a leave of absence from his household duties.

At his wife's insistence, Bala cook had already returned with her to their Kuranko hometown for an extended visit. And to top off an everything-is-going-wrong pattern, our laundry helper became ill for a few days, making it necessary for me to man the washboard.

Everything stacked together amounted to more than my body could handle and the malaria rebounded with hurricane force. I realized I had a high fever the afternoon I turned the thermometer to read it, but never did I expect to see it so high. I called for Harv, who turned a somber white when he saw the red mercury hovering close to 107 degrees.

"What will we do?" he questioned.

"I probably need a doctor," I answered. "But I certainly do not feel up to travel. I've taken all the malaria medicine I can take for a few hours. All we can do is pray."

So trusting the Lord to help, as He had done many times previously, Harv prayed and left the room to look after Jewel. Fortunately, my body had always been able to tolerate high fevers. During childhood, a chronic kidney condition brought on highly elevated temperatures at times, although never as high as what I experienced that day at Ganya.

Continuing to feel even hotter, an unnatural drowsiness began to settle over my body. Alarmed, I rose up from the pillow, rested my weight on one arm, and pleaded: Lord, my babies need me. Please help!

Within minutes, the sensation of losing consciousness began to disappear and I rested back onto the pillow. Soon after that, I started to perspire. The words from Psalm 50:15, "Call upon me in the day of trouble, I will deliver thee," became a wonderful reality.

The following day, after hours of perspiring, I felt as cool as a cucumber compared to the day before. But even so, the thermometer still registered a temperature of 102. Several more hours of dripping pores finally brought it to normal. For the remainder of our stay in Africa, I doubled the amount of my anti-malaria drug, as others in our mission found necessary to do also.

I had been more unwise than practical when we left Freetown without considering the possibility of an emergency with the baby's feeding. The only available, strong-smelling milk powder we used did not seem logical for a young baby, but Joy-Joy consumed it with no complaints. The baby cooperated like a doll through it all. Surely, her heavenly Father took care of that, for had the milk not agreed with her, we would have found ourselves in an even worse situation.

Following my instructions, Harv took care of the water and bottle sterilizing, and with only two bottles, that job came up frequently. But changing diapers and giving baths did not fit him very well. Understanding that, I had him bring diapers, clothing, and water for sponge baths, and I cared for Jewel and Joy on the bed beside me.

I always enjoyed their bath times, and even though weak from the high fever, taking care of the girls provided a lift to my spirits. It provided the therapy to keep mind over matter while waiting to regain strength.

After limping through two days of survival living, I began to feel better. And as strength slowly returned, I appreciated it in a way I never had before. On the third day, I was even able to nurse the baby again. Harv made no objections to giving up his bottle preparation job.

Since Yalunka babies were always small, the townspeople who came to greet us stared at baby Joy, astonished at the size of the second Toosie. The spontaneous response to me when they saw our baby was, "You done born the pickan well."

As soon as I felt able, we set about putting the house in order and trying to make living a little more convenient. Harv played carpenter and finished off a wardrobe for the girls' clothing. He used the wooden box the folding organ had been shipped in, as Grandpa Ford had planned when he constructed the box. We also converted the smaller wooden boxes into toy shelves by covering them with the heavy, green plastic we previously used to protect things during the rain storms.

Harv became inspired to construct bookshelves from the lumber of other packing crates. Those bookshelves! They became a point of conversation soaked with laughter whenever we had visitors, because of the similarity they held to the Leaning Tower of Pisa. Nevertheless, the shelves fulfilled the pur-pose of holding our books.

With an added member to our family and more space needed for drying clothes, Harv climbed a tree one morning to fasten one end of a line to a tree branch. But when he discov-ered he had intruded into a nest of bees, I am sure he never moved faster on a football field than he did getting out of that tree and into the house. And as always, when things went wrong, he declared it to be Devil's Hill, for certain.

Baby Joy was one month old and doing fine. So one day, while she napped, we started going through our drums stored in the outside shelter. When we packed, similar items had been purposely placed in different drums, so in case a drum should be lost in shipping we would not lose everything of the same kind. Therefore, we attempted to reorganize the contents of the drums for more convenience when looking for what we needed.

After we had worked for a short while, I decided to take a break and rest for a few minutes, since I became tired more easily after my bout with malaria. I had just sat down on a box when a helper who had been watching Jewel rushed into the thatch-covered shelter carrying her and told us Jewel had fallen over in the grass. When I looked at Jewel, I froze in fright; she was frothing at the mouth, her body contracting in a convulsion.

Immediately, my thoughts flashed back to earlier that day when a helper called for me to come to the living room. I quickly finished changing the baby and went in to see what he needed.

"Toosie done get seena, Madame," he said, pointing to a bottle of malaria medicine spilled on the floor. Until then, I had felt secure that the medicine stood safely out of reach on a high shelf. Either someone had accidentally knocked it down, or Jewel had performed a seemingly impossible climb. At the time, I did not feel overly alarmed because the pills tasted so bitter, I could not imagine her eating them. Little did I know the habits of some toddlers with medicine.

I also remembered that just a few weeks earlier, Ruth had told me about a similar thing happening with Patsy, which only resulted in an upset stomach for a while. Consequently, I presumed that Jewel would be all right. But looking at her in Mesa's arms, I knew it was something more serious than an upset stomach.

Harv carried Jewel to the house and eased her onto the dining room table. I rushed to the baby book to check first-aid for convulsions. Our helpers stood in the doorway, concerned about their Toosie.

Whenever an emergency arose, a decision had to be made whether to travel over rough roads for help or stay and wait it out with prayer. Decisions concerning our own bodies was one thing, but the responsibility of making decisions regarding the children became more complex.

Little Jewel certainly needed a doctor and emergency equipment. But that day, we had no choice. A section of the road between Ganya and Falaba had been washed out by heavy rains, making it impossible to even consider rushing her to a doctor.

As we watched, the convulsions steadily worsened despite our desperate prayers. In a sense, we began to follow the surrendered course of Abraham as he climbed the mountain of Moriah with his son. It dealt a painful experience as we thanked the Lord Jesus for giving Jewel to us for nineteen happy months. We tearfully submitted that Jewel belonged to Him to take to heaven if that fit His plan. Such a commitment does not come easily, as any parent knows who has experienced that mountain.

After Abraham proved himself willing to give his son back to God, however, God provided another sacrifice. So likewise, the crisis seemed to pass on the hill at Ganya. Within minutes after our prayer, the seizures began to subside. I knew when Jewel started to regain consciousness even before her eyes opened, as her right arm slowly moved up and a thumb slipped into her mouth.

I had tried to break Jewel of thumb-sucking, but at that moment, it looked so beautiful to see her able to suck her thumb again, I never tried with much effort after that. For years, I carried a warm feeling whenever I saw a baby or toddler sucking a thumb.

The ordeal had stretched into an hour-and-a-half, and we felt drained, but rejoicing in our Father's mercy renewed our strength. Baby Joy had continued to sleep through it all, and our workers never left their post at the doorway. They, no doubt, told their families that evening how Yesu had answered our prayer.

All the next day, Jewel could not even keep water in her stomach, and by bedtime, she appeared to be even worse. She was dry-heaving and remained so nauseated that even medication to settle her stomach would not stay down. Realizing it would be a long night, I took her to our bed where I could watch her and still be able to lie down. Sometime later, feeling another flash of fear, I desperately wished there were some way to call for help. Our mission had applied for permission to operate shortwave radios between stations, but for some reason, the government refused. So when bridges washed out or gushing water flushed away dirt roads, as was the case then, we were totally isolated.

At about that time, God's word gently reminded me that even though we did not have the security of communicating with other missionaries, we still had the privilege of prayer at any time, day or night. Heaven knows no night and does not sleep. Sometime during the night, I remember praying, "Father, Jewel is still so sick and I'm so tired—too tired to pray much. Please have someone in the States pray for us."

Occasionally, friends or relatives wrote to tell us they had felt at certain times that we needed special prayer. Once, a pastor friend in Michigan wrote that he had been awakened in the night with that type of urgent awareness. He immediately woke his wife, saying, "Honey, I feel the Aches are in trouble. Let's pray for them." And they did. Not knowing the details or the intensity of the trouble at the mission house at Ganya—yet sensitive through the Spirit of God to perceive we needed help—they prayed on until peace replaced the burden. Thus, prayer operates a marvelous plan from God for His work to be carried out. And so I had confidence in Him as I weakly asked for someone to take over my prayers for little Jewel.

Earlier, Harv had dropped into an exhausted sleep, and knowing we should not both be awake all night, I did not rouse him. Tomorrow would require strength. Besides, creator God seemed to have put within mothers the ability to cope with all-night-care times, and then continue on the next day.

With Jewel restless and only lightly dozing, the night stretched from one long hour to another. Finally, just before dawn, she settled into a deeper sleep—that was the turning point. Improvement steadily progressed throughout that day and the days that followed. There would be no way to measure the gratefulness in our hearts for answered prayers from the Great Shepherd in restoring our daughter.

As soon as the washed-out section of the road had been filled in, Harv took Jewel to Kabala to have the government doctor examine her, only to find that the doctor was out of town. Some days later, when the doctor saw Jewel, he found her central nervous system had been irritated. Otherwise, she seemed fine by that time.

On their way home from Kabala, Harv had an unex-pected encounter with a large python that had crossed the road a short distance ahead. Apparently, adventure started to steam in

Harv as he stopped the Jet, jumped out, grabbed the huge reptile by its tail, and pulled it back onto the road. Because of its slow movements, Harv managed to rush back into the Jet and run a tire over the python, pinning it securely. Enraged at being confined under the weight of the wheel, the python reared up and swung. Each time it moved to strike, Harv gave it a blow on the head with a machete, finally killing the twelve-foot long reptile.

Our helpers chattered excitedly in a torrent of Yalunka words when Harv returned home with the python and dashed it to them. When they requested permission to cook the meat in our kitchen, I did not have the heart to dampen their festive spirits. And so chunks of python boiled in my pans the rest of the day while I attempted to keep my thoughts away from what was cooking in the kitchen. The workers and their families no doubt became the envy of the town that night.

When Jewel Kay began to exhibit an adventurous spirit in roaming away from the house, Harv had the yard workers build a stick fence around the space extending out from the veranda, thinking that would solve the problem. The stockade, however, would not corral our little climber for long. The following day, Jewel managed to scale over the top. Astonished, the helpers laughed each time she did it, saying, "Ah, Toose done savvy de fence."

Since spankings did not seem to correct that particular behavioral problem, the next time Jewel tried to run down the hill, Harv tied her with a rope allowing her space between the kitchen and house. Even though the rope stretched several feet, it spelled confinement to someone in the exploring stage, and consequently became a punishment tool. But that did not succeed in breaking the roaming habit altogether. Whenever an opportunity arose, off she went to see the world.

Ken Rupp and another missionary unexpectedly dropped in to see us one evening on their way to Magburaka. After fixing them a quick meal and making up extra beds, I suddenly realized Jewel was no longer playing with toys in the living room. We could not find her anywhere in the house.

Alarmed because there was not much time before darkness, we immediately went into action. Harv started down the path toward the river, two of the workers went down the back of the hill, and two of us hurried along the path that led to town. We had gone almost halfway to town when a smiling African woman appeared on the path ahead carrying Jewel. It always greatly pleased the Africans that the white child wanted to be with them.

I was so relieved to have her safely in my arms, the only punishment she received for that escapade fell to a weak, verbal lecture as I carried the runaway home. But as with the spankings and being tied with a rope, so the lecture failed to bring anticipated results.

Only a few days later, after her afternoon nap, once again Jewel headed out the door for the path to town. Because I had left her on the potty chair with a book to look at while I prepared her bath water, she had not been dressed yet. African children reached an older age than Jewel before they wore clothing, and evidently she reasoned that when in Rome, dress as a Roman.

Fortunately, I happened to be coming from the kitchen with warm water for Jewel's bath and at the right place at the right time to intercept that missile from hitting town. It certainly would have been a hit with the people, though. They would have loved it, claiming Toosie to be a Yalunka for sure.

From the time she started walking and became steadier on her feet, whenever the word "go" or anything related to it caught Jewel's attention, she headed for the Jet as fast as she could make it down the steps, waving and calling, "Bye-bye!" Harv usually took her with him on shorter trips, but when the time came for supply trips and she found herself left behind, she became an unhappy little girl for a while. Once, as Harv walked past us in the living room, Jewel looked up from the floor where she sat playing and with concern asked me, "Where's Daddy's feet taking him?" She would have been willing to drop the toys in a second if Daddy's feet were taking him to the Red Jet.

Chapter 10: Not a Toy Snake

Trying to help the Yalunka people spiritually could not be accomplished as successfully without showing the compassion of Christ Jesus for their physical needs also. The government operated a medical dispensary at Falaba, but information leaked from one town to another that the African dispenser diluted medicine with water in order to make himself a little richer on the side. As a result, the people chose to seek help from the missionaries who had earned the reputation of being trustworthy and caring. Of course, that influenced decisions to be treated at Ganya rather than to walk the miles to Falaba when not feeling well.

Even though the people had been slow to respond to Ruth Harrigan's medical help at first, as time passed, they gained confidence in her abilities. After she had to leave, Bill continued to treat the more obvious illnesses. Since Harv had been trained to give injections while serving the U.S. Naval Medical Corps, he also followed Bill's suggestions in diagnosing and medicating some of the people who came to the mission requesting *seena* (medicine).

Treating the most common ailments - colds, malaria, worms, skin ulcers, VD, dysentery, etc. bought appreciated relief to those who needed help. Many sufferers reasoned that the more the treatment hurt or the worse the medicine tasted, the more certain the cure. Perhaps that carried over from experiences with the medicine men. The women and children, however, did not feel as eager for injections as did the men.

A European doctor once related to us some of his experiences when going to the villages to vaccinate for smallpox, which is still a deadly disease for Africans. He sometimes had to chase his would be patients to catch them before he could proceed with the vaccinations.

In one village, a girl ran from him and quickly took refuge in a hut, jamming the door shut. The doctor walked away from the door and patiently waited until the girl thought he had gone. When she finally ventured out, the determined doctor captured and vaccinated her. This is not altogether an easy way for a doctor to practice medicine, but he continued his trek of mercy from village to village for the welfare of the people.

One day, parents of small, twin babies appeared at our door from the neighboring country of Guinea. Before the influence of Christianity, newborn twins suffered the fate of being thrown into the bush to starve or be eaten by animals. It was a pagan belief that when twins were born they were demon-possessed and were therefore disposed of. But these parents had walked many miles to seek medical help for their sick babies. With one glance at the labored breathing of their pitifully emaciated chests, it did not require medical training to realize the small infants were in critical condition. While Harv injected penicillin, I brought baby blankets to replace the dirty cloths that wrapped the babies.

Both twins recovered, and the parents came to

show their gratitude in the typical African manner of repeating their word for thank you, over and over. With Bokari turning(interpreting) words, Harv tried to explain to the parents that the medicine alone had not saved the babies. They had been very, very sick and would have died. We had prayed to the Lord Jesus, God's son, and He had helped the babies get well. We never saw the family again after they returned to Guinea, but hopefully, they continued to think about what they had heard at the Christian mission.

An injection had become known as a *chuke*. Watching the Africans receive their shots in the small berry beyond the kitchen seemed to inspire medical inclinations in Jewel. One never knew when a soft voice from behind would say, "You get chuke," as something jabbed your leg. After Bala Cook received his first injection, the can opener never again appeared within reach of little Miss Nurse.

We sometimes caught Jewel chasing young boys in circles trying to practice medicine on them with a stick. The prospective patients had no more interest in receiving a pretend chuke than the girl who had hidden in the hut from the government doctor. Nurse Jewel had the same determination as the doctor, however, and around the top of the hill jogged the noncompliant patients with the nurse in hot pursuit!

Work halted as our helpers became the audience to what their responsive laughter rated as the most comical scene they had witnessed for awhile. Shouts of, "Go, Toose!" inspired the chase even more. The boys could have run down the hill to town, so we knew they were not as concerned as they pretended to be. Nevertheless, we thought it best to ban Jewel's clinical procedures as unethical and forbid further practice.

At one time, we had passed the word around that Dr. Maclure, our mission doctor, would come to Ganya to hold clinics, expecting the people to come en masse for treatment. But the time he spent with us produced only a few patients each day. There could be only one explanation— farming season. The Yalunka people dedicated themselves to their fields during planting and harvesting times. Nothing or no one interferred, not even a doctor to medicate their ills.

Dr. Maclure took it in stride, saying he could use the time to catch up on correspondence. We felt disappointed after he had left his own work and spent the efforts of travel, only to have his offer of help so greatly ignored. From then on, we knew not to schedule anything during the farming season. At least the people ranked as ambitious in trying to provide food for themselves. They realized that even with hard work, food supplies would run short from one harvest time before the next reaping—referred to by them as the hunger season.

It was still dark when we loaded the Jet the morning Harv drove Dr. Maclure to another station following his visit at Ganya. While the men had breakfast and talked, Jewel woke up and called from her bedroom. I carried her out and sat holding her quietly, avoiding any stimulation, hoping she would be ready to go back to sleep after the men left.

Dr. Maclure and Harv carried out the final load,

when suddenly, a movement caught my attention over at the toy shelves. On one shelf, a snake slowly curled in and out among Jewel's toys. Either it had slipped in while the men carried out the loads, or it had spent the night with us. Fearing the snake might slither away into the shadows of the room and hide in the house, I lost not time in calling to Harv. Both men hurried to the house and performed an immediate execution.

After Jewel had been tucked back into her crib and the lamp blown out, I returned to bed with the intention to sleep until daylight. But awhile after the Red Jet faded away in the distance, I realized there would be no more sleep. My mind refused to cooperate with any such notion.

Replaying the incident with the snake in my thoughts caused me to understand how fortunate it had been that Jewel had been aroused before the men left. Otherwise, I would not have been sitting by the table, and very possibly, the snake would have gone undetected. I shuddered to think how usually the first thing Jewel did each morning was proceed directly to the toy shelves to play until breakfast. Certainly, her guardian angel had been on duty.

The first encounter Jewel had with a snake happened shortly after she started walking. Just before dark one evening, I followed a few feet behind as she toddled toward the serving room. At the same moment she started picking up speed, I saw the motion. Creeping across the cement floor in the serving room, a black snake had caught Jewel's attention. Innocent of any danger, she headed after the snake.

Fortunately, Harv came on the scene, and while I grabbed Jewel, he attacked the intruder before it reached the storeroom where it could have been difficult to find. Actually, visits from snakes in the house did not come too often because Bill had trained the yard crew to keep the grass on the hill well-clipped.

One morning, when I went outside to open the window shutters, Jewel followed along behind, jabbering. When I turned to respond, she was standing on a rubber mat on the cement step outside the door. Rain and sun had caused the mat to curl, and there, under one edge, a coiled snake peered out at me! It did not appear large, but size made little difference. My concern dwelt on whether the snake was poisonous or non-poisonous.

So many different varieties of snakes existed, and at times, missionaries, as well as Africans, seemed uncertain about a particular one being venomous. The only was to assure safety, was to treat them all as poisonous—and that, we always did.

With the snake positioned between Jewel and myself, I struggled at how to handle the situation. Should I show alarm, that might cause Jewel to run to me. So, as calmly and with as much authority as I could muster, I told Jewel to stand still.

Calling for Harv in the same tone, he soon appeared behind Jewel. (Although to me, it seemed like a piece of eternity as the snake and I held a nerve-grinding staring contest.) After handing Jewel to Bokari, Harv ended the life of another reptile, and once again, I realized how well the Mighty One had orchestrated the details to provide safety in that encounter.

Once, while visiting other missionaries, I went to locate Jewel and found her sitting on the floor watching older children playing a game. I smiled and started to leave, but at that moment, I spotted a centipede crawling along the floor toward Jewel and the children.

Being engrossed in their game, the children had no idea of danger in the room. The poisonous fangs of a centipede piercing the skin of a child would not be too comfortable. Afterward, I breathed a, "Thank you, Father," for feeling the urge to check on Jewel at that particular moment.

As a missionary mother, I soon extracted the word "coincidence" from my vocabulary. Incident after incident proved the watchful and helpful care of our Guardian. Undoubtedly, many close calls transpired without adults on the scene, proving that we had no idea of the extent of Father God's protection. Children of missionaries need our constant prayers, with some additional prayers for those in developing countries.

Being a typical mother, however, whenever I heard either of the girls start to cry with any inflection of pain, anxious moments followed until I found out the cause to be nothing serious--only the usual mishaps that are expected with children at play. Like all missionary mothers, however, I had to learn to keep the anxiety factor on a guarded level. The fact that danger inhabited the land could not be ignored, but neither could living in constant, fearful suspense be allowed to control life. Faith and practical caution needed adjustment to stand side-by-side in bush country living.

The first time necessity demanded that the girls and I stay alone after the addition of baby Joy, I soon learned it took more managing with two children than had been required with only one. The first day, everything moved smoothly until late afternoon, when I started feeling dizzy and seeing white spots.

The same experience had happened once previously shortly before we left for Africa, so I knew what to expect as soon as symptoms started. The spots would become worse until vision would be totally gone for a half-hour, leaving me with no option but to lie down and wait for it to pass.

It never worked out to see a doctor during such a time until a few years later. After hearing the explanation of it being merely a form of migraine, it became much easier to cope with. It had been one thing to have a brief experience of blindness in the States, which I quickly forgot about due to our busy schedule, but it took a different curve when alone with two small, dependent children in the bush of Africa.

I called Bokari to the house and asked him to watch Jewel and Joy until I felt better. After my vision cleared, a washed out, weak feeling lingered. Feeling uneasy about the situation since it was almost time for the workers to return to town for the night—and I must confess, forgetting to pray for help—I pushed the panic button. I asked Bokari

164

if he knew anyone in town who owned a bicycle and was willing to ride to Kabala with a message for the government doctor. Bokari mentioned the name of a worker with a bicycle but went on to add, "But no person agree to go to Kabala now. It be too late. No one agree to walk or ride bicycle when it be night." I knew he was right. It would be dark within the hour. So I asked Bokari if he would arrange for the person to go in the morning if I did not feel better. Bokari promised he would.

While listening to the workers finishing their final chores out by the kitchen, I dreaded the thought of having them leave that evening. As they treaded down the path toward town, however, a reassuring calmness came to me as I turned my thoughts to the duties of preparing two little girls for bed. During that process, I began to feel better, and by morning, there remained no thought of sending for help. Our unseen Helper had provided all the assistance I needed.

Taking everything into consideration, it usually seemed easier to stay alone at Ganya than to face traveling with small children. But in either case, the assistance of Father God always proved to be faithful. Time after time, travel experiences reminded us of that fact. A letter to my parents related one such time:

"Here we are, back at Ganya. We arrived about nine o'clock on Saturday night. Jewel and Joy were both good on the way home. The farther upcountry we came, the higher the water was rising with flash flooding. We dreaded those last seven miles, especially since it would be

dark by the time we reached there, due to a longer delay than than usual at the ferry crossing at Magburaka that morning.

But it turned out not too difficult except at one place. In a narrow valley, the water gushed so swiftly that one side of the road was being washed away. When the headlights first fell on the disintegrating road ahead, it took our breath! The road was barely wide enough for the wheels of the Jet, which called for very straight driving.

Slowly and carefully, Harv inched the Jet safely past the narrow spot. But then, only a little way up the rain-soaked, dirt hill on the other side, the mud-coated tires could no longer manage the ascent. Even the clutch could not hold and the Jet, and the trailer began sliding back down the hill with the water behind us roaring like a small Niagara in the darkness. Harv turned the wheels to jackknife the trailer, which finally stopped the slide.

We would have hated to had been without a winch right then. Even when the cable had been secured around a tree and the motor started, it seemed we were not going to climb the hill that way either. With mud flying from the spinning back tires, the Jet merely remained suspended on the tensed cable, unable to gain traction. But finally, after many attempts, the Jet slowly inched forward.

We had been silent during the whole operation. Jewel noticed things were not as they should be and clung tightly to me. I think the girls and their Mommy are going to stay in Ganya until the rains are over! Driving through the Ganya valley that night toward the mission hill, we sang the

166

doxology. We were so thankful to have made it through with the heavily-loaded trailer of provisions."

The next afternoon, while Harv was in Freetown, the girls and I enjoyed the fun of opening packages that arrived on a boat from the States. Aluminum lawn chairs for the veranda from his parents, new toys to surprise the girls, canned foods, and even some strawberry jam from Grandma Ford's kitchen in Rosewood all made the day seem like Christmas in August.

Baby Joy faired well with a supply of baby food. After I started her on fruit juices, each morning, Jewel stood by, waiting for the two-ounce mark on the baby bottle to be reached, since she knew the remainder of the juice would be for her to finish. Fruit and juices, whether canned or fresh, tropical varieties, furnished Jewel's "goodies." Unfortunately, she quickly acquired a liking for the candy that came with the packages. What little candy she had, however, never disturbed her strong love of fruit.

From the mail we had picked up, we experienced reassurance through a letter from Bill, which read, "Well, I imagine you are beating your heads against the wall by now. You've been there almost a year and probably can't speak much Yalunka yet. We went through the same thing."

That described our situation perfectly. We could understand and converse only "small small" with the people, but not as much as we had expected or wanted after one year. The long, drawn-out Yalunka greetings spontaneously tossed back

167

and forth when commencing a conversation had been mastered fairly well. Beyond that, catching words and phrases here and there disclosed the extent of our linguistic abilities. I am certain Bill's skills had far advanced beyond our mastery at that point, but his encouragement did help.

Our helpers had picked up additional English words as we taught Jewel to talk. Therefore, their small collection of broken English expressions had developed into a mini language of its own, which sometimes, in haste, we found ourselves reverting to when trying to communicate with them.

The workers took pride in teaching Yalunka words to Jewel. In fact, some words she spoke in their language altogether. That pleased them tremendously, and they would often grin and say, "Ah, Toose now be Yalunka!"

Having no one to interpret in the service after Ali left Ganya created another obstacle. Bala Cook could be trusted with the job when he understood, but with his limited English, only a few, simple sentences could be used. Also, Bala still spoke in his native Koronko, which only some Yalunkas comprehended. So trying to use Bala as an interpreter did not solve the problem.

Suri, a Yalunka who had come in contact with English when he served in the British Infantry in Burma during World War II, had gained a better knowledge and speaking ability than anyone else in the area. But a major hindrance blocked his usefulness to us. Suri evidently set his heart more on the present world than he did on seeking eternal life, and the capital needed to expand his harem each

168

year in order to obtain more prestige.

Consequently, Suri accepted the Old Testament as, "Now that be fine fine." But as for the New Testament and the teachings of our Lord Jesus, he gestured his hand emphatically as he said, "Now that be the white man's Bible!"

Harv used Suri now and then to interpret, but not often, for he could not be certain that Suri would not add his own interpretation to the scripture. Taking everything into account, it seemed better to wait until we possessed a better grasp of the language than chance wrong teachings.

As time passed, Bokari learned more English and could be used more frequently to explain Bible truths. Even though sentences had to be kept in simple form, we felt he could be trusted. Bokari willingly accepted the mark of being known in town for walking the "Jesus way," as the Africans referred to Christianity.

Using a Meneca translation of scriptures and the feeble help of his language assistants, Harv wrote a brief sermon in Yalunka. After memorizing the words, he preached whenever he journeyed to other villages as well as repeating it over and over to people at Ganya. No doubt, many of them knew the message by heart in time also. The essence of the message explained the way to find God the Father (Allah to them) through Jesus Christ, God's Son.

Curiosity drew people to the church services, However, very few wanted to believe and follow Jesus Christ. Between strong Muslim influences and the evil powers of pagan worship, the Word of God seemed to fall on dry, hard soil. But that same Word held promises to break through In-difference. We would have to wait patiently for that to happen.

As each month passed, a greater appreciation developed for daily care and help from heaven. Before retiring each night, it followed routine for me to slip into their bedroom to make a final check on Jewel and Joy. As I stood looking at my little ones sleeping peacefully in their screened beds, I always felt as wealthy as a queen surveying her jewels. The value of human life had taken on a deeper meaning, while things and possessions became less important. Broken-down equipment, discomforts, even fevers and illness all seemed minor when reflecting on our life compared to the lives of the people in the village. Material things would be lost in a forgotten past some day, while my little jewels and the townspeople represented more that just bodies; they depicted beings that would live forever, and they needed the eternal guide to lead their journey on earth to their never-ending life in eternity.

Chapter 11: So Went A Vacation

As I inspected the worn wheel of a rotary beater one morning, I concluded that the life of that beater had expired. Ruth Harrigan had advised me to take more than one beater to Africa, and the wisdom of that advice soon became apparent.

Since our only available milk powder did not dissolve easily in water, mixing the milk required the use of a beater. But it never took long for the person washing dishes to discover the fun of turning the beater at a fast speed in the water to stir up the bubbles. And with that, the dishcloth often became entangled in the wheel, causing damage and a shorter life span to the gears.

No amount of cautioning seemed to stop the dishwater play. Watching the soap bubbles foam brought too much temptation to resist. One advantage came from the forbidden activity, nonetheless, since the beater no doubt ended up in a cleaner state than it might have been otherwise.

My attention then turned to the chunks of fresh meat on the counter waiting to be cut and ground. Obtaining meat at Ganya was no simple procedure, like going to market and purchasing a few pounds. No meat market existed at Ganya, and the cattle owned by the Yalunkas primarily maintained a means for wife-bartering, not for butchering.

A few times, we bought cows that had been attacked by the hyenas, which the Africans considered cursed and would not use for food. But that source of fresh meat came to a disappointing halt after a government doctor censured us for using it, because of the possibility of the hyena having had rabies.

After a while, we found an African man who occasionally liked the experience of possessing cash in return for selling us a young cow. Our helpers looked forward to butchering day with as much anticipation as we did, for they learned to count on a dash of some of the meat for their rice chop that evening.

Full advantage would always be taken of what Western civilization considers waste. With the Yalunkas, nothing counted as refuse. Instead, everything was edible. Each time during butchering, as soon as a knife reached a certain section of the beef, the cutting halted while that small portion was consumed raw. Whatever it may have been seemingly offered a special treat to the person who grabbed it first.

Only one time did I witness something discarded during butchering. While a calf was being slaughtered on the ground back beyond the kitchen, someone pulled a long, thick tapeworm from its stomach. Seeing the workers so delighted with the find, I thought, *Oh no. Surely they will not eat it!* I quickly turned and made a fast retreat to the house, my stomach turning several revolutions with each step. Hearing Sparky being called, I knew the fate of the worm and hoped that Sparky would have enough sense to refuse it. But I certainly did not look back to see.

African beef could be described as 99 percent lean, but through it stretched long strips of tough gristle that needed to be cut away. After slicing all the steaks that could be located, I trimmed the rest of the meat and Bokari ran it through a meat grinder two times. The final, lean ground beef looked Grade

A—at least by African standards. And even though the preparation was a tiring, back-aching task, it brought the reward of having fresh meat again.

Bill had urged us to use their refrigerator until they returned since it would be better for it to be running than to stand idle. The large, kerosene refrigerator ran on an Aladdin burner that did an excellent job keeping the box and freezer compartment cold. The freezer provided enough space to store a meat supply to last several weeks, with some rationing required.

Once, we tried keeping a flock of ten chickens in order to have our own eggs and eventually meat as the flock increased. African chickens were small, with seemingly almost as much bone as meat. Our flock displayed an amazing instinct for safety as they flew up into the branches of the papaya trees by the house to roost at night. The chickens also seemed to sense the animal-lover in Jewel, for they would squat and let her pick them up. But with anyone else, the same chickens ran wildly when approached. Sometimes, they carried on as though they protested Jewel holding them, but never once did they peck her.

After Joy started walking, unlike Jewel, she kept a comfortable distance from most animals. Jewel soon caught on to that fact, and during a frisky, teasing moment one day, she started chasing Joy with one of the chickens. After that, whenever I heard Jewel laughing, a chicken squalling, and Joy crying, the sounds told the story of the scene taking place outside. I automatically moved to the door and called for Jewel to put down the chicken.

Sometimes, a little scratching together and stretching of food had to be maneuvered when we had unexpected guests, as was the case when we were visited by other missionaries one day. After we finished our dinner, Bokari cleared the table for dessert, and as he removed the meat platter, I glanced at the remaining chicken and calculated there would be enough for a casserole the next day. I felt comfortable that the menu plan for the next day would at least be partly taken care of.

But while we remained at the table, visiting and sipping coffee, Jewel Kay, with all good intentions for her pal, fed Sparky his dinner in the serving room—the remaining chicken. Bokari's face remained extremely somber as he later related the news to me of what had happened, but I could see the grin in his eyes. Of course that made meal plans for the next day subject to change.

Also subject to change were our plans for a chicken farm on the hill. Some of the men kept warning us that having livestock around produced too much incentive for leopards to visit the hill at night. Therefore, one by one, the ten chickens appeared on our meat platter.

Whenever we could make connections, an Irish government doctor and his wife bought meat for us at the town market in Kabala. Having a business trip to the Ganya area one morning, the doctor brought along a pan of fresh beef. But before he reached our house, his small car became stuck in a section of mud and Harv answered his call for help in the Jet.

When Harv reached the car, he handed the winch cable to the doctor, telling him to put the cable around the axle. Apparently, the doctor knew much less about automobiles than about medicine, for instead of the axle, he attached the cable to the tie rods. And when the winch began pulling his car, things happened—but not what they wanted to happen!

An African who accompanied the doctor took off the oil pan and pump to inspect the damage done to the rods. After looking, he announced that the rods were indeed bent. Replacing the oil pump, he apparently did not put it back on correctly, and now the car would not start because the timing was off. Before the doctor started his trek to another village to take care of the business he had come for, he sent a messenger to bring an African mechanic from Kabala.

The following day, the mechanic arrived riding a bicycle. A mechanic pedaling a bicycle across the Ganya valley was the equivalent of a lights-flashing, brightly-colored wrecker in America. In fact, it seemed even more impressive to the people since only those belonging to the highest social rank in Yalunka territory could afford a bicycle. Therefore, the mechanic pompously rode over the bumpy, dirt path with his head held high, after a forty-three mile ride from Kabala.

The car had been pulled up by our house the day before to protect it from possibly being dismantled in the valley. After checking it over and not being able to start it, the mechanic concluded, "Now there must be water in de petrol."

His actions moved simultaneously with his words, and what happened next seemed more like a planned comedy than an actual real life drama. As he spoke, the mechanic removed the top of the carburetor and dropped in a lighted match—somehow to prove his point that there was water in the petrol.

Everything happened so quickly and seemed so unbe-lievable. The noise and fire that followed flustered the doctor and Harv so much that it took a few seconds to recover from shock and put out the fire. After the flame had been extin-guished, the mechanic concluded, "Now there must be no water in de petrol!"

The undaunted mechanic then suggested that they push the car down the hill and he would start it with the clutch. That sounded like a sensible suggestion. So, with the mechanic behind the wheel, the men gave the auto a shove and it started rolling down the hill. No one on earth would be able to give a reasonable explanation for what occurred in the descent. To the complete astonishment of everyone watching, the mechanic suddenly turned the steering wheel and swerved the car off the path and into a deep hole Bill had dug to use for a grease pit when servicing the Jet.

By the time the vehicle had been pulled from the pit and back to the lane, the doctor had developed a short circuit in his nervous system. Not in a kindly mood, he told the mechanic to keep away from the car and that he intended to send for an army truck to pull it to an army garage—which he did.

Some African mechanics held a reputation of being exceptionally clever with repair work. Placing banana peels in the cylinder walls to save on oil and utilizing chewing gum for some minor—and well as major —repair jobs were some of the techniques employed to gain recognition for successful work. But the work of the mechanic at Ganya that morning failed to contribute any fame to his success record. As the poor fellow rode away across the valley on his bike, his head took a lower position than when he first pedaled in. Nevertheless, he had tried!

Not long after that incident, we found ourselves with no working lamps. Usually kerosene lamps could be obtained in Kabala at one of the small trading shops, but when Harv went to look, neither parts nor lamps could be found for sale. Resorting to a supply of slow-burning candles, we rationed one candle per evening for each of us, to make the store of candles last longer.

After several nights of burning eyes and headaches from eyestrain, we decided that as soon as the swollen river receded from the bridge, a supply trip to Freetown stood as a must, especially since our shelves were developing that empty look. So each day, Harv checked the river until the bridge finally seemed passable.

For the first time, I suggested that perhaps arrangements should be made for two guards to stay on the hill at night in case I needed help. Therefore, one of our helpers and another man from town agreed to sleep in the outside storeroom. But with that decision, I set myself up to learn a lesson. Because the guards could not have a fire in the middle of the floor to keep away mosquitoes as they did in their mud hut homes, they suggested that they should be supplied with mosquito nets. That seemed understandable, and we provided the nets.

Next, since the cement floor felt harder in comparison to their dirt floors, they decided they needed our camp cots to sleep on. Then, once the cots and mosquito nets were in place, they delivered a lengthy oration proposing that in order to stay, a torch and a gun would be necessary for them to guard properly.

I did not mind giving up my flashlight, but each night, the thought of the workers having a loaded gun haunted me enough to wish that my guards would desert their post and go back to town. With their experience in handling a gun being limited, I could rightly imagine that should they hear something during the night, they could become excited and perhaps accidently send a bullet through the walls of the house.

The watchmen did little sleeping. Maybe they were just performing their duty well, or perhaps being on the Devil's Hill through the night produced insomnia. At any rate, I certainly did less sleeping with guards than when I stayed alone. After a few nights, I became tempted to give each one a dose of phenobarbital from Ruth's medicine chest so we could all enjoy a night of sleep—forget the guarding!

Instead, one evening I treated them to a large bowl of popcorn, which did not prove to act as a relaxant. But they liked the new treat, and the next morning when they thanked me again, they referred to it as "good chop."

The day Harv returned home, the first chance we had to talk privately I stated, "Never again!" During the nights he had been away, I concluded that heavenly angels guard with no disturbances and I always enjoyed peaceful sleep when trusting Father's care. Hence, never again did I issue a request for guards to be on the hill at night when Harv had to be away.

Improvements to the mission house moved along as leisurely as the graceful praying mantis that occasionally took a stroll down and up the dining room wall. In fact, our second November in Africa had arrived before completion of the plastering—almost a year from the time the grass roof had been replaced with metal roofing. That ran true to form with the slow-motion progress we learned to expect and be content with in the bush.

As Harv and I whitewashed the living room and dining area walls in the evenings after Jewel and Joy had entered dreamland, I discovered that the house seemed even more like home when I became involved with some of the actual projects. Covering the walls to a fresh, white appearance proved so enjoyable, we thought nothing of having to use whitewash on mud cement blocks in the house we lived in. In fact, we felt just as proud of the finished work as though it were an expensive paint job on drywall.

Early one morning, as the Jet took us down the hill and across the valley, we excitedly anticipated a few relaxing days at the ocean before shopping in Freetown for provisions. The excitement over a vacation slowly lost its glow, however, as we traveled on. Along the way and including the first day in Free-town, a vexing, all-time record of ten flats and two blowouts set the pace for that particular vacation!

After one forced stop, I jokingly reminded Harv that having tire problems instead of motor trouble presented a blessing, because he could take care of tires more easily. But Harv did not seem convinced about any blessing in connection with the situation, especially after using the last available tire patch before we arrived at the coast and having to rely on bicycle tire repairs to substitute. Top priority after we arrived was getting the Red Jet a new set of much-needed tires.

Arrangements had been made with another mission for us to rent their house near the ocean, about a half-hour drive from Freetown. Unfortunately, it turned out the house stood at a point where the shoreline dipped in, cutting off the incoming sea breeze. With no ocean breeze and no trees near the house for shade, we found the temperature much less comfortable than at Ganya. It required a lot of baby powder to bring comfort for the prickly heat that resulted.

In the kitchen, we found an old kerosene refrigerator that apparently had gone into retirement—or at any rate, needed to. When lighted, the burner only smoked and then went out. Harv spent most of the next day looking for parts for the refrigerator and for kerosene lamps that likewise refused to burn.

After a considerable amount of try-this and try-that, the refrigerator burner finally agreed to operate, which gave us cold drinking water. Harv was proud of that accomplishment. But after not being so fortunate to locate lamp parts, for the first few nights, our only light came from a dim, puffing, smoking kerosene lantern hanging from a nail on the wall.

We had not been at our vacation cove long before we found that Jewel could not be trusted to play alone for one minute. One afternoon, I called for Bokari to bring Toosie to the house for her nap. When he replied that she had already gone inside, a quick search of the house did not locate her. Evidently, Jewel had entered the house, as Bokari said, but then had gone back outside, somehow quietly bypassing Bokari and Mesa, who had been watching her.

With hearts throwing extra beats, all of us dashed toward the shore, which could not be seen from the house. Rounding the bend in the path, there we saw Jewel, fearlessly and happily playing in the sand with the waves crashing in around her. It was certainly not a safe playground for a small child to be enjoying by herself.

After that experience, I kept closer contact with Jewel, even when the helpers were assigned to watch her outside for a while. The incident had jarred them also, for countless times during the following days, they checked to make certain Jewel was with me. "Madame, Toosie no be there?" Bokari called in Yalunka, using the customary negative case when asking a question. Jewel's whereabouts lingered as a constant concern, and only when she rested safely in her screened bed could we relax completely.

Running water did not come with the house. It had to be carried from a well a short distance away, which put the helpers in an unpleasant mood whenever the water buckets stood empty. Carrying water did not come under their responsibilities in Ganya. Soon, the subject became so strained, I merely smiled, looked at the dry buckets, then at my assistants without saying a word. That usually brought sheepish grins and quickly, one would yell at the other to bring more water.

A vacation? Well, it did give us the experience of a change of scenery. Also, the house stood away from the main road, providing a quiet, peaceful atmosphere. On clear days, the Banana Islands could be seen on the horizon. But the nights, with all their penetrating stillness, rather made us miss the night sounds of the bush country.

After a few days of trying to put together a vacation, shopping for provisions to take back home brought the usual complications. We had started to paint the remaining floors of the mission house before we left, but had run out of paint. At each store in Freetown, we heard the same response: "We no get de paint today." So the prospect of the floors being finished would have to be put on hold until the next provision trip. Hopefully there would be paint in stock somewhere in town.

Interior decorating always created a challenge. Some months later, when I included pastel paint for the bathroom walls on the shopping list, Harv returned with the only available color—a bloody red. I imagined I could hear the walls groan as the brush stroked on the red paint, just as I adjusted to accept it.

At least the paint covered only the lower half of the wall, and I had to agree with Harv—it did add color!

On our way home after the vacation, we drove from Magburaka to Ganya with somber thoughts and heavy hearts. As usual, we stopped at Magburaka for a day before going the rest of the way to Ganya. News had arrived that Bill and Ruth would be delayed in the States because Ruth needed surgery. Besides that disappointing information and concern for Ruth, the Field Executive Committee met and decided that due to a shortage of personnel, we would be relocated to another station in the near future.

Had the assignment come a few months earlier, we may have welcomed the idea. During our first year, most of the Yalunka people had remained aloof and suspicious, not seeming to care whether we resided there or not, unless they needed medicine or another favor. Then, as time passed, some began to show signs of acceptance, even friendliness.

As we drove along the dirt highway, we wondered how we could break the news to the people that we would be leaving

Ganya to go to another tribe. Tribespeople did not hold much concern for people of other groups. Not until they became real followers of the Lord Jesus did that develop.

The Yalunka people could understand the necessity of Bill and Ruth leaving because of illness, but never would they willingly accept our going to another tribal area. Without doubt, it would undo the progress made to that point in winning the confidence of the Yalunkas.

The issue of leaving Ganya seemed even more complex since some on the mission staff felt that the work with the Yalunka people should not have been started. Their reason certainly appeared legitimate; with limited staff and finances, our mission already had enough responsibility to operate among two groups in Sierra Leone, without stretching to a third. Yet, there existed a tribe of fifty thousand or more people with no mission and no message of hope. Therefore, the station had been opened with a vision to reach the Yalunka people.

Can a mother forsake a needy child? As plans for the move progressed, my heart hurt as though we were preparing to do just that. Furthermore, substantial fears haunted me that should we move away, and should the Harrigans not be able to return in the future, the work at Ganya might never be reopened. Our mission workers and the people in town reacted to the idea with shock and anger. Then, a resigned gloom settled in causing long faces and dark moods. It seemed that a black crêpe draped the approaching Christmas season that year.

With the innocent, carefree spirit of childhood, Jewel and Joy were the only ones able to prompt smiles from anyone. What a blessing from our great Father to have their cheerful capers bring some sunshine to the mission hill.

Chapter 12: A Christmas Par'Tee

A few days before Christmas, a thought suddenly brightened my mind; we needed to have a Christmas party! And so we proceeded to invite all the men and helpers who had ever assisted us to the event scheduled for the evening of December 23.

On that day, all other work became unimportant as preparations for the party took priority from morning to evening. Tradition usually inspired missionaries to treat their workmen to a rice-chop at Christmastime. But I decided to plan something different to help divert thoughts away from our upcoming departure after the first of the year.

That evening, at lamp lighting time, Harv walked to the outside storeroom, pulled the starter rope on the generator, and instantly, colored lights beamed brightly from the small, artificial Christmas tree perched on a folding table in one corner of the living room. Jewel and Joy stood spellbound, viewing a lighted Christmas tree for the first time. And when a reluctant bedtime arrived, they needed reassurance that the "pretty lights" would be with us for a while.

Apparently, news of the party on the hill had leaked from hut to hut in town. For when I returned to the living room after settling the girls in bed, several pairs of wide eyes peered through the window screens from out of the darkness. They, too, were fascinated at catching their first glimpse of lighted Christmas decorations.

By that time, people had learned to watch activities of the white family with less shock than at first. It came as a surprise, though, that the children standing outside would venture on the hill after dark. Evidently, the taboos connected with Devil's Hill had lost strength with the younger generation. Possibly, the peering eyes belonged to the boys who sometimes came around during the day, and if so, that would bring more courage to come on the hill at night.

Then, suddenly, we heard footsteps ascending the hill, and the spectators instantly vanished into the darkness. Heavy army boots stomping up the path announced the coming of Suri, the ex-soldier. Dressed for the special occasion in his army uniform, Suri proudly displayed medals on his chest awarded in Burma during World War II.

Bala Cook came next, minus his old, brown hat and large, black umbrella. Could it actually be Bala, without those ever-present accessories that claimed such a part of him? Instead, he wore an African gown and a Koronko tribal hat, his black face and eyes beaming as brilliantly as the glowing lights on the Christmas tree.

Anticipation sparked the air as others continued to arrive, all dressed in clean shirts and khaki shorts. Excited Yalunka chatter filled the room until each guest had arrived. A quietness fell over the group as they awaited the unfolding of this new adventure pronounced by them as a "par'tee."

With no Christmas carols translated into Yalunka, Harv told the group I would play a Christmas song that black and white men sing in other countries. As the little pump organ sounded the notes of Silent Night, our African bushmen heard for the first time one of the world's most beloved Christmas carols. Harv then read the Christmas story from the Menkia translation of the Bible, sentence by sentence, while someone turned the meaning into Yalunka words.

Following the devotional time of bringing their attention to God's gift of Jesus to the world, we handed a wrapped gift to each person. As the workers received their brightly-colored packages, they fingered their gifts, shook them, and some even smelled, trying to guess what the presents contained. Each person reacted with the excitement and delight of a child as he clumsily unwrapped his first Christmas present.

Cookies, candy, and plates filled with sandwiches made with homemade rolls brought on more smiling exclamations. A lip-smacking good time followed—their method of showing approval and genuine enjoyment of what they were eating.

This type of hearty endorsement of a new taste reminded me of a woman from town who had brought me two oranges for a dash one morning. Since a dash called for a counter-gift, my mind searched around the serving room for something to reciprocate with, but I kept coming up blank. Finally, remembering a jar of hard candy we had, I offered her some. My guest had never tasted candy before. Etiquette compelled me to sit and wait until the treat completely melted in her mouth, which seemed to take unusually long. All the while, my friend let me know, with the noise from her lips, that she enjoyed the candy

from start to finish. After that experience, I ᵥ
to never again give hard candy for a dash unle
to wait for it to melt away.

As the Christmas party neared conclusioɪ.
from his chair with dignity and ceremony to act as s₁
for the group. Most African men perform ᵥ
spontaneous speeches, Bala being no exception. The ,
would have been appraised as quite mediocre in a develoρ.
country, but Bala's impromptu speech in labored Englisɦ
made it sound equivalent to a royal ball.

I felt humbled and a little tearful as he finished, "Tonight show us how much you done love us. And if you done
love us dese much, we know God loves us much too. We go
love God more." And so ended our little Christmas par'tee on
the hill. It seemed to have accomplished its purpose in making
hearts brighter.

The next morning, Alan Chapman, a manual training
instructor at Fourah Bay College in Freetown, struggled across
the bumpy valley in his small British Austin. During the rainy
season, it would have been impossible for him to make it to
Ganya in such a small vehicle. But with the land dry at the end
of December, Alan managed to maneuver his way over the Jeep
Trail. We also had invited Esther Grody to join us for the holiday and Alan gave her a ride from Magburaka.

Alan, a jolly, wee Scotsman, never failed to brighten
any atmosphere. It did not take long in his presence to recognize
him as a true Christian also. His visit, therefore, granted us a

tual uplift as well as a fun time—a good remedy for our
cumstances right then.

As he entered the house, Alan handed me a package
containing homemade Scotch shortbread, mailed to him from
Scotland. From the package also emerged a pound of butter—
real butter that stood in such contrast to the lard-resembling
margarine we scooped from tins and referred to as "butter."
Pieces of shortbread topped with butter certainly made delicious
gourmet eating in bush country.

Boxes received from the States gave Jewel and Joy
some packages to open Christmas morning. Jewel was so excited trying to decide which toy to play with first. A few times
during the day, I caught myself counting back the hours to State
time to imagine our family gatherings. But the companionship
of our guests, along with watching two little girls having a
happy Christmas, prevented those mind trips from lingering too
long.

The following day, while sitting on one of the lawn
chairs that made up our living room furniture, Alan's carpentry-
inclined mind began to visualize a couch for the room. He
proceeded to plan a wooden framework that he later constructed
in his workshop in Freetown. We ordered thick, foam cushions
from England for the couch. Some months later, after the cushions had been covered with material found in Freetown, the
finished product did not resemble something one would find in
a furniture store in America, but it could be described as comfortable.

For a day or so after Alan and Esther left, the hill became lonely and quiet as our thoughts returned to moving. Through the weeks, reaction against our leaving Ganya had gained momentum, and the paramount chief dictated a letter of protest to the mission officials. Harv also sent a message asking that the decision be reconsidered. We awaited their reply with hope. We did not even start packing, though we knew the conclusion could remain unchanged.

We had just finished our meal On New Year's Eve when we heard a truck in the distance. Since unexpected trucks seldom came our way, we hurried outside to see who it could be. Ken Rupp had been to see his brother, Dave, stationed with his family in Kuranko territory. On his way back to Magburaka, Ken had only reached Falaba when he felt so ill, he decided to drive to Ganya and spend the night with us.

By the next morning, Ken had a high fever and knew he would not be able to drive to Magburaka. Yet urgency compelled him to continue on because he and his family had reservations booked to leave for the States for a year of furlough. Harv immediately went for Dave and brought him back to drive Ken's truck, with Harv driving the Jet along to give Dave a ride back upcountry.

The government doctor at Magburaka found that Ken had a severe case of blood poisoning caused from an insect bite. With treatment from the doctor and answered prayers, Ken recovered enough for the family to fly from Freetown as scheduled.

Harv returned home the next evening after taking Ken to Magburaka with news that the mission officials had reconsidered their decision and consented for us to remain at Ganya for the present. Our workers and many townspeople responded to the news with broad smiles.

Beyond anything we could attain ourselves, the threat of our leaving seemed to have awakened the Yalunkas to appreciate the mission being at Ganya. Therefore, the episode, even though a trial for a while, turned out to promote a better relationship with the people.

Harv also brought another surprise when he returned from Magburaka. Back before Christmas, two boxes received from the States had somehow fallen from the trailer while en route to Ganya. We had no idea when or where it had happened. Disappointed at the time, all we could do was consider the boxes as lost and forget about them. On their way back from Magburaka, when Dave and Harv stopped at another mission, they found that one of the missing boxes had been turned in to the resident missionaries. An elderly Muslim man had brought it to them, saying, "I find on road. Allah no agree for me to keep."

Harv took time to contact the man who had turned in the box and dashed him some money to award his honesty. Because African society considered theft as stealing only when caught in the act, we realized that our heavenly Father had intervened for us to receive that certain box.

From its contents, Jewel and Joy experienced their first taste of graham crackers, and the new treat met with a high approval rating. In fact, they liked them so much that I wrote in a letter to my parents, *"I'll never have the heart to use the graham crackers you sent for the pudding* (a favorite family recipe). *The girls like them too much."* It was interesting to note how special a lost-and-found box of graham crackers could become.

Life on the hill took on a pleasant change after Harv purchased another radio. No longer needing to use the Jeep battery to operate a radio seemed too convenient to be true. The new radio used a smaller battery that had a lifespan of two or three months. Being able to turn it on each day ushered in a major advancement to our living, needless to say. Then discovering ELWA, a Christian radio station broadcasting from Liberia, enhanced our days even more as we listened for a short time each morning. The Sunday afternoon programming, with tapes of American services familiar to us, created a remarkable uplift to those hours that previously tended to drag into a long afternoon.

Dave Rupp had asked Harv to bring his chainsaw to the Monko station to help cut trees for bridge building. So Harv set a day, and while there, he found the talk of the town centered on the destruction elephants had been leaving behind as they plundered the countryside.

Consequently, two weeks later, we arose at five o'clock one morning, boarded the Red Jet, and drove to Monko for the purpose of an elephant chase for Dave and Harv. The British commissioner had loaned a powerful .404 gun to the men and suggested they take down as many of the giants of devastation as possible, considering the trouble they continued to create for the people.

But when we arrived at Monko, we found that Dave had been told the elephants had moved out of the vicinity, making it necessary to postpone the hunt until later when the herd returned downstream to the Monko area again. Our visit that day, however, provided a chance for me to become acquainted with Marie, Dave's wife. Jewel had the time of her life playing with the Rupp children and Joy-Joy beamed her pleasure from the day as well.

On our way back to Ganya later that afternoon, we were fourteen miles from home when the Jet suddenly sputtered to a stop. Harv tried different methods to locate the cause, but after so long, it seemed useless. We prayed. Harv gave another attempt. Nothing happened. Walking the rest of the way appeared to be the only alternative means of reaching Ganya.

I did not relish the thought of walking that far. Jewel, a mere two-year-old, would be able to walk only a short time before Harv would have to carry her. That would leave me to carry Joy. Could I manage such an assignment? I felt doubtful that I could walk even half the distance, even without carrying the baby. But when it came to a choice of walking or spending the night in the Jet at what seemed to be the middle of nowhere with two children who would be hungry soon, I cast my vote with Harv to walk.

We started deciding which things to carry with us and what to leave behind, knowing chances ran strong that anything remaining in the Jet would not be there when Harv returned the next day. In fact, we would be fortunate if the tires remained on overnight. Certainly, we could not expect any loose items to escape being pilfered.

Praying for its safekeeping as we left the Jet, we had walked for only a few minutes down the center of the dirt road when suddenly, the sound of a motor in the distance brought us to a halt. Could a lorry be coming? Thinking perhaps our imaginations had triggered the sound, we started to move again. But before long, we heard it again—definitely the roar of a lorry motor, even though still a faint sound.

We turned and started walking back to the Jet, not knowing whether to expect help or merely a close brushoff from the driver. Many truck drivers seemed compelled to pass as closely as possible when they saw someone parked along the road. For that reason, whenever we traveled and stopped to eat lunch by the roadside, at the sound of an approaching lorry, we quickly prepared for the inevitable shower of dust that would follow. After covering our food, we took shelter as far from the road as possible until the lorry passed and the dust settled.

Surprisingly, this driver did stop—when Harv took his life in his hands by standing in the middle of the road waving both arms. The driver agreed to pull us to Falaba, while, in the same breath, requesting a generous fee for his kindness to the stranded family. We appreciated the unexpected help so greatly that we did not mind paying for it. With the winch cable acting as a tow rope, the Jet lunged forward when the lorry started off. Down the road we bumped and swayed at an unbelievable speed for the condition of the rough, dirt road.

Because of the heat during the dry season, we had removed the side panels from the Jet in to improve air circulation. I tried to protect the girls as a volley of dust poured in from the tires of the lorry. Harv clutched the steering wheel and held his foot ready to brake, not knowing what the driver might do next as the lorry swerved and constantly changed speed.

Our taxicab ride in downtown New York City that I had labeled as "wild" suddenly seemed as mild as a horse-drawn buggy excursion, compared to the ride behind the lorry. But I constantly reminded myself it was much better than walking.

We had gone only a few miles when the Jet's engine turned over and started to run; apparently the hectic ride startled the Jeep into action! Blowing the horn and trying to get the attention of the driver gained no results for quite some time. Finally, he realized the message and braked. Harv paid and thanked the driver, and the Jet performed smoothly on the remaining miles to Ganya, as though nothing had happened. The more we reflected on the incident, the more amazed we became. Only two trucks traveled on that particular road each week, and in the bush of Africa, a lorry schedule could vary considerably, depending on circumstances. Had we stayed a half-hour longer at Monko, or had the lorry been a half-hour earlier, we would have missed the much-needed help. Only divine planning could have managed to bring the lorry at the exact hour of our predicament!

After he installed new plugs and points, Harv presumed that the Jet had been taken care of. But he found that not to be the case the following week. He had driven about twenty-five miles on an errand to Kabala when the motor sputtered and stopped again. Several hours passed by with Harv attempting to locate the trouble. But the Jet refused to cooperate. When an African government official came along, Harv accepted his invitation for a ride to Falaba, and from there, he walked on to Ganya. Since the man had plans to go to Monko, Harv sent with him a message to Dave requesting advice for repairing the Jet. Three mornings later, the official came to Ganya with the information, "Now Pa Rupp be at another village working on a school and no return yet."

The friendly African then offered to drive Harv to the Jet and see if the two of them could discover the source of trouble. By late afternoon, they had narrowed the problem down to the fuel pump—they thought. Fortunately, Harv had a new fuel pump at Ganya. The official took Harv back as far as Falaba. Again, Harv walked the seven miles from Falaba to Ganya that evening and then repeated the hike back to Falaba the next morning, carrying the fuel pump. The same gentleman drove him to the Jet, and they installed the part. Thrilled to have the mechanical work finally completed, Harv moved to the driver's side to start the motor. But after searching in each pocket, harsh reality dawned that he had forgotten to take along the ignition key when he had left home that morning. Later, when Harv described the scene to me, he said, "I felt like sitting down in the road and crying."

The sympathetic African official offered to have a workman pull the Jet to Ganya with a government tractor. And thus, the Red Jet returned home. Harv turned the key, fully expecting results. But the motor still did not respond. Not until later that afternoon did Harv notice the light switch had been pulled out, which explained the reason for the dead motor. While the Jet had sat along the roadside, someone had turned on the lights and ran down the battery. After a recharge of the battery and the running engine sounded healthy again, Harv felt certain problems had been resolved with the replacement of the pump.

We heartily rejoiced to have the tires intact after the vehicle had to be abandoned for so many hours. In fact, seeing the rubber spared seemed quite miraculous since rubber from four tires could be cut to make several pairs of sandals. And who would not like a pair of rubber sandals to wear instead of barefoot walking? Sandals were often acquired in that way.

The heavy canvas roofing on the Jet had not fared as well. Part of it had been slashed away, perhaps furnishing someone with a new pair of shorts. Whatever the purpose was, the canvas had been taken, dooming us to ride without a roof on the Jet until another one could be ordered and arrive from the States. We realized that could talk a long time—and it did. The lock on the hood had been broken, but the motor appeared untouched. How grateful we felt for that, considering all that could have been damaged.

After the Jet started, Harv left to get the trailer, still parked along the roadside. He crossed the river, and part of the way up the hill, the all-too-familiar sputtering started again, followed by silence. Following all the troublesome incidents with the Jeep, exasperation rumbled and mounted as Harv faced yet another episode. When he sent for help in town, several men responded. They met him at the river and pushed the Jet across the valley.

Both Jewel and Joy had been ill most of that week. When they failed to respond to the medication their symptoms appeared to call for, we became more concerned each day. Every time I looked down at the disabled Jet parked at the bottom of the hill, it reminded me that our dependence rested not in man or mechanical help, but in the living God.

Continuing to check temperatures, sponge off hot, little bodies, urge drinks of water, and try to cheer up the patients, I prayed and waited. Finally, the fevers edged away, appetites expanded, and smiling faces returned to brighten the hilltop. We relaxed and rejoiced. To see Jewel and Joy well and playful meant a dear blessing. Father God had been faithful to deliver us out of trouble once again.

Chapter 13: Sammy Chimp

The anxiety of waiting for Dave Rupp to come and repair the Red Jet did not seem so critical once Jewel and Joy had recovered. Nevertheless, our spirits felt brighter the day we first caught the sound of Dave's vehicle climbing the distant hills on his way to Ganya. After a few hours of Dave's expertise work on the Jet, the motor seemed to run better than it had for a long time. The brakes happened to be out on one side, but that would have to be taken care of later, since we did not have the parts needed.

Having everyone well and everything working again seemed great—something like a replica of paradise. But all too quickly, our paradise slipped away, for Dave had been on his way to Magburaka only a few hours when Harv began to feel feverish. Through the night, he became worse, and by morning, he felt too ill to stay up. He suffered body ache, along with painful eyes, a severe headache, and a stiff neck. Since his symptoms differed from those of his previous bouts with malaria, Harv injected himself with penicillin, hoping to strike a defense against any infection. The shot emptied the last bottle of penicillin on the medicine shelf. Dave planned to bring medical supplies when he returned, but that would not be for a few days.

Harv happened to be one of those people who can sleep around the clock during an illness. So while he slept, I rotated between worrying and praying. For three days, he remained the same. Then on the fourth day, he began to show improvement. By the time Dave returned, Harv had passed the need for further medication.

For three days, Harv's illness had appeared to be serious. But without a professional diagnosis, we had no way of knowing what his ailment had been or if there was any need for alarm. At any rate, we realized the Lord had brought us through another distressing time when we had only heaven's help to rely on.

For a few weeks, a little friend lodged on the hill with us, helping prevent even the bad days from becoming too morose. At that time, young chimpanzees were being purchased in Freetown and shipped to the States for use in the experimental stage of the polio vaccine. Therefore, African hunters pursued and killed mother chimpanzees in order to capture their young and sell them to people able to transport the chimps to the coast.

That explained how we happened to acquire Sammy—a cute, curious, funny-faced entertainer who demanded more attention than we had to dote on a chimp. Whenever the

insistent little rascal decided he wanted to be held, which occurred quite often, he jumped up and down, screaming loudly until someone answered his demands. Since Jewel could not endure an unhappy Sammy, she usually ran at his beckon. With motherly concern, she held him until she was too tired to continue. At that point, she called, "Sammy want down." On the contrary, of course, Sammy wanted anything but down.

Loosening Sammy's hold on Jewel usually required two people to prevent him from gripping her too tightly when he saw what was about to happen. The helpers, not being fond of handling the animal, sometimes engaged in a friendly little argument concerning who should help

free Toosie. Finally, as a soft voice continued to repeat, "Sammy want down," two workers would relent and rescue little Toosie from little Sammy.

When not napping or involved in exploring around the storage shelter where he was tied, only one thing diverted Sammy's attention from being cuddled: a banana treat. His

202

fondness for peanuts ran a close second. Teaching the chimp to drink milk from a small bowl seemed impossible for the first few days. But eventually, Sammy caught on, and the milk disappeared from the bowl almost as quickly as it was poured.

Early one afternoon, Harv sat on the back step holding Sammy with Jewel perched beside him. Almost ready for nap time, Jewel's thumb had slipped into her mouth. Suddenly, an expression of surprise mingled with startled annoyance streaked over Jewel's face when Sammy reached over, took hold of her hand, and pulled her thumb from her mouth! How I wished that instant for a camera to capture the scene.

Joy liked to watch Sammy from a distance. If the chimp happened to be close to her when he screamed, little Joy instantly joined in with an alto counterpart. Unlike us, Sparky shared no affection for the new resident. In fact, when Jewel held Sammy, Sparky often turned away in what appeared to be a jealous sulk.

After some weeks, the time came for Jewel to say byebye to her friend, Sammy. Not comprehending that the chimp was starting on a long journey to America where he would contribute a small part in perfecting a polio vaccine and that she would never see Sammy again, Jewel stopped waving to the departing Jet before it reached the end of the driveway at Magburaka. Her thoughts rapidly diverted from the baby chimp to the baby boy living at the Magburaka mission house.

Dave Zimmerman, business manager for the mission, had asked Harv to accompany him to Freetown to purchase food supplies for our annual mission staff conference, since he needed our trailer to transport the load to Magburaka. The girls and I would stay with Imogene, Dave's wife. As soon as we arrived at Magburaka, Dave and Imogene's baby, Terry, had captured Jewel's attention. This explained why Sammy's departure could be brushed aside so quickly. Perhaps a contributing factor for her change in devotion developed because the cries of the human baby failed to be as nerve-racking as the shrieks of the animal baby.

Watching the Jet turn at the end of the driveway and disappear from sight, Imogene and I had no idea of the impending misfortune of what seemed merely another supply trip to Freetown. Instead, we chatted heartily as we turned and walked into the house—two young, missionary mothers with numerous experiences and ideas to share.

While at Magburaka, I proudly reported a positive development in a letter to my parents in the States. *"Imogene helped Jewel with something today, and with no prompting from me, Jewel looked up and said, 'Thank you, Gene.'"* Whenever Jewel heard baby Terry fussing, she told me with concern, "Baby Cry!" Perhaps her young mind reasoned that if she went to Sammy when he cried, Imogene should pick up her baby as soon as he cried, also.

I found myself engaged in fulltime child care during our time at Magburaka. The girls were at a difficult stage to be away from home, and we only had room to take along a minimal amount of toys to entertain them. An extra pair of eyes in the back of my head would have benefited in keeping them in sight and out of trouble. Fortunately, there were afternoon nap times!

One afternoon, I sat outside near the bedroom window listening for Jewel and Joy to awaken from a nap. Suddenly, my attention rested on an African man walking toward the house carrying a white child. And the child looked incredible familiar—something like my own daughter! I could hardly believe what I saw. Unfortunately, because of the Magburaka house being well-screened, I had not closed the lid on Jewel's crib. Apparently, she had woken up, climbed out, walked through the house, and, not finding me, went out the back door and off to find some new friends.

Since the man did not speak English, I could not find out how far the runaway had wandered. I did happen to know "thank you" in his language and repeated it with smiles and

gestures to try and communicate my appreciation for his helpfulness. He appeared overly pleased to be able to return the child who had befriended him with her irresistible smiles and chatter. Needless to say, after that, the crib lid remained down and securely snapped for naps.

Meanwhile, in Freetown, Dave and Harv checked off items on the shopping list one by one as they went from store to store. Their time at Freetown also coincided with the arrival of a new missionary family from the States, Tim and Eleanor Warner, and their two children.

The Warner family had crossed the Atlantic via an American freighter that turned out to be the same ship Dave and Imogene had traveled on. Therefore, knowing the captain, Dave obtained passes for he and Harv to go on board, where they blissfully enjoyed cups of brewed coffee while the captain and passengers ate breakfast.

It took several days of dealing with Customs officials to clear Tim and Eleanor's equipment and Jeep station wagon. Delays stacked on delays, including a stolen trailer hitch, which took some time to replace. Finally, with all the details in order, the day arrived, and the group gladly headed for Magburaka.

Tim rode with Harv in the Jet while Dave followed, driving Eleanor and the children in the station wagon. Pulling an overloaded trailer and a provision trip seemed synonymous in Sierra Leone. In spite of the load, however, the Jet rolled along with no problems. That is, until late afternoon, when Harv steered around a curve and saw a lorry advancing toward them down the center of the road. As the truck drew closer, the driver made no attempt to move to his side of the road. Harv quickly did what the lorry driver assumed he would do and swerved the Jet off the road to avoid a head-on collision. The Jet had barely left the road when the lorry reached the spot. The sudden action had swung the trailer into the path of the reckless driver, and the impact from the truck rolled the trailer over, taking the Jet with it.

What appeared to be a ditch at the edge of the road turned out to be a drop-off that caused the Jet and trailer to continue rolling. After it came to a standstill and Harv's senses cleared, he called Tim's name. There was no answer. Harv slowly pulled himself to a standing position, wincing as he moved one foot, which had the bottom of its shoe ripped off. But immediately, the injured foot was forgotten when Harv spotted Tim pinned beneath the Jet with only his legs visible, extending out from under the vehicle.

By then, Dave arrived, and with a surge of strength from above, Dave and Harv turned the Jet upright. Not knowing the extent of Tim's injuries, traumatic minutes followed for everyone, especially Eleanor and the children. Tim slowly opened his eyes, then moved each arm and leg, checking for broken bones. When he stood and tried to walk, he seemed all right, except for a painful shoulder.

Meanwhile, a passing car stopped, and the driver offered to take Tim and Eleanor back to Freetown to get X-rays for Tim. Since more medical assistance would be available in Freetown than at Magburaka, everyone agreed the option to accept the offered ride to Freetown would be wise.

After seeing Tim and Eleanor off, Dave and Harv walked back down the incline to the wreckage. With their concern having been completely on Tim's condition, full realization of the amount of damage did not strike until then. What a disaster sight! The trailer lay crumbled beyond repair and the Jet looked pitifully disfigured, with scratches and dents all over its red body. Pieces of the windshield frame and shattered glass had left a trail during the rolling fall, while conference food and the Zimmerman's personal provisions had been scattered in all directions. Nonetheless, as they picked up boxes and stacked them by the Jet, they rejoiced that no one had been killed and Tim had been spared further injuries beyond his shoulder. When everything had been gathered, an African man was left to guard, and they drove on to Magburaka with the children in Warner's Jeep wagon.

That evening, Dave and Harv returned in a truck and loaded the boxes of supplies into it. Mechanically, the Jet seemed to be in running order—at least the motor started. But they did not think it advisable to drive it to Magburaka after dark. For the men, it had been a long, weary day, and the night became longer as they tried to sleep in the cab of the truck. The next morning, Harv was none too comfortable driving the Jet with his painful, swollen foot, but he counted it a major blessing to find the Jet drivable.

One week later, having been previously scheduled to speak, Dr. Tim, with one arm in a sling, stood before the missionaries assembled for a pre-conference retreat. Dr. Tim's experience as a Bible college professor in the States helped his lessons abound in depth with a comprehensible simplicity. Hence, the retreat achieved its purpose as mission personnel felt refreshed and renewed to return to their work at each station.

Following the conference, we rode to Ganya convertible-style in the Red Jet, which had taken on a better appearance after the dents had been worked out with a rubber mallet. During the ensuing months, a new windshield and top that had been ordered from the States seemed to take forever to arrive. After riding through a few soaking showers and drenching downpours, we learned to not be caught on the road without rain gear.

The morning after returning from the conference, we found time to unpack things our families had shipped to us with Tim and Eleanor. After Harv pulled pieces of a red wagon from a shipping container, Jewel stood by, fascinated, watching each nut and bolt being tightened to assemble the shiny, new wagon. The maiden ride in her new red chariot enchanted Jewel Kay so much, she did not want the fun to end.

The wagon arrived at an opportune time for Joy, because with the trailer demolished, there had not been enough space to bring back everything with us, so the stroller had to be left at Magburaka. Therefore, the little, red wagon turned out to be a very serviceable piece of play equipment, requiring only one person to pull and entertain both girls at the same time.

The arrival of a small, one-quart, ice cream freezer perked up our late Sunday afternoons from then on. We froze extra ice cream the day before in preparation for what developed into a family tradition. Jewel and Joy immediately acquired a strong, American liking for the ice cream treat. Once, young boys from town happened to be outside when Harv emptied the crushed ice on the ground. The youngsters quickly grabbed for it and received the shocking sensation of holding ice for the first time. In a few moments, their fingers stiffened and the mysterious objects fell back to the ground while the boys yelled in Yalunka, "It burns! It burns!" They then hurried to town and returned with other children to show them the cold fire discovery. But by that time, all evidence of what they had experienced had melted away.

The confusion of the children regarding the cold and hot was similar to the foreign culture impact that a group of our workers displayed one afternoon as they huddled around an object on the veranda. Stopping to observe the scene, I remembered a speaker in an anthropology class I took explaining that invariably, illiterate people will hold pictures upside down as they look. I watched as the workers paged through a Sears catalog that Jewel apparently had carried out from the house. Having the catalog in an upside down position, they pointed to an item they recognized and chattered vivaciously. Now and then, their voices lowered in serious discussion as they tried to determine the function of some of the items pictured.

When the workers came upon a section of men's shirts, excitement mounted and words tumbled from each mouth even faster. Yalunka males belonging to the younger generation had become very fond of shirts, so seeing such a variety caused quite a commotion. Eventually, I walked over and casually turned the catalog around. But by the time I reached the door and glanced back, they had turned it again—a live rendition of the anthropologist's statement.

Plans for Dave and Imogene Zimmerman to visit the upcountry stations in the near future prompted a detailed cleaning of our house and grounds. As I worked on that project, I remembered some words of wisdom from a neighbor in the past: "It's a good thing to have company once in a while, because you take care of doing things you don't find time for otherwise." The hilltop did benefit from the busy preparations. Things were accomplished that had been on hold for some time.

During that time, both Bokari and I ran into some snares with our work. After spending most of one morning roasting and shelling peanuts, Bokari dropped the nuts into a wood mortar and started pounding.

I usually had him prepare peanut butter using the meat grinder, but that day, he wanted to do the job Yalunka-style, after promising to clean the mortar well before using it. Everything went fine until Jewel walked over to Bokari and released a handful of sand into the mortar. What had prompted such an action, we could not surmise. Was it the beginning of the terrifying twos stage? Perhaps she thought Bokari was pounding dirt in the mortar. Much of her playtime consisted of helping the workers with their duties—or so she thought she was helping.

Apparently, she considered her act as helpful that time, according to the hurt expression in her eyes as Bokari scolded her. His reaction was as near to being angry with Jewel as he had ever been, as he said, "Toosie, you done spoil de konstitu-dina!" It took only seconds for Bokari's flare-up to subside after I had dealt with Jewel, although I heard some deep sighs uttered as he went back to step one in cleaning the mortar and preparing more peanuts.

My setback came when we went away for a while one evening and left a recently-acquired dog in the house, thinking he might run away otherwise. Friends in Freetown had present-ed the dog to Jewel and Joy for a pet. Walking to the living room when we returned, I stood in the doorway speechless as my eyes took in what seemed to me, with company coming, nothing less than a calamity.

Being left alone, the dog must have panicked, jumped at the windows trying to escape, and tore the curtains. Perhaps curtains were not a "must" in the bush, but the yellow sheers certainly helped to create a cheerful atmosphere. I felt like crying, but since that would not repair the damaged curtains, I searched for yellow thread instead. Fortunately, there happened to be a spool of yellow that matched perfectly. Consequently, all the next morning, I mended curtains while trying to practice patience each time I recounted the many other things I had planned to do that morning.

Not only did we have a new dog on the hill, but also a new cook, who proceeded to bring about more complications than the dog had. At Magburaka, someone had recommended this worker to replace Bala, who had gone back to his own people several weeks earlier. In his oral resume, the new cook had assured me, "I savvy de cooking fine-fine."

But after a few days on duty, it turned out that he understood neither the basic art of cooking nor the English that he pretended to know. And since he did not understand Yalunka, Bokari could not help explain directions to him. Overall, communications between the cook and myself totaled to only a shade above zero.

It did not take long to realize the new cook had mastered one art quite well, however. In thievery, he could be classified as skilled! The sugar bowl began to empty all too quickly, as well as the salt box. Other things began to disappear, but the most upsetting was when I discovered that ten spoons could not be accounted for. If any more vanished, there would not be enough spoons to set the table when other families came.

The fact remained, in Yalunka culture, no person could be accused until caught in the act; even strong evidence of guilt meant nothing. Therefore, I tried to play detective in an attempt to end the stealing. But try as I would, the thief proved more cunning than the detective. Finally, when we began to notice a deteriorating attitude among some of our workers toward us and their work assignments, we realized the influence of the down country cook needed to be extiguished. Therefore, Harv drove the chap to Falaba one morning and presented him with one-way lorry fare back to Magburaka.

Some weeks passed before we found a Yalunka person who provided tolerable help in the kitchen. I tried to keep in mind that even learning to fire a wood stove actually pushed our helpers forward in progress amounting to centuries. And so cooking lessons remained rather difficult for a worker, as well as for myself, considering the desired goal was to produce a dependable, clean worker to manage the responsibilities of the kitchen—keeping within reasonable expectations.

We had been at Ganya almost two years when one morning, we found ourselves once again with no help. Bokari became ill for a few days, and the worker who did the laundry had given notice that he would be helping his family farm. Straightening up from bending over the washboard, I said to Harv, "The only thing that keeps me going is knowing the washer is on its way."

In the last mail, we had received word from my parents that they planned to ship an electric washer with a missionary couple returning to Sierra Leone. The news had left me ecstatic for a few hours. But when I remembered that no one else in our mission owned the luxury of an electric washer, my rejoicing subsided, and I felt selfish. Yet, as my lot fell to using the washboard, anticipation returned again for the future help of an electric washing machine.

Weeks later, when we heard that the washer had finally arrived in Freetown, plans for a supply trip took shape. The empty shelves in the storage room had been reminding us for days that a trip to the coast could not be postponed much longer. Hopefully, there would be a trailer available for Harv to replace the one lost in the accident. When Jewel woke up the next day and discovered her Daddy and the Red Jet were missing, she carried a smile-free face the rest of the morning.

The rainy weather that kept her inside added another trial to her young heart. That evening, I started a letter to my parents: *"Remember the toy cooking set you sent along with us for Jewel? It rained hard all morning, so after lunch, while the girls napped, I looked in the storage drum for a new toy for entertainment. I found the cooking set and also the toy dishes and silverware. It was a big hit; Jewel cooked and fed dolls the rest of the day. At times, she ran into trouble with little sister when she tried to set the table (a box on the floor) and Joy-Joy came along and pulled things off."*

Chapter 14: A Jittery First Election Day

While searching in the drums for toys, I also discovered a supply of paper and pencils I had forgotten about. Suddenly inspired to start our employees on a learning experience, the next day I handed each worker a pencil and sheet of paper with his name printed at the top to practice copying. When the crew returned to work that afternoon, they hurried up the hill and proudly showed me their first copy work. Evidently, Bokari had been thinking about it for a while, and the writing lesson provided the occasion for him to tell me, "Now when de mission go get Bible school at Kabala, I want go there."

In the pioneer stage of mission work, hearing such a statement coming from a young person compared to the thrill of listening to the final measures of Handel's Hallelujah Chorus! I did not know if he had already told Pa Harrigan of that desire, but considering the time and effort Bill and Ruth had invested in training Bokari, I knew they would be pleased if he carried through with such plans.

Our only weather forecast at Ganya amounted to standing outside and watching black clouds and rain roll in over the distant hills and then across the valley toward us. I never failed to be captivated with the sights and sounds of an approaching storm, then to feel comfortably snug inside the house as it reached our hill.

I had no forewarning, however, of the storm headed our way as I went to bed one night during Harv's trip to Freetown.

216

But a few hours later, as claps of thunder roared, synchronized all too closely with bolts of blinding lightning, I failed to realize any cozy sentiments connected with that particular storm. Above the forceful wind that beat gusts of rain against the house and lashed furiously at the aluminum roofing, I faintly heard Jewel's cries. Joy slept in her crib as though it were a quiet, peaceful night. Mommy's arms brought immediate comfort to a storm-frightened little girl as I carried Jewel to my bed. Once in, she snuggled against me and relaxed into sleep within seconds. The security I brought to Jewel reminded me of the privilege I had to experience the same calming presence of Father God. And before long, even though the storm continued, drowsiness overtook my thoughts and I also slept.

The next morning, when I went to open the back door, to my surprise, I found it already opened. Sometimes, the lock on the door did not catch well. Apparently, that had been the case the night before, and the strong wind had blown it open. So in addition to thanking the Lord for protection during an angry storm, I also rejoiced that the open doorway had been guarded. After that, I made certain to check the lock nightly, since I really did not care to sponsor an open house for any prowling animals or reptiles to come inside for a look around.

On the sixth day after Harv left, we began to listen for the sound of the Jet, even though that seemed somewhat unrealistic, considering provision trips seldom ran on schedule. Also, with the rivers high, he could possibly be held up with washed-out bridges. It was not until the ninth day, as the helpers prepared to leave for the night, that we heard the distant, familiar sound we had been listening for.

The noise of the Jet as it mounted and descended the hills beyond the river turned on smiling faces and an outpouring of animated chatter among the helpers. Then, as the Red Jet approached across the valley, Jewel started running in circles, squealing with delight. Toddler Joy tried to mimic her sister, became dizzy, and fell. Laughing and struggling back to her feet, she tried again. The stimulated performance of the excited little girls gave us all a dose of relaxing laughter.

I realized that Harv had good news—behind the Jet rolled a trailer. But obviously, it was not all good news; the top for the Jet had not arrived yet, as we had hoped. Harv related the long story of the difficulties he encountered attempting to find a trailer in Freetown. As he reached the point of giving up, some- one suggested that since the Army often helped missionaries, he should contact them. The advice proved fruitful. As for the top, at least the rainy season would be over before the next planned trip to Magburaka.

I eyed the box of mail in Harv's hand as he walked toward the house. It had been almost six weeks since the last mail delivery to Ganya, but I realized that treat would have to wait until later that evening, after the girls had been settled into bed.

Jewel trod as close to her Daddy's heels as possible, with Joy-Joy trying to keep up, but having difficulty. Before following the others to the house, I took another look at the large wooden crate that held the washer; it seemed too good to be true. The next day, following morning devotions with the workers on the veranda, preparations took shape to try out the new washer. Someone carried water to the kitchen to be heated on the stove. Every now and then, hands reached to shove more wood into the glowing flames, causing flickering ashes to sift through the grate onto the cement floor below. Outside, the yard workers helped Harv uncrate the Maytag washer and carry it to the veranda, while I grated a bar of lye soap—our bush country detergent.

Finally, with everything ready, Harv walked toward the storage room by the kitchen, unrolling a long, heavy-duty extension cord as he went. After plugging in the cord, he called to me, "Don't turn on the switch until the generator warms up. I'll tell you when."

With anticipation mounting, we heard Harv say, "Okay, now." I pushed the switch on the washer—nothing happened. Harv came to examine the silent washer motor to check if something had loosened during the shipment. Then he noticed the motor voltage marked 115.

"That's the problem," he said. "I'll turn the voltage higher."

When the needle on the generator gauge reached 115, Harv called to turn the washer on. No sooner had he spoken than I quickly acted, but again the motor did not respond. I felt heartsick, reflecting on the distance it had traveled, only to not work. I had been praying silently all the while, but there seemed to be no ready answer to the perplexing situation. When I heard Harv say that he would turn up the voltage beyond 115 to see if that would jump the motor, I asked, "Is there danger of burning out the motor?"

My apprehension increased all the more when Harv responded, "I suppose it could, but it's the only thing left to try." Anxiously, I listened to the generator rev to higher pitches as the revolutions increased speed. Higher and louder it continued to whirl until suddenly, another sound joined in.

"It started!" I joyfully shouted. Harv then lowered the voltage to 115 and the washer continued to run. How we rejoiced! Even though our helpers and others who had gathered from town did not understand the complexity of the starting operation, they shared in our delight at the noise coming from the large, white box perched on four legs.

In the next letter to my parents, regarding culture shock in reverse, I wrote, *"You should see the Africans when they first glimpse the agitator swirling around the clothes. They also stand astonished as they watch the wringer squeeze water from the clothes passing through the moving rollers. I believe I'm just as amazed as they, after not using an electric washer for over two years. Jewel Kay doesn't understand why I refuse her pleas to help put laundry through the wringer. She wants to help with everything."*

I relished the experience of pushing the washboard to the back of a shelf, placing it on reserve for emergency use only. Yet at times, the theory that modernizing methods might place more barriers between the people and the missionary hauntingly recurred to my thoughts. Certainly, I did not want that to happen. Then, after a few weeks of chasing the idea around, I finally rested on a conclusion my conscience could live with.

But before that came about, we spent a weekend visiting a couple from another mission. While there, we observed that the nicer-than-usual mission house apparently had not hindered their mission achievements. A neatly-constructed meeting place, as well as a town well, conveyed to the people that the hard-working white man cared for both their spiritual and physical welfare. The church had grown.

As I witnessed the exchange of warm smiles and fond glances between the Africans and missionary family that Sunday at the morning service, I realized that Chapter 13 of 1 Corinthians provides the answer: "Love never fails." Above everything else, true, genuine love and concern that originates and radiates from Christ Jesus is the master key.

Therefore, the morning after our visit to the Little America station, as I poured melted soap chips into the agitating water of our new washing machine, I happily concluded my new tool would not hinder the Ganya work. To the contrary, by having it—especially during farming season when invariably, help became scarce—more of my time and strength would be conserved for mission work. Before long, electric washers started to appear on other stations also. And some years later, our faithful Maytag continued in service at the mission boarding school, helping to keep clothes clean for the children.

Starting to pave the way for future independence, the British government scheduled the first election in Sierra Leone to vote for representatives of the government in Freetown. With upcountry citizens being illiterate, a picture to represent each of the five candidates (a cow, goat, cooking pot, lantern, and hoe) appeared on each of five boxes for the voter to know in which box to cast his ballot.

To avoid duplicate voting, each man had to use his tax receipt for a ballot. It would be marked with his fingerprint just before it was cast into one of the boxes. Only males paid taxes, so only males voted. The District commissioner had requested that Harv supervise and help keep order at Ganya on Election

Day. Fingerprinting 776 people made Harv feel more like an FBI employee than a missionary.

Up on the hill, I found myself occupied by making certain Jewel remained on the premises. Knowing that Daddy had gone to town, along with the sound of many voices floating our way, served to lure her attention in that direction. I managed a tight security on Jewel all morning and through her afternoon nap. When the workers reached the bottom of the hill upon returning from their break in town, as usual, I let Jewel run down to meet them. Then, relieved the helpers were back to help watch her, I turned and walked to the house.

Not until several minutes later did I learn what happened when one of the workers picked up Jewel to carry her up the hill. As she pointed toward town and said, "Daddy," he turned and strolled off to town with her. Mother lost. Daughter won.

Presuming that I had sent Jewel to town, Harv let her stay, although he was none too happy about it. I waited for Harv to have Jewel brought back, but when they did not come, I assumed Harv decided to let her stay, which in turn, I was none too happy about.

Not until late afternoon, when Harv returned with Jewel after the voting had ended, did we both learn the facts of what had happened. Even though we had not considered it wise for Jewel to be in town on Election Day in case trouble erupted, the people grinned with pleasure at her appearance.

"Toosie now come to town to vote!" or "Toosie now be fine Yalunka!" were some of the comments. Who knows? Perhaps the Lord used Miss Toosie to help in her small way to lighten the tenseness of that first voting occasion at Ganya. In some towns, voters took the election of their desired candidate so seriously, fights broke out and voting had to be called off. Such was the case in Falaba.

Following the election, we found another challenge upon us. Without vaccines, an epidemic of smallpox in Africa sometimes proved fatal. No sooner had Joy been vaccinated then a mild epidemic of smallpox commenced in town. Only three days after her inoculation, Bokari came down with the disease. The timing came too close for comfort.

When the government doctor at Kabala received Harv's message that cases of smallpox were showing up in town, the doctor rushed to Ganya as fast as the roads permitted. Even with medical help, one young man died during that time.

In the weeks that followed, each time church services assembled, children with telltale eruptions attempted to join the congregation. Consequently, before each service, an inspection evaluated which sore had dried enough to consider the child non-communicable. With sores so encrusted with dirt, how any escaped infection failed to make sense. Perhaps a sufficient amount of friendly bacteria existed in the dirt to counteract the germs.

One Sunday morning, a naked chap decided he was not about to be sent home. Sores or no sores, he had come to church, and he was staying. Some of the older workers who understood the danger of exposing others, dragged the boy from the shelter. But when we opened our eyes after prayer, the pox-covered body had returned. Another slight delay followed while the boy had to be bodily ushered out again, with another reminder that he may return as soon as his sores healed. We rejoiced after the final smallpox case cleared and the services resumed without forced segregation.

After the site of the future school for the missionaries' children had been chosen on a hill overlooking Kabala, Dave Rupp became responsible for starting the building project. So with Dave and Marie living near Kabala, the girls and I tagged along more often when Harv traveled in that direction.

Jewel thrilled at each chance to be around people, adults as well as children. She developed attachments quickly. Once, after a visit from Dave, Marie, and their children, Jewel stood at the edge of the hill watching as they drove away across the valley, her doleful eyes moistening with brave, unshed tears.

Ken and Dave's parents—the Rev. and Mrs. David Rupp, Sr., missionaries to Africa for nearly a half-century—still maintained unusual vitality for their seventy-plus years. For some time, they had resisted retirement. But eventide for their career ultimately arrived. Before leaving Sierra Leone, they planned a final visit to some of the interior stations.

Since neither had previously visited the Yalunka work, the Rupps chose Ganya for one stop. Soon after they arrived, Mr. Rupp and Harv began to discuss an overnight trip to another village. Listening to their plans, I experienced a mild anxiety attack while wondering how I would entertain Mrs. Rupp by myself. How could I, a first-termer, initiate conversation for two days with this well-seasoned, veteran missionary? And even of more concern, how would active Jewel and Joy fit into the picture?

Silvery-white hair and a dignified, straight posture perfectly complemented Mrs. Rupp's nature. A woman with strong faith, fortitude, and perseverance to match that of her husband, she had encountered a life packed with devoted service to her heavenly King during their many years in Africa. After the men started on their trek, any reservations I had held about hosting a mission dignitary quickly vanished. From morning until evening, one happening after another poured from Mrs. Rupp's lips as she recounted experiences from her past. Our conversation never lagged for a moment.

But just as I began to feel more comfortable with Mrs. Rupp, I spotted a potential problem developing. As Jewel walked past, she suddenly stopped, squatted down, and peered at the nylons on Mrs. Rupp's legs. This provided a new adventure for Jewel, and for some reason the hosiery really sparked her curiosity. I started pumping questions to Mrs. Rupp, hoping to keep her distracted from the inspection of her legs until Jewel went on her way. But Jewel continued to stare, and eventually, Mrs. Rupp became aware of her and stopped talking. I hurriedly suggested for Jewel to go play with Joy. Mrs. Rupp, however, smiled at Jewel and invited her to touch the stockings. And as her little hand softly stroked over the nylons, the beginning of a friendship launched. Rather than being annoyed, as I had feared, Mrs. Rupp enjoyed the girls and urged them to call her "Grandma."

Before the Rupps departed, Mr. Rupp expressed his gratitude that the Ganya station had remained open. He thought the Yalunka work held potential for the future, and assured us that Ganya would be in their prayers as they returned to live in the States. We felt secure they would not forget that promise because they strongly believed in the results of praying. Consequently, their visit left us encouraged and more expectant.

Once again, Jewel Kay looked sad as her newfound grandmother rode away. Later that day, I overheard her explaining to Joy, as she pointed to a picture of my mother, "That's Mommy's Grandma." The concept of a grandmother remained confusing to a little girl who could not remember her two grandmothers, an ocean away. But for a few days, the Lord had provided her some happy moments with a substitute grandmother.

Chapter 15:   To Catch a Leopard

Seldom did we hear wild animals near our hill, making it easy to forget such things existed. Leopards sometimes roamed the valley, but usually kept their silence. One evening, just before dark, the sound of baboons barking at the back of the hill caught our attention because they sounded so close. But they soon moved away, deeper into the jungle.

The call of hyenas in the distance could be expected on any night. Once, however, a hyena came out from the wooded area on one side of the hill and stood howling, quite loudly. Harv and I woke up startled at first, and then waited for the eerie calling to stop. Instead, it continued on and on.

Like some jungle animals, a hyena is usually harmless unless previously injured by a human. None had come that close or behaved so boldly before and we did not know what to make of it. One thing stood certain: if the commotion continued, the girls would probably be awakened and frightened. So Harv, armed with his rifle, and I with our high-powered lantern, marched out the back door around four o'clock in the morning to stage an attack. I quietly suggested to Harv, "Maybe we shouldn't move too far from the house just in case we need to make a quick retreat if you miss him." But Harv continued to edge forward. "And there might be more than one hyena out there, you know!" I added in a whispered warning.

By that time, Harv whispered back, "Spot the thing with the light; I'm ready to shoot." The instant the lantern went on, the sound of breaking sticks and rustling leaves sent the mes-

228

sage that the bold one of minutes before had reverted to his cowardly reputation and retreated, afraid of the light. Harv fired into the woods several times to help discourage a return visit.

Back inside the house, Harv decided, "Since I'm going to Kabala this morning, I might as well stay up and get an early start to beat the heat." So after a cold shower and breakfast, he went on his way and I returned to bed to sleep the remaining time until dawn.

It soon became evident, however, that sleep would be difficult to recapture as the hyena incident continued to replay in my mind. An argument began to clash in my thoughts. Common sense reasoned that the cowardly hyena would never return after being frightened away. But the opposing side forcefully suggested that since the animal had acted so strangely, he just might return. And what would I do if he did?

Finally, a pre-dawn stillness settled over the sounds of the outdoors. Not even an owl or cricket could be heard. And when the first welcome hint of daylight crept through the window, I knew the hyena would be bedding down somewhere for the day. Relaxing, I dozed off for a short time, and when I awoke and remembered what had happened, I laughed at myself for not falling to sleep sooner instead of listening for the hyena to return. Daylight always seems to assist in placing circumstances into better perspective.

Our ex-soldier friend, Suri, also had been encountering an animal problem. Suri had settled his own small village a few miles from Ganya on the way to Falaba. Family members comprised most of the population of Suri Town—as Harv called the small village. With plans to purchase additional wives year by year, Suri offered the reason for developing his harem: "Now Suri get more wives and someday become Ganya town chief."

Even though he did not want to change his lifestyle by becoming a Christian just yet, Suri seemed interested in learning more about God's Word. And since it is the holy Word that persuades people, Harv started going to Suri Town on Saturday evenings to have a short service. As chief of his own town, Suri demanded all his clan attend the meetings—and they did.

One Saturday evening, Suri poured out his concern that a leopard had been thieving their chickens and asked Harv to kill the animal. We wondered why Suri, who owned a gun and was an experienced hunter, would ask Harv to kill the chicken thief. The explanation soon came forth.

Each Animism family unit had its own animal in which they thought spirits of dead kinsmen lived. The Yalunkas held three animals in such respect: the bush foul, leopard, and croco-dile. The animal for Suri's family happened to be the leopard, which explained the complex situation Suri found himself in regarding the safety of his remaining chickens. Even though the flock of chickens made a valuable possession, how could he level his shotgun at a leopard that might be housing the spirit of a dead relative?

Regardless of the circumstances, taking pity on the people in Suri Town who needed chickens more than the leop-ard did, Harv promised to return in a few nights and try to end the leopard dilemma. Thus, as Harv cleaned his gun early one evening, he visualized the strategy he and Suri had planned to do away with the leopard that intimidated Suri and his clan. A small animal would be tied to a tree, and Harv would perch on a branch high up in the tree to wait for the leopard to move in on the bait. No doubt, he could almost feel the thrill of watching the shadowy figure of a leopard sneaking closer to the animal, making a lunge at it, and then he would pull the trigger. Not only would Suri's chickens be safe, but Harv would possess a leopard skin for his reward. He could hardly wait for night to come so he could drive to Suri Town for the real action.

Harv sat halfway up on an attic step in the storeroom while he worked on his gun. Then, with cleaned rifle in hand, he suddenly tripped as he reached the bottom step. The gun fired. Part of the bullet rocketed up through a rafter and out the aluminum roof, leaving a tiny hole to commemorate the incident. Somehow, a portion of bullet lead ripped across the palm of his other hand. Hearing the shot, I had already started toward the storeroom when Harv called, "Jane, come here!"

Since we had no emergency room to rush to, it was fortunate that Harv's hand did not bleed excessively, even though the gash seemed deep. After I cleaned around the wound and placed a sterile bandage over it, we decided Harv should see the government doctor in Kabala the next day. Of course, the appointment in Suri Town to kill the leopard that night had to be postponed.

Fortunately, the doctor happened to be in town, and after examining the bullet wound, he decided it needed stitches. The doctor did not want to give a local anesthetic however, since Harv had driven to Kabala alone. As soon as Harv arrived home, he quickly swallowed pain medication the doctor had sent along to ease his throbbing hand.

While the hand healed, the leopard could not be forgotten—Suri made certain of that. Finally, the night came when they proceeded with their original plan. Hour after hour dragged by without an appearance from the hunted, while the patience of the hunter slowly drained away. As Harv quietly shifted position on the tree limb from time to time, he became more resigned that it did not appear to be the night—or perhaps the way—to catch a leopard. Either the animal had found a meal elsewhere, or he had too much discernment to fall for the trap placed by humans.

Instead of shooting a leopard and obtaining a skin, spending the night in a tree only resulted in a tired body and a case of malaria. Suri soon found it useless to beg Pa Ache to stay in a tree all night again. Pa Ache encouraged Suri to shoot the leopard himself, reminding him that he would not be shooting the spirit of a dead kinsman. It initiated an excellent opportunity to instruct from God's Word that one of two places receives the spirit of a dead person, not the body of an animal.

No other trip to Magburaka had become more tedious to prepare for than the one I tried to concentrate on one day during our third November in Africa. While attempting to decide which clothes and other necessities to take along for

232

our family, Yalunka words and phrases constantly spun back into my thoughts, interrupting packing decisions. Not only did we plan to go to Magburaka, but en route, we faced the inevitable language exam that every first-term missionary must encounter and pass. Dave Rupp planned to administer the exam the next day in Kabala. By evening, my mind and body were so exhausted, I felt I could neither make the trip nor take the language exam. But morning delivered a fresh start and renewed energy from the giver of strength.

I still dreaded the language exam, yet as we climbed into the Red Jet and set off, excitement started to generate with the thought of seeing missionary friends again. Until then, I had been too busy to think of that aspect of the trip. Jewel beamed a smile when we discussed spending the day with the Rupp family.

"Now what's wrong?" Harv uttered, as a sudden sputter interrupted the loud, but previously smooth sound of engine parts working under the hood of the Jet. When the malfunction lasted only a few seconds, he added, "Must be a little water in the petrol."

We happily accepted that explanation. But a mile later, the choking noise occurred again, but lasting longer this time. Harv and I looked at each other with dismay as he pulled the Jet to the side of the road. After a surface examination of the motor revealed no clue to the cause of the trouble, we decided it would be wise to return to Ganya.

We had gone only a few miles, but it took the Jet a long time to limp back those same miles. The amount of time mattered little, though. We centered our concern on making it home and not becoming stalled along the road with the girls and a loaded trailer.

The morning certainly had not turned out as expected. Yet, we felt protected as the Jet struggled up the mission hill, and we both breathed a sigh of relief as we pulled to a stop at the top. Disappointed by not reaching Kabala and too young to understand the circumstances, Jewel found no reason to rejoice over being back home.

"Daddy will fix the Jeep and then we'll see the Rupps," I reassured her, while silently hoping and praying Daddy would be able to come through with a mechanical surprise. Later that afternoon, brimming with delight, Harv turned on the ignition to demonstrate the Jet actually had been repaired. But since only a few hours remained until dark, it seemed best to spend the night at Ganya.

By the time we reached Falaba the next morning—with the Jet receiving a high grade for performance—we thought the rest of the way to Kabala would pass quickly. But it soon became evident that the Sierra Leone Public Works Department had been at work.

Since paved roads could not be afforded in the interior, an alternative method for road improvements meant that loads of fresh dirt had been dumped over the road and manually graded. Unfortunately, however, a rain the night before had played havoc with the fresh highway, leaving a thick layer of slippery mud that challenged even a four-wheel-drive.

"What's going on?" Harv mumbled as he started braking. Apparently, a lorry driver had not respected the treacherous mud in gauging his speed. The large truck had gone out of control and landed across the road in front of a bridge, completely blocking traffic. After watching the driver for some time make no progress in solving his predicament, Harv walked over and offered his help in directing the operation of inching the long vehicle around on the muddy road. Finally, after our patience had been properly tested for the day, we moved on our way again.

By then, we happened to be over twenty-four hours late for our language exam, but we knew it would be waiting for us. To be sure, Dave swung into action soon after we entered the house, taking us individually to another room to test our Yalunka-speaking abilities. Not understanding Yalunka, Dave used Koronko and worked through an interpreter, who spoke both languages, to give our oral exam.

As we left Kabala the morning following the language exam, we felt somewhat akin to the two birds in a homemade cage that had been brought to our door at Ganya one day and offered for sale. The Yalunkas called them rice birds because they fed on grains of rice. Delicately small and beautifully colored, it did not take long for us to decide to purchase the adorable little birds.

We placed the cage on the veranda ledge where we could enjoy watching our new pets. Jewel found them fascinating at first, but lost interest as the birds remained totally inactive. Even though we did everything possible to make the little rice birds content, including keeping rice grains in the cage, they obviously responded negatively to their confined captivity. After a few days, we conceded, opened the cage, and watched the beautiful creatures flutter away to freedom.

With the language exam completed, our hearts felt just as free as the released rice birds that morning, even though we realized language study remained far from over. Swiftly-spoken Yalunka conversations did not sound as jumbled as they had at first, but much study and work remained in the future to conquer the Yalunka tongue. Even though we had merely scratched the surface, we at least felt we had put the first milestone behind us, and that created an achievement to happily enjoy as we turned on the road toward Magburaka.

Not until that moment did I have time to give full attention to and begin to sense excitement concerning the reason for our trip to Magburaka. With one girl on my lap and Bokari holding the other, I smiled as my mind flashed back to an incident that took place on our initial journey to Africa. In Liverpool, as a British Customs official looked over our papers, he declared, "Oh, I say. American missionaries…and only one child?"

Still amused at the bluntness of the official, I thought of how well we had progressed in living up to his observations, with our third child soon to be born. Facing the reality of another baby did bring sobering thoughts at times. Trying to keep up with the boundless energies of Jewel and Joy, along with fulfilling mission responsibilities and managing a household in the bush, already burned all the strength I could pull together some days. Except when napping, both little girls had the capability of keeping the pace of lively puppies. Though not destructive, the puppies were extremely energetic, and we never knew what to expect next.

Only a few days before, hearing hilarious laughter outside, I hurried to the door to investigate the cause. Out beyond the storage shelter, Jewel and Joy were playing in a pile of cold ashes where wood had been burned to make charcoal for the iron. Apparently, both thought it the funniest game they had ever played, according to their delighted, spirited giggles. Soon, everyone on the hill had stopped all tasks to see what the two Toosies were up to.

Joy stood with arms folded while Jewel showered gray ashes over her head. Looking much like a miniature clown, with her mouth open in gleeful laughter, ashes coated her body from head to feet. Within moments, everyone had joined in laughing, the merriment of the girls being too contagious to resist.

Even during the subsequent scrubbing of two heads and bodies with soap and water, I realized that such sunny moments furnished a healthy sport for everyone on the hill. Therefore, so what if we had another child coming to join our family before

Jewel had turned three and Joy eighteen months? After all, I comforted myself, the more the merrier!

Chapter 16: An Unsolicited Adventure

As the Red Jet rolled along the bumpy road to Magburaka, Jewel snuggled against me and relaxed into a nap. I turned to see Joy also sleeping on Bokari's lap. Suri often chided me for holding Jewel instead of the younger *pickan* when we rode in the Jeep. But with no sides on the vehicle, I felt more in control to have Jewel within my grasp since she moved quicker than Joy. Accustomed to African children not being as active, sometimes our helpers found it difficult to keep up with Jewel's acceleration.

Waiting at the river for the ferry to float us across to Magburaka, we found ourselves reminded of the stifling heat in that part of Sierra Leone. I chose to believe we would not be at Magburaka long. The baby would hopefully come on time, or perhaps even early, as Joy had, and we would head back to our more comfortable Ganya hill. I could entertain those thoughts, since we had no idea how events were to tumble around in the coming weeks to sabotage such optimistic dreaming.

As we unloaded the girls' beds and our other gear into a small house at the Magburaka station, we felt satisfied with the arrangements planned for us. To have a house and do our own cooking certainly would keep living more natural and settled for Jewel and Joy while away from home. A British doctor in Magburaka had agreed to deliver the baby, with a mission nurse assisting him. Then the nurse would stay and help with baby care for a few days. For Africa, the plans sounded great to me—much better than to have another delivery at Freetown.

By the time Thanksgiving had come and gone, it became apparent the baby would be neither early nor on time. And as the days dragged into December, everyone became more and more anxious to have the baby make an appearance and allow us to return to Ganya. Bokari's smiles appeared less frequently, Jewel talked about "Mommy's other house," and little Joy suffered from a scalp peppered with heat rash. Day and night, the heads of the girls remained damp from the sweltering temperature. Their pink, plastic tub became a favorite resort to bring temporary relief.

Each time I saw the doctor, his standing comment remained, "Any time now." But after more than three weeks of expecting to hear from the procrastinating baby, even the doctor began to show signs of becoming edgy. Finally, he sent medication home with me one day, hoping to prompt the baby into action. The pills caused pain, but failed to bring the desired result.

Regardless of the uncomfortable heat, Magburaka provided pleasant times with the resident missionaries and other families as they stopped on their way to and from Freetown. One evening, a group of us gathered in the large room at the main house to sing Christmas music.

Singing carols helped divert my attention from the growing discomfort of another try by the doctor to induce labor. This time, he had increased the medication and I felt certain the real thing seemed to be underway. By morning, there could be a newborn to name and become acquainted with. But when morning dawned, the news bulletin going out from the little house followed the same tone as before—labor pains stopped during the night. And once again, disappointment had to be patiently dealt with.

Later that morning, when answering a knock at the door, I found the doctor and district commissioner standing on the other side of the screen. It did not take long for the D.C. to state their purpose for the unexpected visit. "We both feel that you should go to Freetown where you can be under the care of a specialist," he abruptly announced.

With memories of my former experience at Freetown when Joy came, I quickly responded, "I really would rather stay here." But the faces of both men made it clear that the matter had been decided and settled.

I began to adjust to the idea as the doctor went on to explain, "Princess Christian Hospital has been opened recently by the Church of England to care for European women and the wives of government officials. In fact, only one child has been born there to date. The doctor is from Europe. She will take excellent care of you."

So once again, the girls' beds were folded, wrapped in blankets, tied with rope, and packed into the trailer with our other belongings. Heavenly planning had managed for Pauline Wanner to be in Magburaka at the time and available to go with us to Freetown. After hurried packing, an instinctive nurse nature prompted Pauline to tuck a pair of scissors in her pocket as she left her room, just in case of an emergency along the way.

Needing a ride to Freetown, Esther Grody also climbed into the back of the Jet with Pauline. Not knowing what the hours of riding in the Jeep might bring on, having two experienced midwifery nurses aboard certainly helped relax the situation. Along with the concern of an overdue baby, the clutch had been sending signals that it might retire very soon. Therefore, Harv shifted gears cautiously and we stopped for necessary reasons only.

Hence, we found ourselves in an experience none of us ever would have requested. Trying to brighten the situation, we joked and made light talk as we rolled on our way. Jewel and Joy helped with that project even though innocently unaware. Silently, I continued to "Amen" the prayer back at Magburaka when we committed our way to Father God before leaving.

As we passed from one landmark to the next along the way, it brought reassurance to know we had made it that far. At one point, a popular song from World War II came to my mind, "Coming In on a Wing and a Prayer." I smiled as I likened our circumstances as coming in on a worn-out clutch and a prayer.

At last reaching the outskirts of Freetown, the trip had finished without one incident. And despite the failing clutch and all the bumps, the Jet had successfully outrun the stork. It seemed impossible to tell the Lord how grateful I felt. Yet I knew He understood my feelings ran deeper than words could express at that moment.

Not until I eased into bed that night did I realize how exhausted my body felt—too weary to find sleep. Being the week of Christmas, my thoughts turned to Mary and the night Jesus was born. How extremely tired Mary must have been from her long journey to Bethlehem, after either walking or possibly riding on the hard, swaying back of a donkey. The thought reminded me to be thankful to have had the Red Jet to ride in.

Life in Africa had taught me to appreciate God's grace by maintaining a rule regarding adversity: always speculate on how each problem could be more severe, and be thankful it is not. Throughout the night, as I turned again and again trying to relax on the hills and valleys of a straw mattress, the adversity rule stepped in to help. Something more uncomfortable than a straw mattress, I reminded myself, would be a grass mat on a mud floor, as was the lot of the African mothers-to-be. I tried then to be thankful for the straw mattress. But if graded, my attitude score probably would not have made an "A."

The next morning, Harv and I met the obstetrician that the doctor at Magburaka had referred me to. After a brief examination, she briskly gave instructions, "Report to the hospital this afternoon. If the baby has not arrived by tomorrow morning, I will proceed with a caesarean late that afternoon." Pauline, Harv, and I climbed the stone steps of an older building that had been renovated into the Princess Christian Hospital. We planned for Pauline to stay at the hospital with me. Once inside, however, we quickly detected our proposal did not agree with the African nurse in charge. "Since you are the only patient," the nurse emphatically stated, "we can very well take care of you." As Pauline and Harv were leaving, I heard the same nurse say to them, "You may come back in the morning, if you wish."

At that moment, "morning" sounded years away. It seemed absurd for them not to be permitted to return for at least a while that evening. But that marked only the beginning of several things that appeared difficult to understand before the night ended.

A heavy lump started to form in my throat as I faced the fact that Pauline had to go; I had been counting on her support. But the lump had no chance to linger. Seconds later, the nurse appeared in the doorway. I instantly felt an inward restraint, remembering that a missionary not only represents the mission, but also Jesus Christ. And with that thought, I knew that even though this African nurse had dismissed the American nurse I wanted to have present, I would have to accept the situation and forgive.

Then, as Miss Nurse walked toward me, I noticed how her spotless, white uniform contrasted with her clean, black skin. Already impressed with the cleanliness of the hospital and now with that of Miss Nurse, I began to be a little less apprehensive about being alone in strange surroundings. Subconsciously, I must have associated cleanliness with competency.

The pills Miss Nurse held out looked familiar—like the ones I had taken at Magburaka, only there were more of them.

This doctor means business, I thought, as I put them in my mouth. Miss Nurse played her professional role to the highest degree. She did not engage in casual conversation, and as soon as she made certain the medicine had been swallowed, she walked from the room.

Picking up a book that I had fortunately taken along, I stepped from the room onto an adjoining veranda overlooking the ocean. Sitting in a wicker chair, I watched the waves rolling and tumbling in the distance. Feeling very alone, I reminded myself that Jesus promised to be with us always. He could not be sent away by the nurse. Gradually, a tranquility settled over me that remained during the trying hours that followed. The experience on the veranda could only be explained as "the peace of God that passes all understanding" (Philippians 4:7).

I thought about Jewel and Joy; I missed them, but was grateful they had been cheerful and cooperative when we left for the hospital. Opening the book, I found it difficult to concentrate at first. But soon, I became absorbed in the story and did not notice anyone near until a uniformed waiter spoke, "Madam, your dinner is here. Meals are served from a restaurant across the way."

As soon as I finished eating, Miss Nurse stood over me holding out another set of pills. On into the evening, the pills continued to come. Later, I explained, "The contractions are getting so strong, I don't think I need to take any more."

To that, Miss Nurse merely replied, "The pills are on order by the doctor," and motioned for me to take them.

As the pain increased, I felt more uneasy about continuing the medication. Once, I tried holding the pills in my mouth, with the intention of getting rid of them after she left the room. But sharp-eyed Miss Nurse must have been on the alert for that strategy, and again, she forcefully reminded me, "The pills are on order by the doctor!"

Two nurses comprised the only personnel on duty in the hospital that evening. Both were large, for African women. I realized I stood no chance between the two of them and their pesky slogan, "The pills are on order by the doctor." One thing appeared certain: those nurses had been trained to follow written orders, and they did not intend to be diverted by any development, not even increasing mega labor pains.

Since I had been endowed with a fairly high pain tolerance, I decided that perhaps it might be best to continue the medicine—not that I had any choice in the matter. I certainly did not want this to end up as another false-labor affair. Evidently that had prompted the doctor to order such frequent doses. With that in mind I tried not to be overly anxious.

The thought of the doctor, however, led to another concern. I wondered why she had not stopped in to check on me. *She probably kept in touch with the nurse*, I reasoned. That, however, turned out to be a miscalculated assumption.

Eventually, the pain became overwhelming, and my endurance began to quickly weaken. Miss Nurse happened in and found the patient with teary eyes. That did it! It was as though she had caught me lighting the fuse to a stick of dynamite, and we had to evacuate before the explosion. She moved me to the delivery room so quickly that, regardless of the circumstances, it struck me as amusing. Hurrying past the other nurse standing by the desk, Miss Nurse ordered, "Call the doctor!"

So that was what they had been waiting for, I thought. If only I had known, I would have pulled out some tears much earlier. But it happened too late. From the delivery room, Miss Nurse called, "Have you reached the doctor?"

"Not yet; I cannot find the number," came the reply.

Oh no, I thought, remembering the time the phone number of the doctor could not be located when I arrived at the hospital for Joy to be born. *But the doctor did arrive in more than enough time for the delivery*, I reassured myself.

This, however, amounted to another time, a different hospital, and perhaps an overuse of labor-inducing drugs without proper monitoring. In a few minutes, Miss Nurse anxiously called again to the other nurse, "Let the phone go. Come quickly. I need you here!"

It was December 20. Counting back to Ohio time, I knew my brother Joe's family were probably in the midst of celebrating the birthday of their oldest child. And the following day would be Joe's birthday. At the end of each contraction, which continued to intensify, I looked at the large, round clock on the wall and wondered if the baby would arrive on Danny or Joe's birthday.

In fact, it turned into a diversion activity to help keep my thoughts from totally dwelling on the situation I faced—apparently, a delivery without a doctor. When both hands of the clock joined at twelve, December 21 had arrived with baby still en route—Uncle Joe's birthday had won.

Throughout the evening, Miss Nurse had emphasized that she also had midwifery training. Shortly before midnight, I began to experience difficulty breathing toward the end of one contraction. From then on, the attacks continued, lengthening in time and leaving me struggling for air. After Miss Nurse checked my blood pressure, her former self-confidence quickly withered. Eyes registered fearful panic, and her hands trembled as she lifted my head and held a medicine glass to my lips, telling me to drink. Repeatedly, she tensely asked, "Are you all right?"

My senses had not been dulled with anesthesia—there was none. And even though I realized the developments seemed serious, not one second did I experience any fear. Nor did it occur to me that with my lack of oxygen, the baby could possibly be having distress also. Instead, my mind remained encased with the same peaceful calmness the Comforter had reinforced me with that afternoon on the veranda. I realized He had prepared me then for the coming events of that night. As a result, instead of panic —which only would have worsened the situation—I concentrated on seeing the baby.

For over an hour, the delivery room drama turned topsy-turvy, with the patient attempting to reassure frightened nurses she was all right after each episode of gasping for breath. It seemed too incredible to believe; I had been sent to Freetown for special care, but there was no doctor present for the delivery. Then, suddenly, at one o'clock in the morning, the atmosphere in the delivery room transformed in a flash with the appearance of a baby. Both nurses excitedly talked with relief and pride, taking full credit for the perfect-looking baby boy.

From then on, during our remaining time at the hospital, every time the little master made the least whimper, eager hands immediately reached for him. While walking the baby to sleep, one nurse always sang and hummed as her feet took each step in time to the music. This usually continued long after the baby fell asleep, I noticed. Apparently, to the nurses, caring for the baby resembled more fun than work. I agreed with them on that.

Later, after we had been taken back to my room, I looked at the newborn sleeping in the basket beside my bed and reflected on how much the heavenly Father had watched over this little life, protecting him not only during delivery, but also in Ganya when, during the first weeks of pregnancy, there had been a threat of losing the baby. And then, because of living in the bush and travel conditions, the following months went by without medical checkups. Everything considered, I knew the Lord had been so wonderful and capable in divine overseeing.

When the doctor arrived the next morning, she offered no explanation or apology for her absence the night before. Instead, she looked at me and said, "My, you look tired." Then, observing the baby, she added, "Well, he certainly is post mature. Just look at those long nails!" That constituted the extent of her call.

After the doctor left, I thought I could have voiced the reasons of my exhaustion: a fatiguing trip from Magburaka, two sleepless nights, mega doses of medication, and delivering a baby without an attending physician had all taken a toll. Earlier that morning, however, I had decided to file away the events of the previous day and night under unfortunate circumstances. I felt too happy and grateful for a safe arrival of the baby to bother posting complaints or accusations. There could also be the possibility that the full account of the night before had not been recorded for the doctor to see. Since she had not been summoned, perhaps she thought the delivery had been a quick, smooth process. Some things remained a mystery, but most importantly, we had our baby.

Since the house our mission rented in Freetown did not have a telephone, it was not until Harv arrived at the hospital that morning that he heard the news that he had a son. So happy with the long wait over, we laughed about the fact that we had come all the way to Freetown for a midwife to deliver the baby. "Next time, we'll stay at Ganya and use a midwife from town. It will save wear on the Jeep tires," Harv joked.

Three days later, Andrew Joe and I left the hospital a few hours before Christmas Eve. With the Calcutts out of town for the holidays, they insisted we stay at their comfortable house on the Forrah Bay hillside, overlooking Freetown Harbor. Their offer appeared too tempting to pass by.

A friend of the Calcutts had arranged to drive us from the hospital. As he opened the car door on my side, he offered his opinion about missionary women having to ride around in Jeeps. Until then, I had never thought of it as something degrading to womanhood. I did not take offense at his remarks, nor did I dislike riding in a Jeep after that. He meant well—simply characterizing a true, British gentleman.

Pauline, Jewel, and Joy greeted us at the door with a hearty welcome. Two big sisters took turns brushing a gentle kiss on baby brother's forehead. With no hesitance, the new baby met their approval and was accepted into our family.

After the girls had been bedded down that evening, Harv and I opened a box of gifts from his parents and prepared for Christmas morning. A dock strike prevented other Christmas packages from arriving from the States until two months later.

"See what I bought today!" exclaimed Harv as he held up a miniature toy train. He then wound the little engine and demonstrated how it pulled two cars around the small, circular track. Harv had found his treasure at a British department store. I somehow doubted that the newborn would respond with equal enthusiasm as that of his elated daddy.

Apparently, I had become overly tired, because later that night, I began to feel lightheaded and weak. Then, discovering excess bleeding, I could think of only one thing: I certainly did not want to go back to the hospital! Therefore, I kept the problem to myself, went to bed, and prayed. When morning dawned, I felt much better. My appreciation for that answered prayer, along with all the other help from heaven that week, made the day a very special.

Meanwhile, in the States, my family puzzled over the cable they received from Harv: "ANDY JOE BODEC 21 NINE POUNDS MERRY CHRISTMAS LOVY TOOSIE." Of course, they realized that correcting the typing error made the end of the message read, "Love, Toosie," and that the baby weighed nine pounds. But it took a little longer to decipher the rest of the message the African operator in Freetown had squashed together.

The telegram cable did not mean twenty-one inches, as they first thought, or that the baby had been given a third name of Bodec. Rather, "BO" stood for "born" and "DEC" for "December"—born December 21. Later, when Uncle Joe saw his little nephew, he could not resist teasingly calling him "Andy Joe Bodec" from time to time.

Chapter 17: A Live Jungle Zoo

Attempting to slip out of Freetown unnoticed in the noisy Red Jet seemed futile, but we tried nevertheless. After driving away from the house, Harv shifted into neutral gear to coast quietly down the long hill. Knowing the British friends living on Forrah Bay Hill would be disturbed by us making the trip to Magburaka with an eight-day-old baby, we had no desire to encounter any of them that morning. We respected their concern in thinking we should remain in Freetown longer, but mission circumstances urged us to leave a thank you note with an appreciation gift and hurry off before Dave and Eileen Calcutt returned home. We would never forget their thoughtfulness in insisting we use their house.

One person, in particular, we did not want to meet as we drove away was the British professor who had transported baby Andy and myself from the hospital to the Calcutt house. *Thankfully, the kind gentleman cannot see us now*, I thought, with the wind blowing against our faces and hair in the open Jet as we left Freetown behind. Picking up what speed was possible, we no longer felt concerned about the Jet's boisterous nature.

The few days of comfortable living on Forrah Bay Hill had been great, but the time had come to draw a curtain on soft living. Our annual mission staff conference starting the next day at Magburaka was another contributing factor to our rush. Along with our not wanting to miss the conference, Pauline's assignment to chair the medical committee that year made it vital for her to be present.

I turned to look at baby Andy cushioned atop the pillow on Pauline's lap as she held up a blanket to protect him from road dust. The sight served to remind me we were not doing what would be termed as sensible with such a young baby. Nonetheless, experience and necessities had taught that missionary living could not always be governed by logic, since many circumstances differed greatly in a developing country. Therefore, unavoidable diversity from the norm had to be committed to the Lord at such times. Regardless of the heat and dirt, Andy Joe stood the trip like a pro. As soon as we arrived at Magburaka, baths did wonders in restoring all three children to clean, sweet-smelling, little beings once again.

Later that week, Ruth Schierling baked to help celebrate Jewel's third birthday. For lunch, Imogene Zimmerman had arranged at each place a lighted birthday candle floating in a bread cube. Tall candles flickered cheerily in the center of the long table surrounded with mission personnel and their families. Burning candles always captivated Jewel, and she enjoyed the celebration until everyone sang "Happy Birthday" to her. Then, she sat quietly, embarrassed with the attention focused on her, trying to suppress a slow grin from progressing any further. How quickly three years had hustled by since the time Jewel Kay made her appearance into our world.

On Sunday morning, African Christians stretched to catch a glimpse of the new missionary baby as Gene

Ponchot, acting Field Director, dedicated Andy to the Lord during the worship service at the local church. We had been blessed with another good baby who was doing well—how grateful we were.

The next morning, as the baby reached the two week mark, we prepared to leave for Ganya. In a letter to my parents that evening, I expressed thoughts of concern for the trip. *"Jewel, Joy, and Andy kept both Pauline and I busy coming from Freetown. I don't know how I'll manage tomorrow, but guess I will in some way. Jeeps certainly weren't made for small children."*

With much heavenly assistance, we made it to Ganya. No one fell out of the Jet, no flat tires, and even the ailing clutch held on to what life remained. I am certain that this was the result of answered prayers, since as usual, the trailer carried a heavy load. We continued to wait patiently for the new clutch to arrive from the States.

After being away for two months, I was thrilled to see familiar sights of home territory as we neared Ganya. Even the Jeep Expressway was a friendly welcome when we turned onto it at Falaba late that afternoon. The townspeople seemed to share the pleasure of us being back. Whether their warm greetings resulted from our long absence or the fact that we had returned with a baby boy, we were not certain. Whatever the reasons, more encouraging friendliness generated from the people than at any previous time.

A few days after our return, a messenger arrived at

our door and begged Pa Ache to take medicine to the sick people at his village, about five miles away. "Many people done be sick. Now de men done make yeepina [Jeep] road for you de come." Bokari interpreted.

We had been fighting malaria symptoms since returning home, so Harv did not feel up to a ten mile trek. But since a path had been cleared and there was only one river to cross, he decided to chance driving the Jet to the village. Later, Harv discovered that even the town chief had left his hammock to roll up his sleeves and help cut away a path for the white man's vehicle.

When Harv arrived at the village of approximately 150 people, he told the chief he wanted to hold a service before giving out medicine. Except for emergency cases, mission policy required presenting the Gospel of eternal life prior to dispensing medications. Otherwise, many would receive help for their sick bodies, then shuffle away still unaware that their souls needed healing also.

The people in the village did not seem to mind the delay. In fact, everyone that was physically able gathered for the short service. Harv recited his Yalunka sermon that explained why God's son, Jesus, came to earth. Later, the men and women expressed their gratefulness for the much-needed medicines with a Yalunka thank you repeated over and over. They also presented Harv with dash of one chicken and three stocks of bananas. It always disturbed us to take food from people who had so little, yet protocol demanded it, lest the people be offended. As Harv left, the villagers begged him to return, saying they all wanted to go the "Jesus way." The visit brought a heart-warming response compared to the indifference in some other villages.

On the way home, in the middle of the river, the inevitable finally happened—the clutch died! With help from some Africans, Harv worked until almost dark trying to pull the Jet from the river, but without success. The next morning, perspiration beaded on many black faces and backs as they rendered wrecker service at the river. Some men tugged on the winch cable while others pushed against the back of the Jet. Freeing the mud-bogged hostage from the river was not an easy operation. The men laughed and chatted with delight once the vehicle sat on dry ground at the top of the bank. Harv felt just as happy with the accomplishment, even though he realized the Jeep would remain inoperative until Jake could come our way. And that might be a while, since Jake kept a busy schedule with building projects.

Living without transportation could be tolerated as long as no emergencies occurred. But trying to exist without kerosene would be a major catastrophe—or so we thought. Therefore, after draining the last of our kerosene supply, Harv borrowed one of the few bikes in town and pedaled to Falaba, only to discover no kerosene available. Finally, he convinced one Syrian trader to sell a small amount from his personal supply. Even though we had to prudently ration the precious oil, we appreciated being provided with some. At least our lamps could be lighted at night, even though the Jet remained useless.

It was nearing the middle of February when the distant sound of a Jeep shifting on the hills beyond the river announced the coming of Jake in his Yellow Peril to work on the lifeless Red Jet. Jake had previously stopped by on his way home from a business trip to tell us he would return in a few days. We also made plans for Ruth and the children to come along for a visit. As soon as they pulled to a stop, Harv and Jewel moved in to greet the Schierling family. When I met Jake and Ruth at the door, they had difficulty keeping composed faces as Jake asked, "Whatever happened to you?" The explanation for my unusual appearance originated some years earlier when I suddenly developed a food allergy to cherries and chocolate.

Since that one miserable experience, I carefully avoided that food combination. But the previous afternoon, as I scraped fudge frosting from the sides of a bowl after frosting a cake, one taste called for a few more. Not once did I think about the cherries I had sampled that morning while baking cookies. In fact, it never occurred to me what I had done until I awoke the next day, swollen and itching, plastered with hives from head to feet. When the cake was served that evening, I jokingly reminded everyone to enjoy it; I had paid a price for that chocolate dessert! By the following morning, after suffering through a sleepless night, I began to feel eligible for appointment to Job's League of Sufferers. And I realized that without medication or a miracle, I could expect one or two more days of torment.

During breakfast, Jake and Harv decided to drive to Falaba and check if any kerosene had been delivered. At Falaba, they not only found oil, but also learned that a British doctor had been working in the area for a few days. The doctor happened not to be in town that morning, so they left a message. Fortunately, the dry season made the Jeep Expressway passable for a small vehicle, and that afternoon, the doctor drove to Ganya with medication to treat the hives. After introductions, he handed me two pills, saying, "Here, take these for the first dose."

Holding the medicine, I asked, "I'm nursing the baby. Will this upset him?"

The doctor assured me it would not. But as I walked to the serving room for water, I remembered how additional malaria medicine I recently needed to take did appear to bother Andy. With that thought, I quietly slipped one tablet into my pocket. I reasoned that it was better to have hives than have medicine affect a seven-week-old baby. That decision proved to be God-directed.

I swallowed the pill and returned to the others who were visiting with the doctor. Before long, I started to feel drowsy, then dizzy and sick. After I had been helped to the bed, the doctor joined Jake outside and reported I had an elevated fever and a fast pulse. Under normal circumstances, there probably would not have been much concern—just a reaction to the medicine that would soon pass. But the doctor obviously felt uneasy because he had no medication to counteract the reaction, should it become worse.

Between his trips to the bedroom to check on me, the doctor paced about the hilltop smoking cigarettes. Meanwhile, everyone else sent prayers to the throne and I concentrated on deep breathing, hoping that relaxing would help end the embarrassing performance my body persisted in staging. The cuckoo clock, however, announced an hour had passed by the time my heart settled to its normal pace again. It had seemed even longer.

As he walked to his car, the perplexed government doctor looked as though he had made a strenuous house call. He planned to return to Falaba and take some of the pills himself, to determine if something had gone wrong with the medication. "They are old, but I cannot understand how two pills could cause so much disturbance," he repeated in a British accent.

I did not confess to him that I had taken only one tablet, since he specifically had ordered two. We did not hear the results of his personal experiment with the medicine, but neither did we hear of a government doctor succumbing in Falaba. Our paths never happened to cross again.

On his last visit to the bedroom before he left, the doctor had advised me to stay in bed and rest. A little later, surprised at how limp my arms felt when I tried to rise to a sitting position, I realized I had no choice but to wait for strength to return. Having Ruth there to take over made resting much easier as she supervised meal preparation and bathed the girls before bed.

That night, as the adults sat around our lamp-lit table, "Thank the Lord," crept into our conversation more than once as we relived the events of the afternoon. And by then, some amusing sidelights began to surface. We even found a laugh in the fact that after all the trauma the medication caused, it still had failed to cure the hives. I no longer complained about the hives, however—not even to myself. For once again, the lesson, "Things can always be worse," had clearly struck home. And as a result, my tolerance level for the burning itch had risen many degrees.

After Jake and Ruth left, we considered ourselves back to civilized living again with a repaired Jeep and a supply of kerosene. Going for rides with Harv when he had short trips provided tremendous enjoyment for Jewel. And when Joy no longer remained content being left behind, she sometimes accompanied them.

On their way to Falaba one day, Harv heard the chatter of a pack of chimpanzees. As he pressed the brake pedal, he caught a glimpse of dark, hairy bodies moving among the trees a short distance from the road. When the motor stopped, the chimps quieted, hiding behind branches. Then, as soon as the motor started, they peeped out and commenced screaming again. Harv played the game with them for several minutes. Jewel and Joy delighted in the entertainment of a live jungle zoo where the animals roamed free from captivity.

Another time, we spotted a family of gorillas along the same stretch of road. When we slowed for a better look at them, they turned our way. But the gorillas did not hide behind trees as the chimps had done, nor did Harv turn off the motor to play games with them. With our curiosity quickly satisfied, we drove on as the gorillas appeared only mildly interested in our presence.

When the mission assigned a national Christian to help at Ganya, the work soon began to take on more activity. Being from another area, Sabu neither understood nor spoke Yalunka when he first arrived. But he plunged in and started to learn the language quickly. Sabu seemed to enjoy teaching, and he felt concerned that the children should learn to read. Therefore, he tackled holding simple reading classes for the children who wanted to learn.

A small hut in the valley between the mission hill and town, constructed for Ruth Harrigan's medical clinics, served as Sabu's living quarters and classroom. Sabu taught reading lessons in vernacular, and then, to satisfy the children's eagerness to learn English, he trained them to sing a few choruses. It brought a smile to my face each time I heard the joyful enthusiasm of the children ringing out in their Yalunka-accented English, as the music floated up to our house. Even though the

children had little concept of the individual words, they loved singing in English. What a pleasure to have some positive activity taking place in the small, thatched, one room school. *Things are certainly looking up*, I often thought to myself.

When Sabu requested me to read with him in English every day, I gladly consented. He insisted that we read theology books because he wanted to learn more about God. I honored his wishes, but listening to him slowly stumble through pages of reading far too advanced for him became tedious. Sabu pressed on, however, continuing to attack the many words he did not understand. With Sabu's limited English, trying to explain the meaning of certain words proved to be no easy task. Our brain cells received a strenuous workout during those reading sessions on the veranda of the mission house. Undaunted, Sabu soon requested to come twice each day for reading, but before many days passed, I wondered why I had consented to that request. Nevertheless, watching Sabu's relentless perseverance in trying to learn to read served as recompense for the time and effort spent in the reading sessions.

When we had Sabu start a series of lessons on the life of Christ on Sunday evenings, interest picked up and more people began to attend. Until then, because of strong Muslim influence, the Yalunkas accepted accounts from the Old Testament. But when lessons about God sending His own son to earth to become the Savior were delivered from the New Testament, they categorized such teaching as the "white man's Bible."

Therefore, hearing the New Testament taught by an African started to smother that long-standing argument with some of the people who listened out of curiosity. And even though he was from another group of people, Sabu gradually gained respect with the people in Ganya and they became somewhat more willing to listen to his teaching from God's Word.

Amazed, I watched daily as Sabu displayed sweaters and socks he had knitted. Sometime in the past, a missionary had taught him the art of manipulating knitting needles, and his workmanship had been cultivated almost to the extent of looking professional.

Another surprise came when Sabu talked about boiling his drinking water. Someone he had worked for had been able to convince him of the health value of boiled water. When he tried to persuade Bokari and the other workers that they should do the same, Bokari immediately vetoed the idea with a laugh, saying, "Cook de white man's water be plentee trouble. I no do cook more water!" So Sabu failed to convince our helpers on that issue.

Massive results did not come in the Yalunka work, but at least things had started to move. It was exciting. But as the mission work improved, our family life seemed to be tested at an increasing rate. Problems with the Red Jet were enough to cope with, but our difficulties did not stop there. When I walked into the living room one day and saw Jewel Kay holding and empty baby aspirin bottle, I froze in my steps. Recalling that the bottle had been approximately half-full, my mind flashed back to the other time when malaria pills had flung her into convulsions and unconsciousness. I realized that baby aspirin did not compare in any way to the strength of malaria pills, yet that did not settle my apprehension completely.

Taking precaution, I moved into action and tried to induce Jewel to vomit, with no success. On Harv's last trip to Kabala, there had been no petrol available and the Jet only had enough gas to drive back to Ganya. Once again, we found ourselves unable to escape for human help. As always, recalling promises from God's Word for help in trouble brought a calming reassurance that remained.

I continued to watch Jewel closely, even taking her to bed with me that night. She snuggled tightly, enjoying the intensive care treatment. An upset stomach for a while the next morning appeared to be the only reaction to the baby aspirin snack. By the time the Jet had petrol and Harv took Jewel for a checkup, the doctor pronounced, "She's fine."

How Jewel acquired the aspirin bottle remained a

disturbing mystery. We had found the cupboard door open where the bottle had been kept on the top shelf, totally safe—or so we had thought. Considering the possibilities, we concluded that perhaps someone could have knocked it off without noticing. This was not too likely. Perhaps someone could have given the bottle to Jewel when she begged for it, not realizing the danger. Whatever happened, we were not to find out. It seemed more important to make certain of no repeats. Harv planned to have a talk with the helpers and try to explain the hazard of children eating pills. But to them, medicine made people better. How could it make someone sick? And didn't the Madame give medicine (vitamins) to the children every day? Harv had a difficult assignment.

As for Jewel, she always had been cooperative in taking medicine. My assignment resembled Harv's. How could I make a young child understand that the same helpful pills also could be harmful? I tried, and Harv attempted the same with the helpers, but neither of us felt certain of success at the time. At least we had no further episodes of overdosing after that.

Chapter 18: A Bush Hospital
In Action

We would have liked to close a door to all problems that called our time and attention away from mission work and language study, but that seemed impossible; the trials and tribulations continued. Little Joy suffered the next assault. She and Jewel had been outside playing one morning, when a yard employee came rushing to the house carrying Joy. I could recognize from her screams that it was more serious than an ordinary fall.

"Toosie Fidina done sit on de grou when she done start cry," he explained as he pointed to large, red welts on the back of her upper thighs.

"Snake bite?" I anxiously asked Harv as we examined the area.

"No, but I don't know what it is," he answered. None of the puzzled crew of helpers recognized the welts as anything they had seen before, although they could usually ascribe a name to everything. Not knowing what we were dealing with made treatment more difficult. I applied a medicated lotion to help soothe the discomfort. Joy even woke up crying during the night—quite unusual for our little sound sleeper. It seemed to be only a local irritation with no fever or other symptoms, and two days later, the redness had disappeared. Joy had become "Joy-Joy" again.

Obtaining dental care in the bush often became complicated, and sometimes problems would not be solved even when the service of a dentist could be had. Such facts I became acquainted with in a personal way. While in Freetown the previous time, I had lost a filling from one of my teeth. When it happened, I considered it most convenient to be at the coast, where I could make an appointment with a dentist. The Indian dentist worked faster and cut procedures shorter than any dentist I had seen before. Getting the work over in a hurry suited me fine, yet I began to wonder where the dentist had received his training. Could he merely be a self-proclaimed dentist in an African country?

When the filled tooth continued to be painful the next day at Magburaka, someone suggested pain was not uncommon following a filling, and it would stop in a day or two. That may have been the experience for others, but some days later at Ganya, my endurance reached its peak. Deciding to practice dentistry myself, I proceeded to remove the filling from the hurting tooth with an ice pick. It brought blessed relief, though only temporary.

Two months later, after putting up with not only one, but two aching teeth, we went to Kabala to see if the government doctor would pull them. But he happened to be out of town; the day had not been successful. That night, we decided that since Harv would be going for supplies soon, my only resort would be to go along and seek help at Magburaka. It would be the last major provision trip before our furlough to the States, which was less than four months away. Keeping the three children at Ganya seemed much easier, and it had not been my intention to go along. But considering the circumstances,there seemed to be no alternative choice. If we had known how the trip would turn out, however, I certainly would have remained at home.

The British government doctor at Magburaka looked in my mouth then sorted over some dental instruments on a shelf. Turning back to me, he said, "Sorry, but I do not have the proper-sized instrument to pull your teeth."

The doctor did not seem to display any disappointment that he could not take care of my teeth. After all, he was trained to be a doctor, not a dentist. And even though he extracted teeth for African patients, perhaps mine held too much of a challenge on that day. Disappointed, we headed back to Ganya with the annoying teeth. At least they did not cause constant pain.

A week later, hopes for relief surfaced again when we heard that a dentist would be in Kabala for a one-day clinic. For certain, we planned to grab that opportunity. In fact, it seemed too good to be true—a real dentist actually visiting Kabala!

On the day prior to the scheduled dental clinic, Joy awoke with a high fever. And by evening, a rash covered her body with what appeared to be a case of measles. As far as we knew, the dentist held the clinic, but plans for me to be one of the patients vanished like a dream—just too good to be true.

After that help fell apart, my thoughts started wandering to the tool chest and the pliers inside. One morning, I had finally had enough of the pain. Gathering enough determination, I walked to the storeroom, opened the toolbox, took out a pair of pliers, scrubbed them, and called Harv. When I made known my intentions, Harv took the pliers and appeared much more willing to come to my aid than the doctor in Magburaka had been. But as soon as his hand closed around the pliers, my predetermined courage instantly vanished.

"On second thought, I think I can tolerate the pain a while longer," I said, backing away. From then on, I made little mention of the hurting teeth. Harv seemed too convinced of his capability once I had planted the idea in his head.

One early evening in May, thunder rumbled in the distance, forewarning a coming storm. Rains were becoming heavier, washing off the land and starting to swell rivers. Consequently, the unhealthy river water hosted even higher levels of bacteria, amoebas, and other water infestations that caused a greater amount of illness for the people.

While Harv made his way around the house closing and securing the window shutters, I sat on the back step waiting until he finished. Jake had stopped by to visit and had just left. Listening to his new Land Rover putting distance between us as it climbed the hill across the river, I began to sense a heavy loneliness surround me.

Events had moved so rapidly during the past two days. It had been only the morning before that I happened to step on the bathroom scale and saw that my weight had dropped over thirty pounds. I was startled to see the extreme weight loss in less than three weeks. Only then did I begin to realize that the repeated sickness I had been experiencing for several weeks could be more than a recurrent virus, as I had been presuming.

Keeping busy with mission duties and caring for our three-bed nursery—as one woman called our young family—evidently had worked too well at maintaining a mind over matter attitude for me.

When we had gone to Magburaka to seek help for my teeth, I had also mentioned to the doctor that I had not been feeling well at times. He would not examine me without first having lab work. But when I returned to see the doctor the day before we were to go to Ganya, he had not received the lab report yet and did not know how soon it would be available.

Thinking my problem to be something that would clear up with more rest, I decided to float along with Africa and not pursue the issue further. Since we had no assurance when the report would reach the doctor, nor the accuracy of it, it seemed more important to return to Ganya the next day as planned. But the attacks had grown more frequent and severe, especially a recent bout that started with palpitations and numbness over my body. I became weaker, until at times, it exhausted all my strength just to walk across the room. After discovering my recent extreme weight loss, we decided things had gone far enough and we should seek proper medical help. Harv sent a messenger the sixty-seven miles to Jake and Ruth requesting them to come and take the children in order for us to go to a hospital.

Harv finished closing the shutters, and as I rose from the step and slowly walked toward the house, I pictured those ominous, narrow stick bridges the Land Rover would have to cross before reaching Kamaron. I thought of the rising, swirling rivers; unless it blew over or changed course, Jake was headed in the direction of the oncoming storm. The road to Kamaron had never been an easy drive even in daylight and dry weather.

But in the midst of those worrisome thoughts, a gentle hand seemed to brush away the concern from my mind with one thought: *You must not spend your strength on being worried. The Lord will take care of the Land Rover and everyone in it.*

Inside the house, quietness loomed like a morgue. This time of the evening, I always spent a happy and leisurely hour with the children before their bedtime. Reaching a chair at the table, I sat down to rest before going to the bedroom to pack, wishing I were reading books to Jewel and Joy as usual, instead of the unwanted circumstances we found ourselves in.

I remembered the relief that had moistened my eyes two hours earlier when we first heard the Land Rover coming. Sitting on the couch at the time, I struggled to persuade baby Andy to forget his former method of feeding and drink from a bottle. But the baby was not readily accepting that change. Being almost too weak to continue to hold him, yet not wanting my little one to go hungry, I kept trying to convince Andy to give the bottle a chance.

Unbeknownst to us, Tim and Eleanor Warner were visiting Kamaron that week and came along with Jake to help with the children. When I saw Eleanor walk through the doorway, she seemed on par with an angel direct from heaven. At a glance, Eleanor comprehended the situation; she quickly walked over and took the baby and the bottle from me. Soon, everyone went into action packing the children's clothing, emptying the refrigerator, and taking care of everything necessary to prepare for our departure the next morning.

As they were leaving the house with the children, we paused at the door and Tim prayed. Listening to his words, I thought, *Why is he praying so long for me? I'm not that sick.* But realization of the seriousness of my illness would come soon.

Rounded peaks of Ganya huts silhouetted against the dark, gray sky when we drove across the valley soon after four o'clock the next morning. The scene remained quiet and still except for the Jeep motor, which undoubtedly had awakened many in town by the time we reached the river. As the Jet slowly inched across the sticks spanning the river, apprehension began to creep into my thoughts. I wondered how long it would be until I would cross the bridge again. Talk the evening before had indicated that with our term almost over, perhaps we would be sent to the States from the hospital. Suddenly, I felt a surge of affection for that primitive bridge in spite of all the countless times it had caused trouble by marooning us helplessly in the bush. Regardless of being ill, I did not want to leave behind what had become "home."

On the other side of the river, the Jet's headlights beamed up the familiar hill. As we climbed upward, my thoughts turned back to the darkened village we were leaving behind. It seemed we had done relatively little to help the people, since so much depended on communicating in their language. Yet maintaining daily existence still commandeered our constant attention away from the many hours needed for proper language study.

Learning the lesson that time and patience play a necessary role in a pioneer ministry with an unwritten language remained difficult at times. But again, as the night before, the Father's kind grace cleared away troubled thoughts, making space for hope to calculate something better. I reasoned that on our next term, the children would be older and not require as much of my time. When we returned, gaining a conversational control of the Yalunka language would be much easier with more time available to study. Also, Bill and Ruth would probably be back by then. With those thoughts, the future appeared brighter. Not all of those dreams were to come to pass, but at that moment, it proved a blessing not to know the future. The present furnished enough to cope with.

Instead of going to Freetown, we had decided to go to a Wesleyan mission hospital in order to see an American doctor. The trip to Kamakwie Hospital involved a 200-mile drive over roads that gave a constant, jolting motion inside the Jet. We had not been on our way long that morning before I began to realize how really ill I was. Only then did I start to comprehend why Tim Warner had prayed so intensely the evening before.

Not only mission personnel who knew about my condition prayed, but someone else also interceded for me that week. Back in Ohio, my dad became heavily burdened with apprehension for me. Mother later told me how he prayed long and fervently, as though pleading for my very life. And that he actually did, even though they knew nothing about the emer-gency drive to the hospital until they received a letter from Harv weeks later explaining my illness.

Months later, as a doctor in the States looked up from reviewing my medical record, he asked, "How far did you travel to the hospital in Africa?" After hearing the answer, he shook his head in amazement and declared, "You could have died on that trip!" But not once did the possibility of dying enter my mind that day, nor during the days that followed. The Spirit of Christ graciously maintained my attention to concentrate on getting well.

The same doctor reacted even more when I answered his next question, "How did you get to the hospital?" To be sure, a Jeep substituted only so far for an ambulance. The front seat allowed only a small space to curl up on, and the jar from each bump seemed to become more unbearable as we drove. By early afternoon, I thought could not endure another mile. Struggling against an inward sinking sensation, I forced my eyelids to stay open and continued to watch the numbers on the odometer slowly count off the miles.

Finally, after twelve weary hours, we came to the end of the last mile. As the Jet slowed to a stop at the mission com-pound, the first person we saw was Dr. Marilyn Birch, the American missionary doctor in charge of the hospital. Coming from the construction site of an additional building where she had been taking pictures, Dr. Birch walked over to greet us. After introductions and an explanation of why we had come, we saw a bush hospital scurry into action.

Dr. Birch took us to the house occupied by herself and two American nurses. Directing me to a bedroom, she told me to lie on the bed. But looking at the clean bed, I hesitated, saying, "I'd better wash off some of the road dust first." Within seconds, however, the doctor started an examination, seemingly more concerned about my condition than with the bed becoming soiled.

At times throughout the day, I had been bothered about intruding upon the busy medical missionaries with no way to alert them of our arrival. But those troubled thoughts quickly vanished. From the first moment, genuine hospitality and concern made us welcome and very glad we had sought their help. The two nurses even took turns sleeping on a camp cot so I could have a comfortable bed. Before I went to sleep that night, and at more times in the following days, Dr. Birch reminded me, "You can be thankful you are here and not back at Ganya!" And indeed I was.

Dr. Birch diagnosed me with an advanced case of amoebiases that had enlarged my liver well below the ribs, with another abscess mass in my lower right side. Since the hospital did not have X-ray equipment at the time, whether or not to surgically remove the lower mass posed a complicated decision. But feeling reluctant about surgery with my weakened condition and enlarged liver, both doctors decided to try medication first.

After a few days, the abscesses began to decrease in size.

When the nurses came to my bed with the many pills, they often joked that if the disease did not kill, the cure might. Some truth hid folded in that statement because of the potent drugs I needed. One day, an allergic reaction to a combination of medications gave me a few hours of added discomfort. Malaria in my system required treatment, along with a shot of penicillin every day for over a week to fight infection from the abscesses.

Amoeba required intensive treatment with a potentially toxic medication called emetine. An ex-army doctor who had been stationed in the tropics later told me he would not have considered giving the drug emetine without an electrocardiogram each day. But that equipment was not available in every mission clinic, and one missionary nurse had a male patient drop dead as he left the clinic after having received an injection of emetine from her.

Due to the toxicity of the drug, Dr. Birch ordered a barbiturate to be given awhile before the shot each evening. One night, it had been accidentally forgotten by all of us, and soon after the emetine injection, I quickly found out the reason for the mild sedative prior to the injection. It required two shots of another drug to counteract the reaction before I began to feel better. Unfortunately, that canceled out the emetine for that night and we had to add one more day to the time of treatment. None of us forgot the pre-medication again as we counted off the ten days of injections.

I tried to eat to regain strength, but my digestive system remained too upset to find any food it could cope with. My body nature seemed to have been composed so that I very rarely—almost never—vomit when sick. Therefore, eating even a small serving of food made me feel sick as it struggled all the way through the irritated route. It tempted me to forget about eating, but I knew I had to keep trying.

Reading helped to pass the time and keep my mind occupied, but weakness and drugs affected my vision, making it difficult to focus for very long. Even though my situation did not make for an easy time, the Lord God did supply grace, and at no point did I feel depressed.

In spite of everything, being able to witness the inside story of the medical missionaries in their home brought about a valued experience I have never forgotten. No matter how busy or rushed, following breakfast every morning, Dr. Birch and the nurses faithfully observed a devotional period together. Their prayers revealed a complete dependence for the Great Physician to guide the day before them. And listening to them pray for my recovery each day gave me a comforting reassurance.

The other two meals usually came late for the medical team—sometimes very late. And yet, when returning for a long-delayed evening meal, they consistently maintained a pleasant nature, even though weary after spending many hours in a clinic flooded with suffering humanity and taking care of surgeries, treatments, and emergencies in a poorly-equipped hospital.

During the day, Harv tried to be useful by driving a truck to help the workers at the construction site. When he was struck with malaria our second week at the hospital, everyone teased Harv about becoming the first male patient in the yet uncompleted women's ward of the new building. The American construction supervisor and his wife had set up living quarters in the new building, and Harv had been sleeping there on a cot.

Within only a few days of joining the hospital staff, the other American doctor and his family found themselves plunged into missionary pressures when one of their children developed acute appendicitis. The episode unfolded quite differently from what it would have back in the States, as the father of the patient assisted Dr. Birch in the operating room that relied on an open window for ventilation and light. What concerns one, concerns all on a mission compound. Hence, everyone prayed before and during the surgery. We all then expressed prayers of gratitude when the news passed among us that the surgery went well and the young patient was doing fine. Even though it was only an appendectomy, everyone sympathized with the doctor and his wife about the strain of surgery at a hospital in the African bush.

My awakening, though, on our sixth day at the hospital centered on it being our Joy's second birthday. A little girl would be having no birthday celebration since neither she nor Jake and Ruth would realize it was her birthday. Sentimentally, I thought about the cake mix on the shelf at Ganya reserved for the occasion. But forcing aside those thoughts, I reminded myself to be thankful the children had good care during our separation time. There would be other Joy-Joy birthdays to celebrate in the future. Tim and Eleanor Warner had taken baby Andy home with them to help relieve Ruth Schierling, realizing she had enough to handle with Jewel and Joy in addition to her own children—what a tremendous help and blessing.

Not knowing that Tim and Eleanor had an appointment to see Dr. Birch one day, they surprised me when they appeared in the doorway with Andy. While they went for their appointment, baby and I enjoyed an affectionate reunion. How wonderful it felt to have his head cuddled against my neck for a nap.

Andy was still sleeping when the Warners returned for him. Wisely, Tim whisked the baby from me and left before I had time to realize it. Being exhausted from sitting up and holding Andy made the parting a little easier. Soberly, I returned to the bed, realizing I had far from enough strength to care for the baby, and wondered how long until I would be able.

The day following the last emetine shot, I moved to the building where Harv stayed. As soon as Dr. Birch thought my liver would handle the morphine—which was to be substituted in the absence of Novocain—the infected teeth scenario came to an end as she extracted them.

During the long days, while everyone else busily worked, I passed the time with reading. Now and then, when tired, I put the book aside and my eyes traced around the many rows of large hands and the words "Hand Brand" imprinted on the new aluminum roofing above. While doing the eye-tracing activity one morning, I became aware of someone standing at a nearby window opening. When I looked his way, the African man introduced himself as the local pastor and then gently stated, "I am so sorry you have become ill while trying to help my people." With that, he turned and walked away just as quietly as he had appeared.

As I reflected on what had just happened, I realized the pastor had not said "the Yalunka people," differentiating between the Yalunkas and the local people the pastor belonged to. Instead, he had swept the Yalunkas under his wings as "my people," forgetting tribal barriers, which can extend deep in Africa. I knew I had just witnessed the transforming power of the Lord Jesus functioning in the heart of an African. What a miracle of love! Being in the bush, having visitors or get well cards to raise my spirits was not customary. But that one short visit from the African pastor sufficed and will always remain a cherished memory.

Never will I forget our days spent at the bush hospital at Kamakwie. The kindness of the doctors and nurses extended far beyond duty. To witness the devotion of the medical missionaries to the Master Healer and their Christ like love and dedication to the Africans inscribed a lasting impression.

Chapter 19: Gay Ole Paree

During my childhood years, I would sometimes sit at the piano and play the melody notes and sing the words to a song entitled, "Gay Ole Paree." It was found among sheet music from a previous generation in Mother's piano bench. With youthful fantasy, Paris became an enchanted city of glimmering lights and lovely ladies in flowing gowns, as it was pictured on the front cover of the music.

Never once did I ever dream of actually seeing the fairyland city someday. Unfortunately, the day we spent in Paris on our way to the United States from Africa did not fulfill my childhood imaginations derived from the song of a colorful, merry-minded Paris. From the mission hospital all the way to Paris, obstacles cluttered our course. After leaving the hospital, I stayed at Magburaka while Harv went to Ganya to pack our things for storage and then pick up Jewel and Joy from the Schierling's home at Kamaron. At Ganya, Harv met with delays, and the packing took longer than anticipated.

On his way to Kamaron, a flash flood forced Harv to spend the night in the Jet between two washed-out bridges. The Jeep managed to ford the first river, but not the second. By morning, the water had subsided enough to make a temporary crossing with rocks and sticks. At the final river before Kamaron, another bridgeless river greeted Harv. Leaving the Jet at the riverbank, he swam across the river and walked the rest of the way. Early the next morning, two excited Africans came to the mission house with news that the Jeep had been pushed into the river. Jake and Harv dashed to the river and found the report to be accurate; the Jet stood on end in the water.

Their first thought focused on finding the culprits responsible. Instead, becoming more practical, they turned their attention to the task of gathering together a rescue team. And with the muscles of several African men, the help of cables, ropes, logs, and shouted instructions from Jake, the Jet finally reached dry land. The rescue team thought they had not worked so hard for "plenty long time!" No doubt they were right.

Then came the job of getting the Jeep back in running order. Again, Jake's mechanical expertise saved the day, and Harv left Kamaron with the girls by mid-afternoon. After spending that night at Ganya and bidding farewells the next morning, one term with the Yalunka people ended as Harv locked the door to the mission house on the hill and drove across the valley.

Meanwhile, at Magburaka, I could only wait and wonder what challenges the unpredictable bush country held this time. Each day of delay brought a little more concern. It became more difficult to not drift into moments of anxiety, since Harv had to manage two spirited little girls by himself.

With the boarding school at Kabala under construction, Tim and Eleanor were living on the other side of the river at Magburaka in a rented building, temporarily house-parenting the children of our missionaries. They continued to take care of Andy.

One afternoon, Tim came and took me to spend some time with the baby. When I lifted Andy and held him, I quickly realized that I had regained very little strength, if any, from when I had held him at the hospital. I had expected to rebound much quicker, but since I was still unable to eat much, that was not happening. After returning to Magburaka, a bout with discouragement followed until I remembered the Lord Jesus and tried to relax in His promises.

Finally, the wait ended as the Red Jet came down the palm-lined driveway one afternoon. What a beautiful sight for me! As soon as Jewel and Joy bounced from the Jet, they ran toward me shouting, "Mommy, Mommy!" Uncertain that I could withstand their enthusiastic greeting, I quickly sat down on the step to receive their hugs. How we rejoiced to be together again.

Since our passports needed to be updated with the addition of Joy and Andy, they had been sent to the American Embassy in Monrovia, Liberia. But for some reason, we met an unexplainable delay in the return. Each day, we waited and hoped as the date of our flight to the States came closer. Finally, the plane tickets had to be canceled and the next connection would be eleven days later.

Additional urgent requests sped by wire from our mission to Monrovia. Still, no passports appeared. Convinced we needed to leave on that second date, Tim Warner drove us to Freetown strictly on faith. Not only had I not gained weight or strength, but malaria had attacked twice within two weeks. It seemed leaving Africa tormented us, and yet this place would not loosen her hold on us. The situation looked hopeless, to say the least, when the passports still had not arrived on the morning of the second scheduled flight.

Therefore, Tim and Harv went to the Air France office to explain the circumstances and cancel the flight again. Before long, they rushed back to the house and excitedly shared the news that the Air France representative said he could get us out of Freetown. He felt certain we would be taken care of in Paris with a temporary passport to go the rest of the way.

Jake, Ruth, and Esther also happened to be at the mission guesthouse and that brought a very helpful blessing. It took all of us working together to get last minute details in order and final packing done. We had tried to maintain readiness to leave in case the passports suddenly arrived. But with three young children—one being a baby in diapers—that goal was easier to plan than to achieve. During the flurry of racing against time, Esther remarked, "This would make a story to publish!"

It seemed a dream when we finally boarded the launch that would take us across the bay to the airport. Remembering the wild ride on the launch when we first arrived in Sierra Leone, I had been dreading the bay crossing. But apprehension immediately dissolved as the launch skimmed across a bay of smooth water, and I watched Jewel and Joy each happily clutching their new dolls we had saved for the trip.

Harv's shirt pocket held the paper we thought would be our magic ticket to substitute the missing passports. It gave the explanation for our not being in possession of passports and informed that we had received permission from the Principal

Immigration Officer at Freetown to travel by air to Paris without passports. The paragraph ended: "This authority is valid only for two days from the date of issue, and is issued only because of a serious state of illness of Mrs. Ache."

At the airport, the paper worked fine; no difficulties at all. I did begin to see other difficulties emerging, however. While Harv took our luggage through inspection, I began to calculate that the trip would not be nearly as easy as making hay on a hot summer day!

Stepping out into civilization marked a new adventure for three-year-old Jewel and two-year-old Joy. Trying to keep them under control while holding Andy left me almost as perplexed as though I had the responsibility of corralling two young colts just turned loose in a pasture. How nice it would have been to have Bokari within calling distance.

While I went to the restroom to change Andy, Joy took off her shoes and waded in a puddle of water in stocking feet. Fortunately, our luggage still remained open on a counter and I had a chance to grab another pair of anklets for her. Even though oblivious to their audience, the girls provided ongoing entertainment for other passengers as we waited for our late-arriving flight. The show continued on unrehearsed, but could end none too quickly for me. At last, the plane circled above and landed.

We were so happy to be on our way at last that we did not take much notice of the plane we boarded until takeoff. We then realized that we were on an airplane apparently overdue for retirement. It roared, rattled, and shook not only during takeoff, but also after we were airborne. In fact, the plane vibrated so much, it was impossible to use the armrests. The two Africans at the controls in the cockpit were the only crew members. Harv and I exchanged concerned glances, not wanting to say anything that might frighten the children. After landing at Conakry, Guinea, we gladly changed planes for a Super Constellation for the rest of the flight to France. A stop at Dakar and the evening meal provided a chance for the girls to burn off some bottled-up energy. Then, following the next stop at Casablanca, all three children settled into sleep for the rest of the night.

After landing at the Paris airport the next morning, a damp wind greeted us that chilled us through the sweaters. But an even more chilled atmosphere awaited us inside the terminal when Harv revealed that we were traveling without passports. Immediately, we found it not to be the most desirable way to enter a country. The paper from the immigration officer at Freetown seemed to hold no authority whatsoever, and we were placed under house arrest with the stipulation we could go to the American embassy only.

Breakfast had not been served on the plane, and it was too late for it in the terminal. While we wondered where we could find food for Jewel and Joy, a beret-capped, jolly-faced Frenchman walked past. Unlike everyone else we had encountered to that point, he flashed a friendly smile and asked, "Have you eaten?"

After hearing that we had not had breakfast, he said, "I think we can find cookies and milk on the next floor." To avoid sick spells while we traveled, I did very little eating. I knew my stomach would not tolerate cold milk and cookies, nor would my legs manage the long flight of steps the man motioned for us to follow him up. So I opted to remain with our luggage and give Andy his bottle while Harv took the girls.

Feeling the isolation of being in a strange country, I remembered the assurance others in our mission had given us that once we reached Paris, everything would be fine. When traveling to the States because of illness, they had been given the red carpet treatment with a private room to rest. Of course, they had traveled with passports; those necessary papers made a world of difference.

When Harv returned, he phoned the American embassy, and after retelling our problem many times to a higher personnel each time, he finally reached the top. At first, the American at the other end of the line responded reluctantly, but finally said he would see what he could do for us. After a long bus ride to the downtown terminal and a hurried lunch—minus drinking water—we found our way to the American embassy. For over five hours, we wrestled for passports in order to catch our flight that night.

We soon realized we had gained the title of "nuisance of the day." Taking care of us obviously disrupted the work schedule of more than one person. But knowing we had passed the point of no return, we ignored their annoyance and continued to persevere. Needing pictures for the passports, a man from the embassy guided us to a photographer a few blocks away. From the start, he set out at a pace I could not maintain. Harv carried Andy and went ahead far enough to keep the man in sight. Holding the hand of a girl on each side, I struggled to keep Harv in view, thinking how amusing we must look with our try-to-follow-the-leader hike down the streets of Paris. But when the distance between Harv and I kept widening, and then he turned a corner out of sight, things no longer seemed as amusing. However, a short distance from the corner, Harv stood waiting at the door leading to the photography studio.

The session with the photographer that followed could not remotely be described as pleasant. Again, we had cut into the schedule of another person without a previous appointment. Being tired and thirsty, Jewel and Joy begged for water, which they had not had since the night before. And when they would not cooperate with happier faces, the photographer did not attempt to cover his irritation. He finally had to settle with a picture of the girls looking just like they felt—miserable!

Back on the street, we stopped at a sidewalk cafe for an ice cream treat that helped to quench the thirst of Jewel and Joy for a while. Opening my purse, which I had not used in three years, I spotted a bottle of Dramamine that had helped to prevent motion sickness when needed on our way to Africa. I reasoned that if Dramamine helped the rolling days on the Atlantic, why not use it for a turbulent day in Paris? It did bring some relief from the nausea that had been hounding me all day.

Back at the embassy, Andy began to fuss for his long-overdue bottle. Before we left Freetown, someone had thoughtfully reminded me that water would be scarce in Paris. So to avoid so many changes for him, we had made up enough bottles to last throughout the trip. Unfortunately, we had left all the bottles in refrigeration at the air terminal, having no idea it would take so long at the embassy. It mattered little to the baby whether we had passports or not; he just wanted his bottle. Leaving the girls with Harv, I took Andy out into the corridor and tried to coax him into forgetting about his empty stomach and get him to go to sleep. At least as long as I walked with him, we snuggled and he kept quiet.

Now and then, I went to the door to see how Harv was faring with the girls. Each time I checked, it became more similar to a comedy scene. I cringed when I saw Harv tugging at Joy to pull her away from investigating the telephone on a desk. With his other hand, he made attempts to pull Jewel from her squatting position as she inspected the nylons of a secretary, just as she had done to Mrs. Rupp at Ganya. I desperately hoped she would not start to touch the woman's leg, as Mrs. Rupp had invited her to do.

Looking at Harv from a distance, I realized how much like refugees we really did appear. When he brought our things from Ganya to Magburaka, rain had seeped into one drum and the coloring from a red notebook had faded into Harv's travel suit. The new suit he purchased in Freetown to replace it turned out not to be wrinkle-free, but wrinkle-full.

Harv also needed a haircut. His hair length would pass today, but not in the fifties. Even without a mirror, I knew how I looked in the same nylon dress I had worn to Africa when over thirty pounds heavier. Certainly, no Paris designer would be impressed with my appearance in spite of the heels I wore for the first time in three years, trying to look more tastefully up to par for travel.

The next time I glanced through the door, Harv held the hand of Jewel on one side and Joy on the other while they turned him in circles. Oh no! Knowing how easily Harv became dizzy in circular motion, I quickly closed the door, not wanting to witness the outcome of that entertainment.

As I paced in the corridor with Andy, two American servicemen walked by, then turned to inquire where I was from. They started making over Andy and he grinned at them. When one asked to hold him, I gladly handed over my little load.

Since the corridor had no benches to rest on, I leaned against a writing shelf attached to the wall and tried to relax.

I am convinced our Lord had those two servicemen in the embassy corridor at the right moment, just as he had the friendly Frenchman at the airport that morning. Not only did I have a little rest from carrying the baby, but seeing Americans and talking with them somehow helped to bolster my courage and strength.

At 5:15 that evening, we walked from the embassy with passports finalized, extremely grateful to have that struggle finished. Later, our mission office in the States informed the Office of Public Affairs of the National Association of Evangelicals in Washington, D.C., who, in turn, reported the difficulty we had encountered to a United States government office, attempting to prevent a repeat of our experience for any other missionary in the future. Whether it had any influence or not, an American ambassador was eventually placed in Freetown.

Six hours after we left the American embassy, our plane climbed upward into the night sky and banked in a turn above Paris. Below lay the enchanted, glimmering city of my childhood visions. It really did exist after all—the charming city of sparkling lights. The day we had just spent in Paris had camouflaged any beauty, but it instantly became bygone as I viewed the scene below. *Bonsoir, Paris!* You are, indeed, beautiful from up here. I can never recall our day in Paris without deeply marveling at the miraculous manner the Lord aided us. I easily could have qualified for a wheelchair, but that, of course, would not have been possible with three children and all the events of the day. But our Great Keeper had supplied sufficient grace and made His strength perfect in my weakness, just as the promise states in 2 Corinthians 12:9.

Fatigued, the children soon settled into dreamland, but sleep dodged my grasp in spite of exhaustion. The deep, dark Atlantic below seemed foreboding during that night flight. Sparks flying from the engine on our side of the plane did nothing to increase my security level. Finally, I nudged Harv and whispered, "There must be something wrong with that engine." He reassured me it was nothing. After a while, when no fire developed, I decided Harv must be right; sparks flying from plane engines must be normal.

Whenever my attention turned to the hammocks hanging from the top of the cabin where the children slept, over and over, words from Scripture repeated in my thoughts: "The eternal God is thy refuge, and underneath are the everlasting arms" (Deuteronomy 33:27). And even though my body did not feel well, my heart and mind had peace from the Comforter within.

The Emerald Isle slept soundly as the landing gear lowered and we touched down at Shannon, Ireland to refuel. We saw nothing of her but lights. Harv left the plane with some other passengers to be able to say he had walked in Ireland. The children continued to sleep during the landing and takeoff.

Drowsy passengers were served breakfast over the snow-capped mountains of Greenland, but I had to decline; no help came from Dramamine that morning. Finally, New York came into view and soon, the first bounce of contact with a runway at Kennedy International brought a special thrill. When we walked away from the ramp, certainly no one has ever been more overjoyed to stand on American land and have a trip concluded.

With no chairs or benches in the area where the children and I waited while Harv took our luggage through customs, I passed the point of being conventional. Finding an empty corner, I spread out a raincoat on the floor and sat on it with the children. Right then, I considered it fortunate to be in the midst of a rushing throng

of busy, self-involved people, since no one seemed to notice us and our wearied appearance. When Harv returned, we moved on and found his parents waiting for us. My parents, involved in evening Vacation Bible School at their church that week, drove all night to be in Allentown by the time we arrived there from New York. My brother Joe and his wife Jane had traveled with them to bring a used car so we could have transportation. After all the hugs and greetings, the four grandparents and other family members spent the rest of the afternoon focused on Jewel Kay as well as Joy and Andy, who they were seeing for the first time.

Mother later told me that my appearance shocked her so much, she could not sleep that night, even though she had been up all the previous night. They knew I had been ill, but not until they saw me did they realize how serious it had been.

Harv, the children, and I had no problem sleeping that night after not being in a bed for over sixty hours. Just being back in America and surrounded with family gave me a comfortable feeling that all would be well. I reassured myself that I would regain my health quickly and in a year, we would return to Sierra Leone.

Chapter 20: On the Move

After being with Harv's parents for a while, then visiting my family in Ohio, we set up residence in an apartment our mission provided in Fort Wayne, Indiana for our one-year furlough. Harv soon became busy with mission speaking assignments. Two years later, after my health had not made the progress we had hoped for, Harv accepted the pastorate of a church in Illinois.

Located on a country road in a farming area, the church and parsonage seemed to hold a quiet, more conducive atmosphere for me to relax and gain strength. The children relished the freedom of a yard to play in, and for some reason, the cemetery behind the church quickly became a drawing attraction to the three explorers. Once, Harv peered around a corner of the church and saw Jewel standing atop a tombstone "preaching" to her congregation, which consisted of her younger sister and brother. Before long, however, fearful the sanctity of the graveyard may be disrespected, we had to declare it an out-of-bounds area. In moments of weakness, I think the alluring cemetery still may have received some occasional visits.

In the years that followed, Harv always laughed heartily when relating the time he officiated at the graveside service of an elderly person who had returned from a distance for burial. Andy had followed Harv to the cemetery and stood beside his daddy during the brief service. But while Harv prayed, Andy moved back a few steps and dropped into the open grave. The solemn service took an unexpected break while mortician and pastor struggled to suppress a mounting impulse to laugh as they rescued the unharmed little boy from the dust of the earth.

Even though he was a quiet child, more than once during his early years, Andy innocently became involved in troublesome situations. The embarrassing episode that occurred while we still lived at the apartment housed in our church headquarters in Fort Wayne started the chain of events that followed. One morning, Harv's reporting of a suspicious smell brought the busy president from his office to our basement apartment in search of the origin of the odor. Caution demanded alarm, since the building not only housed offices and many records, but also a bookstore, and apartments on the second floor for missionaries to live in while on home assignments. There were also storage areas in the basement for missionary supplies and equipment that would be shipped overseas. A fire breaking out in the building certainly would not be wanted.

We finally located the source of the smell in the oven where a plastic toy had been rolled too close to the pilot light by toddler Andy. How he had managed to open the oven door seemed surprising. My face burned red as the president returned to his office with a dark smear on his otherwise spotless shirt, although he had coped with the incident with an understanding spirit. The following summer, we had moved from Fort Wayne to a second-floor apartment owned by our denomination in Berne, Indiana. Soon afterward, one quiet day suddenly turned alarming as I attempted to explain to Andy how to unlock the bathroom door after he had somehow maneuvered the sliding bolt to a locked position. Amazingly, he had reached the bolt even though it seemed too high for him to do so. Instead of the door being unlocked as I attempted to get the message across, from under the door came the sound of water being turned on in the bathtub. A small child and running water behind a locked door could hold the potential for developing into something more serious. Consequently, in order to end that dilemma, someone had to be called in to remove the bathroom door.

One other day, Harv had taken Andy with him to pick up some things in downtown Berne. As they walked, Andy's shoe became caught in a grating along the sidewalk. It had wedged into such a position that Andy's foot could not be pulled out of the shoe. Soon, a small crowd gathered, which in turn drew the attention of a police officer. After some time and much effort, the shoe eventually became dislodged. During all major and minor childhood misfortunes, our blond, blue-eyed Andy always remained patiently calm and collected.

But that did not hold true with Joy the day a door behind her blew shut and locked, after she had gone out to a screened porch off the same second floor apartment in Berne. Jewel came running to the other side off the house where a neighbor lady and I stood visiting to tell me about Joy. Before I could arrive, frightened Joy panicked at being locked out, removed one of the screens, and dropped to the ground. Fortunately, she landed in bushes that broke her fall and she suffered no injuries.

So for the most part, we found country living in Illinois taking on an easier format. In September, Jewel enjoyed her half-days in kindergarten, and then proudly climbed aboard the yellow school bus the following year to enter first grade. Her face beamed in a grin each morning when the door swung open and the bus driver greeted her with a loud, cheerful, "Good morning, Jewel."

Later that year, when Jewel became somewhat handicapped with a broken leg, and then another broken bone that occurred the following year, bus driver George quickly rose from his seat as soon as the bus stopped to assist her up or down the steps. Jewel remained a good sport with the bothersome casts both times. In fact, with pain, she always came through as a non-complainer, to the extent that we failed to realize her shoulder had been broken until she could not move out of bed one morning. When asked by the doctor when she had fallen, how do parents explain it had occurred two days earlier?

As my health began to improve, I became involved in more and more church responsibilities. Busy with duties of a pastor's wife, plus caring for my family, I failed to take seriously the warning signals that my activities had been exceeding my strength until too late. Once again, I found myself down—weak, unable to eat, and losing weight. Someone recommended I see a doctor in the area who had had experience with tropical diseases while serving with the U.S. Army overseas. The doctor sent me from his office directly to the hospital and started tests that seemed quite extensive for my weakened condition. Without doubt, the doctor possessed experienced knowledge in searching for evasive tropical bugs, but I realized my hope rested only in the Lord.

As in Africa, I went through several days of treatment again, but with another drug that supposedly had been improved to be not as toxic. Nevertheless, my body recognized it as a strong medication from start to finish, and I had to remain quiet to avoid heart palpitations. Then, on the final night of treatment, my heart reacted with a message that it had had enough, and another drug had to be used to temper down the racing pump in my chest. For many weeks after, there were times when it throbbed too rapidly and other times it slowed below a normal beat. As I prepared to leave the hospital, a nurse wisely advised, "Don't measure your progress by days or even weeks. It may take months, but have patience." Her sound words of wisdom often helped during the months that followed.

When I saw the doctor for a post-hospital appointment, he strongly urged me against returning to the tropics. The doctor gave suggestions to help avoid another recurrence and told me what foods to exclude from my diet. But inwardly, I refused to accept his prognosis as final and kept praying and striving for better health to be able to return and work with the Yalunka people.

There were not many African-Americans located in the area where we lived. But whenever I happened to see one, I was reminded my heart still longed for the people we had left. Not that serving churches in America brought misery, but to work in a developing country trying to help people who had no yellow pages with listings of churches, clergy, schools, local doctors, and hospitals, and who remained virtually undeveloped, had become the most valued years of my life. It brought too much heartache to even think about the possibility of never returning. The reason why David Livingstone wanted to be buried in the soil of the Dark Continent can easily be understood once Africa or any third-world country captures a heart for service. In Yalunka it would be expressed, *I x la n suxu.* This means, "Desire for you holds me."

After three years in Illinois, we moved to Michigan where Harv became the pastor in another country church not far from Saginaw Bay. That fall, Jewel entered third grade, Joy became a second grader, and Andy started kindergarten. With school well advanced into the second month and the children having adjusted to the changes, we had seemingly become settled in at the parsonage. Since Harv enjoyed teaching, he obtained permission from the church board to become available to do some substitute teaching in the local schools.

One evening in October, following a phone call, Harv had gone to the home of a teacher to pick up lesson plans for the next day. As I sat at the table sewing on drapes, an ambulance sped by outside with its siren blasting. Jewel, Joy, and Andy were in bed sleeping and I hoped the noisy siren would not startle them awake. Without a doubt, adjusting to living in a house so close to the highway would take a while. I do not remember if I did that night, but the sound of a siren usually caused me to pray for the person involved, since it always denotes some type of trouble.

Sometime later, responding to the doorbell, I saw two patrolmen standing at the door. "Your husband has been in an accident," one said. "You should go to the hospital right away. Do you want us to take you?" I explained I would find another way because I had children and would need to locate someone to stay with them.

Stunned, I walked across the room and picked up the phone book to call someone for help. But to my dismay, I found my mind totally blank and could not think of the last name of one person in the church who might be available. Fear moved in and I began to panic. But as I called on the Lord Jesus for help, a calming voice spoke in my mind: *Jane, you have the Lord.*

Praying while scanning down the columns of names, I finally recognized the name of one family. The wife immediately said she would come and take me to the hospital, and she also knew a girl she could pick up to stay at the house with the children. While I waited for them, I went to the basement to put coal in the furnace and bank the fire for the night. As I watched the flames shooting, once again, the Lord touched my mind and heart with His miraculous, calming peace.

When we arrived at the hospital, they were ready to take Harv from the emergency room to surgery. A nurse said to me, "Go ahead and talk to him, he might hear you." Even though Harv's pale, still form did not look able to comprehend anything, I bent over the cart and with assurance, said what came to my lips: "You are going to be alright."

After Harv had been wheeled from sight, a nurse tried to reassure me by saying, "We're in luck. A highly-qualified surgeon from this section of the state happened to be available and has been called in for the surgery." I knew, of course, our great Shepherd, not luck, had arranged for the surgeon to be in the area.

As the surgeon walked toward us following surgery, his face revealed the situation to be serious. The doctor explained that Harv had several internal injuries. His chest had been crushed so severely that his heart had been moved out of place and would have to remain in that position. He added, "The next forty-eight hours will be crucial. We have done all we can. It's up to the man upstairs now." My trust rested in our great, loving, all-powerful God, not just a man upstairs, yet I appreciated the doctor's willingness to acknowledge a higher power. Already, the Lord Jesus had shown His providence in having a car drive past sometime following the accident. In the darkness, the son of the woman driving spotted Harv leaning over the hood of his car. They could have driven past with no one noticing.

The accident occurred at a T intersection in the road. With no warning sign posted in advance and being unfamiliar with the country road, Harv had kept going straight and plunged into a deep ditch. The doctor concluded that if Harv would not have been found when he had, he would not have lived much longer. Time was running out as the ambulance reached the hospital.

Walking into Harv's room, I found myself unprepared for what I saw. Bare to the waist, the claws of a large hook had been planted into the skin and up under his rib cage. Attached at the top of the hook, a rope went up through a pulley on a frame above the bed. It traveled the length of the bed, through another pulley, and down where it fastened to a weight that raised his chest with each breath.

Still semiconscious, Harv tried to talk, but the tangle of drugs, weakness, and coping with a tracheotomy made talking difficult. Harv lived through the night, and by late morning, our district superintendent had notified several churches, and many people started praying for his recovery. During the following days, complications brought some concern, but by the time a week had passed, Harv appeared to be on the way to recovery.

Meanwhile, another problem reared one morning when Joy complained that her legs hurt. I looked and found both legs firmly swollen from the knees to her ankles. After the doctor examined Joy, his orders kept her home from school and off her feet. I appreciated visiting grandparents being in the house to help with home care service. Keeping a seven-year-old down with legs elevated when she did not feel ill required expert entertainment at times.

Not wanting to put that concern on Harv, everyone made sure not to mention to him about Joy. The swelling went down in a few days, and the cause remained a mystery. Since the blood work had not revealed anything, the doctor decided to wait and see if there would be a recurrence before having further tests.

People inclined to superstition often believe traumatic situations strike in triple blows. I am not superstitious, but the third strike arrived. One afternoon, after being motioned from Harv's bedside by an employee from the hospital accounting office and hearing her tidings, I thought, *Oh no, what next?*

After we moved to Michigan, we changed our hospitalization to another company. As far as we knew, the transaction had been completed and we were covered. But the new insurance company had rejected the claim submitted from the hospital, and likewise, the former company refused responsibility. As I walked back to Harv's room, I could not imagine what a huge sum the surgery and hospital care would amount to. Having lived on a hand-to-mouth income since we returned from Africa, naturally, we had no savings. I tried to block out the enormous problem from my thoughts for the rest of the day to keep Harv from recognizing that additional trouble existed. Before I fell asleep that night, helplessness and exhaustion forced me to commit the outcome totally to the Lord Jesus.

The next morning, a man from our congregation suggested I see the lady who worked in the office of the insurance company we had transferred to. He referred to her as being a Christian and assured me if anything could be done, she would certainly help. That turned into good advice, and before many days passed, the problem was resolved with all hospital and surgery bills completely covered.

Harv steadily improved and left the hospital in record time, considering the severity of his injuries. In a few months, scars remained the only visible evidence of his having been in a serious accident, as life settled back into a normal pace. Jehovah-Jireh had not prevented trouble, but He had guided the way through a difficult maze. His strength had been perfect in our weakness.

The following summer, three lively kittens brought a new dimension into the lives of Jewel, Joy, and Andy. Each child adopted and named one of the kittens as their personal pet. Sounds of happy laughter often rang from the backyard as the children watched the three little kittens romp and play. By winter, the kittens had grown and found shelter in the garage to protect from the cold Michigan climate. In January, after her kitty came up missing, Jewel became more and more sad each day when it did not return. A Michigan snow lay deep one afternoon when Joy and Andy arrived home from school with the news that from the school bus, Jewel had spotted her kitty on the snow several feet from the road. After getting off the bus, she had walked back for it.

Standing at the kitchen window, I watched as Jewel trudged along the side of the road, struggling with the dead weight of the frozen cat held out in front of her. With the distance she had to walk, it painted a touching picture of loyal devotion to her pet. Once she found her kitty, Jewel accepted the loss bravely, and when Harv arrived home a little later, he helped her place it in a box to wait until the ground thawed to bury it.

A highlight of our family memories came the following summer when we attended an annual evangelistic crusade sponsored by churches in the area. At the close of one evening service, Jewel, Joy, and Andy walked forward on their own initiative to give their hearts to Jesus. That evening remains a precious memory, when our three children became babes in Christ. Even though young in years, apparently each made a meaningful commitment to the Savior that kept them from the rebellion that seemed to stampede upon so many in their generation.

After two years in Michigan, we changed course and moved back to Indiana for Harv to be free to travel as an evangelist, since he had been receiving requests from churches to minister in that way. The following year, when my parents moved to Wellington, Ohio where my dad had accepted a church pastorate, we decided to migrate with them so that we could have family in the same town while Harv was away so much.

Harv had accepted an invitation from churches in Hawaii for a preaching tour and left in late August, prior to the start of school. Mother and I took the children to school on opening day to help them find their classrooms. This was the fourth state for them to enter a new school system since the girls first started kindergarten in Illinois. Even though they seemed to be adjusting well to another change, I did feel some concern for them.

As we drove past the front of the school one day, many excited, energetic children bustled about on the playground equipment until the bell rang. Then, I noticed a small, blond-haired boy standing back by the building watching the other children playing—it was Andy. I realized he would have friends in a day or two, but for the moment, he looked so all alone. My heart hurt for him and the girls as they experienced the loneliness of being strangers in a new locality. Realizing the Lord might have other plans, I did not make it a prayer, but in my thoughts, I wished the children might be able to finish their school year in the same system, unless a miracle happened for us to return to Africa.

When Harv returned from Hawaii, he brought orchard leis and a variety of beautiful tropical flowers ladies at one church had carefully packaged and sent to us. The leis and some flowers went to school with the children the next morning to give to their teachers. Jewel's sixth grade teacher became inspired and planned a Hawaiian luau for the following day as an extracurricular experience for the class to learn about Hawaii. Jewel beamed with delight when she came home with the news that afternoon.

Once we became settled, the children found interest in two new pets. Instead of kittens, we embarked on a venture with a parakeet named Sweetie and a Peruvian guinea pig named Rusty. They belonged to all three children, but Jewel usually held Rusty more often, stroking his long hair while he nestled his head against her neck.

Over a year after our move to Wellington, when a small church within driving distance needed a pastor, Harv took the position and also started teaching school part-time. Then, with Kent State University close enough for commuting, he gradually took classes, gained a bachelor's degree in education, and began teaching full-time. More education followed in the form of night classes and summer school until Harv received his master's during a graduation ceremony at Kent State, where peace symbols decorated the caps of several seniors protesting the Vietnam War.

Even though our country was seemingly becoming more unsettled, for a time, our family life began to take on roots in Wellington. From then on, the children enjoyed relatively normal lives through the remainder of their school years. Apparently, the Lord had taken note of that silent wish I made on the day the children enrolled in school at Wellington; Jewel, Joy, and Andy each graduated from Wellington High School.

Chapter 21: Little Africa

The elementary grades, junior high, and then high school years seemed to brush past our family so quickly. During high school, Jewel participated in several different activities, but music remained her favorite pastime. She enjoyed playing Christian records on the stereo and taking walks with music provided from a small radio she carried. The girls had taken piano lessons in Michigan, and Jewel delighted in being able to resume lessons during high school. She progressed well, and when a small church in Wellington needed a pianist, Jewel filled in for some time.

Jewel also became a candy striper at Oberlin Memorial Hospital in nearby Oberlin, Ohio, where she completed over 500 hours of service. Many Saturday afternoon and evenings found her faithfully walking the corridors of the hospital delivering trays, filling water pitchers, and helping wherever needed.

Achieving a goal she set during her sophomore year, Jewel saved enough money from babysitting jobs to fly from Cleveland to Dayton the following summer to visit a girlfriend she had met at church camp. Even though it was a short flight, venturing out on her own and the time enjoyed with Beth made that week a very special memory in her diary. Airplanes remained a fascination to our children, especially Jewel. Driving to Cleveland Hopkins Airport to watch planes land and take off supplied an inexpensive family entertainment we all enjoyed.

On one occasion, when the kids were younger and I had a lengthy hospital stay after our return to the States, Joy and

Andy were cared for by grandparents in Ohio and Pennsylvania, while Jewel stayed with friends in Fort Wayne. The husband happened to be a pilot and at times, he took Jewel with him to the hanger when he had no flights scheduled. That, of course, provided neat entertainment for a preschooler captivated with planes and airports.

With such an interest in airplanes, Jewel decided she would become a flight attendant when she grew up, and one by one, the number of planes representing major airlines increased on her charm bracelet. But during her mid-teen years, that dream began to fade as a desire to become a missionary nurse took over her life plans. Perhaps the seed had been planted by watching her Daddy give shots at Ganya and then trying to play nurse as she chased African children around the Ganya hilltop with a stick trying to give them a "chuke." Cultivation probably continued along the way with family conversations and reading missionary books. At any rate, a drive from the Lord to serve as a missionary began to churn in Jewel's heart.

During the summer before her senior year, an opportunity opened for Jewel to spend nine weeks with a missionary nurse in Haiti. Excitement, elation, ecstatic happiness, and more emotions gleamed in Jewel's eyes as we stood with her at Cleveland Hopkins airport on a mid-June day in 1971 waiting for her plane. It was a beautiful, dream-come-true experience for Jewel after several months of waiting from her initial application to the mission. It was now reality as she found herself actually on her way to visit a medical clinic in the interior of Haiti.

312

When boarding time arrived, Jewel wanted me to accompany her onto the plane. I never knew her reason, unless she wanted me to share her happy experience all the way to her seat. Before a parting kiss, with a teasing grin, Jewel assured me she had the safest seat on the plane. As I walked back to join Harv, Joy, and Andy at the gate, my sunglasses conveniently concealed warm tears I struggled to blink away. I was certainly grateful for Jewel's interest in missions and for her eagerness to see missionaries in action, yet my maternal instincts brought on apprehension concerning her traveling alone with a change of airlines and a two-hour layover in Miami. At that moment, she seemed too young to thrust from our nest to travel alone as an adult.

313

As we watched the United jet lift up, bank, and fly south until it became only a speck in the sky, I knew the heart of seventeen year old Jewel Kay was pounding with excitement. What soothing comfort I found as I committed Jewel to the care of our great Father God. I had requested Jewel to call from Miami after she found the departure gate for her flight to Haiti. I could detect from her voice that she was enjoying the time of her life as she described the happenings in her journey to that point.

A missionary met Jewel at Port-au-Prince, Haiti and gave her an informative tour of part of the city. She looked on with astonishment at the elegance of the presidential palace compared against the slums, shanties, and begging children. For the first time in her life, when they went for a walk that evening, Jewel saw homeless people sleeping along the streets. During the drive inland the next day, Jewel discovered the beauty of the Haitian countryside and admired picturesque views as the vehicle followed the road up, down, and around mountainous terrain. For various reasons, Haiti is sometimes described as "Little Africa."

Jewel's letters confirmed that similarity as she wrote about the excessively rutted and rock-scattered roads, waving children calling to them as they drove by, a sudden downpour when they could hardly see the road, and then being stranded a mile or so from the mission with motor trouble. Thus, the gal from America checked in as a weary traveler ninety miles later when they finally reached their destination after seven hours on the road.

Jewel immediately felt at home with the friendly, family atmosphere among the three missionary couples and their children. After reporting about each family, her letter went on, *"And I must not forget that character Zelda—the nurse I stay with. She jokes and is easy to get along with. I liked her at once."*

The following nine weeks were not exactly a leisurely vacation in the Caribbean for Jewel. She had gone to be helpful, and her letters depicted the busy days on a missionary compound. Describing the first morning after arriving, she wrote, *"Woke up around five this morning. After breakfast, I went with Zelda to the clinic. To get to the clinic, we had to walk through a wooded area. When we got there, another nurse and a Haitian worker were taking out maggots from a sore on someone's head! My first job was washing out a bunch of new syringes. Later, we went over to the maternity building that has twenty-six beds. Besides being a nurse, Zelda is also a midwife. She has delivered over 2800 babies. I was impressed with the clean delivery room. It was 95 degrees in the shade today, but it didn't feel that hot."*

Jewel spent many hours at the clinic doing what she could to help overworked nurses dedicated to the care of hundreds of patients. She learned to operate the sterilizer, weigh patients, take blood pressures, give worm medicine, bandage sores, help care for newborns, and trotted along with Zelda whenever she was called to deliver a baby, even during the night calls.

Jewel wrote about her first walk to the clinic at night,

"The woods seemed very dark against the small beam from our flashlight." A few weeks later, when an emergency came up one night, Jewel experienced the adventure of taking that walk through the woods by herself. Of that, she described, *"It was sort of spooky."* In a land of voodoo and spirit worship, being out alone for the first time in the night darkness undoubtedly carried a challenge to a teenage girl from the States. But she did her assignment willingly, although no doubt praying as she went.

Due to working with limited equipment, many tense situations emerged for the nurses to cope with. Two sets of twins were delivered during Jewel's stay, and she became involved in the fight to save one twin that Zelda took to the house for more intensive care. When all efforts failed, Jewel helped prepare the little body for burial.

In spite of some unpleasant aspects in Haiti, Jewel's letters remained positive: *"Prenatal clinic is held on Monday, general clinic on Tuesday and Friday, well baby clinic on Thursday, and on Wednesday, Zelda has a service for the children. Today was general clinic. I got to weigh two babies. One three month baby weighed only four-and-a-half pounds...I bandaged a dressing today...Zelda showed me how to sterilize...I tore 1,200 pills from individual wrappers to put in bottles...My fingers were sore for a while.*

I also got to bandage the sore on a man's leg today... Tuesday, Zelda saw 230 people in the clinic and pulled teeth for five people. We didn't eat lunch until two o'clock. One day, we didn't have lunch until 4:30...Yesterday, Zelda had to treat one of the mission pigs for bites and worms. Yuck! The unexpected really happens around here.

Every morning before clinic starts, Christian Haitians have a church service for the waiting patients. After the service, the Haitian workers try to teach the people about cleanliness, disease, and proper nutrition. Some people travel as long as three days. Others sit on the hard benches all night for clinic the next day.

Each Sunday, the missionaries spread out to different churches. The church where I went with one couple was twelve miles from here. Another bumpy ride! The church had a dirt floor. They had communion and the bread was a little dry and they used grape pop—the only thing available. Sunday night, we walked to another church about a mile down the road. The church used a kerosene lamp. It made me sleepy. The stars were beautiful that night.

Today, I went with Zelda to hold services with the school children. I've worked quite a bit on VBS material. Getting ready for Vacation Bible School is a big job since they prepare for 2,000 children. I can see why Zelda needed help.

I broke 1,000 crayons in half and distributed them in the right sack for each church. I ran off over 7,000 sheets of paper for VBS. That was a job, but the toughest is yet to come; we have 2,000 sheets of material to staple. Oh, did I tell you I have forty bites on my legs? They itch like crazy and they've turned red. It looks like I have measles on my legs.

The compound is such a peaceful place to live, especially in the morning, when I can hear the chattering of the Haitians. You never hear airplanes, only crickets. There are plenty of little flies. Hardly any snakes. I have seen two big spiders the size of my palm. I would not attempt to kill them.

Little lizards crawl on the window screens. In a way, they are cute, and they eat the flies and bugs. A lot of pretty flowers grow here. While we were at another missionary home yesterday, we watched a rat crawl across the ceiling. It was funny.

Zelda has a big German shepherd dog that has two pups. There is also a cat that stays under the roof. Anytime, day or night, you can hear it chasing rats and mice. I must sign off now because in twenty minutes, the electricity goes off."

Chapter 22: Haiti or Heaven

Before Jewel wanted it to happen, the nine weeks in Haiti ended and she boarded a plane to fly north. Even though she was glad to be home, she remained noticeably melancholy for several days—homesick for Haiti. Her diary told of being sad the last few days in Haiti because she did not want to leave. The diary also recorded how happy she felt each time she dreamed about being back in Haiti. Of one such dream, she remembered, *"A missionary family from Haiti was in church this morning, and when I saw them, I jumped for joy."* Quite obviously, Haiti, the Haitians, and the missionaries had captured Jewel's heart.

Jewel returned from her trip with the information that a nurse at the clinic had discovered amoeba when giving her a checkup before leaving for the States. The nurse had sent along medication for Jewel to treat herself. But knowing the potency of amoeba drugs, and the fact that Jewel had a heart murmur, I hesitated to have her take the treatment without being under the care of a physician.

After explaining the situation to our family doctor, tests were ordered at the hospital. The results turned out negative— no trace of amoeba. That brought little consolation, however, considering an amoeba infection can elude detection at times. We wrote the nurse in Haiti, and she returned a written report of her findings. After further testing with continued negative reports, our family doctor referred Jewel to an internist. Then, when lab reports remained the same, not knowing what else to do, we let things ride.

When Jewel became ill during Christmas vacation, we thought it to be a virus. But as she continued to feel sick and missed several days of school during January, we decided to make an appointment at the Cleveland Clinic. After the doctor read results of Jewel's outpatient workup, which only established that her food moved too rapidly through her body, he suggested the digestive problem and sick feelings could be psychological; perhaps she did not like the food in the school cafeteria or something to that effect. I knew Jewel well enough to find it difficult to accept that diagnosis and felt that something must be going undetected in the labs. Prior to her return from Haiti, Jewel always enjoyed a healthy appetite with no digestive problems.

Understandably, the doctors could not treat without finding a cause. But diagnosing tropical diseases not only requires book knowledge, but also experience in a tropical country learning to recognize the symptoms of these diseases which are not always apparent by laboratory testing. Therefore, I called different mission agencies attempting to locate a mission doctor on leave within driving distance. Encouraged, we learned of two doctors who met those criteria. But after calling each doctor and finding that neither would be able to see Jewel because they weren't affiliated with a hospital while in the States, we found ourselves disappointed once again. Both doctors reminded me that amoeba can be difficult to detect at times. How well I knew. That remained a strong concern for Jewel, because once the disease spreads beyond the colon, it becomes all the more difficult to cure.

So it seemed we had arrived at a dead end in trying to obtain medical help. We continued to pray for Jewel's health. With her not being a complainer, I never knew until later from her diary how much Jewel suffered during those weeks, and also how greatly she matured in her walk with the Lord Jesus. She penned the following excerpts in her diary on different days:

"Wow! Can't believe it's New Years! Didn't feel too well last night and I had trouble sleeping. What a day. Was really sick all day.

"Maybe it has been good that I've been sick because it has brought me closer to God.

"Will I ever enjoy good health when I get it back?

"I am so thankful that Jesus is here with me to stick by me as I try to get better.

"I've given my whole body over to the Lord. He can do what He wants with me.

"When I woke up this morning, I was so very tired. So I asked for strength from the Lord and I got it!

"I went over to the church to practice piano. Had a wonderful chat with the Lord.

"I think I walked too fast this morning because I had one of those spells in homeroom. But with the Lord's help, I could fight it off.

"I never will leave the house in the morning or prepare for school without praying to God first. It's really great, I was tired all morning but it didn't make me sick.

"Today, I vowed to God I would give at least fifteen minutes of my time at night to prayer.

"I felt sorta nauseated this morning and afternoon."

On Good Friday, Jewel wrote, *"Kept thinking how much God has brought me through. Thank you, dear Jesus. I love you so much!"*

On Easter Sunday, Jewel recorded, *"Thank God Christ arose and is coming again. Oh what a glorious day that will be! I wanted to feel so close to Jesus all day."*

Jewel always appreciated the small things. She reported in the diary about get well cards and letters sent to her. About one, she wrote, *"That was nice of her to write."* Later in the spring, she expressed, *"Thank you God for the sweet rain."*

Shortly after Easter, she wrote, *"I vowed to the Lord I would give up rock music since I believe it is coming between God and me. It takes away Bible reading and prayer."* The following day, *"I was disgusted hearing that music today. Now I know why people call it trash. After giving up that music, I feel different already. Stronger in Christ, I mean."*

The last entry in her diary, made on May 4, 1972, declared, *"I am tired of writing in this diary. All I do is talk about myself, and it doesn't seem right."* She ended with, *"When we accept Christ as our personal Savior, then trust in*

Him daily, He gives us unusual peace. This fortifies us against much emotional stress."

High school graduation day dawned bright and beautiful for Jewel in June, 1972. Since commencement at Wellington High School took place on the athletic field in order to permit more guests to attend, we had  prayed for a clear day. And the Lord abundantly provided.

Two things had bothered Jewel about that special day. Since relatives had to travel a few hours, it concerned her that something might turn up to prevent them coming. Her grandmother, aunts, uncles, and cousins all arrived on time, however, generating a happy graduate as Jewel marched across the field with her class.

Fear that she might become sick during the ceremony had also promoted some concern. But her heavenly Father likewise took care of that prayer. Except for being obviously pale as compared to her classmates, Jewel appeared to be having no trouble. Following commencement, she enjoyed a great time at her open house with relatives and friends. And although very tired that night, it marked the end of a perfect day that had meant so much to Jewel.

No one but the Lord knew the extent of the struggle that life had been for Jewel from January on. I continued to silently observe and remain concerned for her. But after taking her to the Cleveland Clinic, we felt we had no other options at the time. It seemed our only hope remained in the Lord, so we continued to pray. Jewel was determined to keep active whether she felt well or not, once doctors had convinced her they could find no physical cause for her problems.

As her digestion continued to remain upset, Jewel and I worked out a diet similar to the foods I could eat. This seemed to help some, but that meant eliminating many foods she liked. From babyhood on, she enjoyed almost all foods, with the exception of her adamant rejection of the pureed baby food served on the ship during our Atlantic crossing. But Jewel courageously accepted and adhered to the restricted eating plan in order to avoid feeling sick as much as possible.

Warm weather and a relaxing summer brought some improvement, and Jewel seemed stronger. She spent some time with her Grandmother Ford during the summer, which proved to be good medicine for both of them. Following the death of my dad four years earlier, Mother had returned to their home in Rosewood, Ohio, and had been living alone.

Mother and Jewel worked on projects together and also spent time reading and visiting on the front porch. They cooked jam one day after Jewel had a fun time picking blackberries with her cousins. A friend had told Mother about foot massage therapy, so the evening we arrived, she and Jewel jovially demonstrated how they had been massaging their feet each night.

Jewel enjoyed being with her grandmother and seemingly could bring a smile to her face quicker than anyone else.

Perhaps a special bond had been cemented years before during those nightly rocking sessions while Grandma Ford helped a colicky baby get to sleep. At any rate, it seemed evident Jewel's visit had been a special time for both of them.

In the latter part of August, Jewel packed her things and left for college at Fort Wayne Bible College, later known as Taylor University Fort Wayne Campus. I suppressed deep misgivings regarding how she would manage college life with her health and diet problems. But I lacked the heart to place a damper on Jewel's enthusiasm and excitement at entering college to prepare for a career in missions.

Letters arrived from Jewel telling about classes, chapel services, new friends, and a fun-filled dorm life. Apparently, adjustment problems did not exist, except for learning to manage study habits with so many girls in the dorm to enjoy being with. By November, after hearing a report of Jewel's grades and fearing she was not giving enough effort to her studies, I gave a gentle warning that if she did not improve her grades, she might have to drop out. At the time, I thought it might shock her into working harder, since she enjoyed college life and the peer fellowship so greatly and would not want to leave. But later, considering her physical condition, I deeply regretted having added another burden to her life.

The day before Thanksgiving, Jewel had a ride to Rosewood where we met her that evening. When we arrived, we found her on Mother's couch with a fever that she had had for three days. By Saturday, she seemed better, and we proceeded with plans to take her back to Fort Wayne before we drove home. I felt uneasy about leaving Jewel at college that day. But after purchasing a new pair of high boots she needed and reminding her to dress warmly so she would not catch more cold, I tried to console myself on the drive home that she would be alright.

The week before Christmas break, Jewel called collect one evening to describe in detail the Christmas decorations on campus. From the time of first seeing the small, lighted tree at the Ganya house and on through the years, Christmas decorations had always fascinated her. Even though the pinching of dollars in our family budget hardly allowed for chatty, collect phone calls, later it occurred to me how thoughtful Jewel had been in wanting to share what she was enjoying. We celebrated Christmas with family in Rosewood, where Jewel, Joy, and Andy always prized the time spent with their cousins. That day delivered the usual happy memories to drive home with.

Jewel had been experiencing reservations about her hopes of becoming a nurse, since she realized her grade level the first semester had not been high. But on the second of January, she went to the doctor's office to have a physical form filled out for entrance to the nursing program which would begin the following year in conjunction with her missionary nursing course. She soon returned home from the appointment with instructions to go to the hospital for admission.

The doctor met us at the hospital, and after taking a lengthy oral history from Jewel, he explained that her blood tests in his office showed extremely abnormal readings. It amazed him that she had been able to keep going, considering her blood report. As the doctor talked, I realized Jewel's physical condition no doubt had accounted for some of her problem with grades.

After being admitted, the former candy striper settled in her room and felt comfortably at home in the Oberlin Hospital where she had spent so many hours in volunteer service. The following day marked Jewel's nineteenth birthday. Since angel food cake remained tradition for birthdays in our family, I prepared the cake and wrapped gifts to celebrate her birthday at the hospital that evening. When a call came the following morning that the doctor wanted to see both Harv and I in his office, we feared it could mean something serious had been discovered from the blood tests. But the words "acute leukemia" struck a blow we had not been prepared for.

As we walked to our car, tears flowed from the anguish of finding out our daughter faced a terminal illness. But by the time we arrived home, we had chosen to follow the course every follower of the Lord Jesus has the privilege to pursue; we started asking for a miraculous healing, provided that would coincide with our Lord's plan for Jewel.

The doctor arranged to meet us at the hospital so Harv and I would be present when he told Jewel the diagnosis. At the hospital, a nurse sent us to a waiting room to be called when the doctor arrived. Since he was held up at his office longer than planned, minutes ticked on far past the appointed time, making it more and more difficult to sit and wait. Meanwhile, Jewel happened to take a walk to the end of that corridor and saw us in the waiting room. She asked, "What are you doing here?" and the expression on her face told me she realized something was wrong. As we walked toward her room, I decided to tell Jewel myself and be able to give instant support with a reminder of our hope in a powerful Savior.

Jewel probably had no idea of the full implication of acute leukemia nor the short timeframe expected in the 1970s, but she accepted the unpleasant news bravely. Not having felt well for over a year no doubt helped buffer the shock of being told of a serious disease in her body. She confessed for the first time how difficult it had been the past few weeks to find strength to walk across campus for classes and meals.

After the doctor arrived and explained the situation more fully, he told Jewel an internist would take over her treatment. When the doctor had left, without even a quiver in her voice, Jewel said, "I wanted to go into the mission field, and I got to be in Haiti for nine weeks. And I wanted to go to Bible college, and I was able to go for a semester." She even smiled some, fully at peace. Jewel's calmness seemed astonishing. How marvelously the grace of our Lord operated for Jewel as she faced death at age nineteen. From that moment on, we took one day at a time.

At the suggestion of her new doctor that Jewel get away from the hospital for a while, Joy and I took her to a department store to browse around one afternoon. Knowing Jewel's weakened condition and the potency of her drug therapy, I found myself wanting to keep a constant vigilance on her without her being aware, since she preferred not to be pampered.

At one point, after she had been out of sight for a while, I finally spotted her with Joy, standing by a rack admiring frilly, ruffled baby dresses. Both girls loved babies and taking care of them. Watching them, it seemed not long at all since they had been my babies wearing ruffles and bows. And how well I remembered the time twenty-month-old Jewel had pulled baby Joy-Joy from her basket in the Jeep as we loaded for a trip, and to our shock, sat holding "My baby," as she called Joy, when I returned from the house. Leukemia had probably strayed far from Jewel's thoughts as she and Joy continued to happily admire each little dress. But the scene reminded me that except for a miracle, Jewel would never enjoy a family and babies of her own. I turned away and let the girls enjoy their time together.

Returning to the hospital, we found a large dog stationed by the doors quite determined to enter. Even though the dog appeared friendly, because of his size and strength, we could not pass until someone came along to hold him back while we entered. Since she liked animals, that topped the afternoon outing as Jewel returned to her room with giggles and a happy smile.

Jewel's leukemia did not respond to therapy and enter remission as everyone hoped. Blood transfusions failed to strengthen her; instead, she started having high fevers and became weaker. Even though Jewel wanted to remain at the

Oberlin Hospital, when the doctors decided to transfer her to the Cleveland Clinic, she cooperated with a brave heart. A retired pastor who had visited Jewel at Oberlin later told us she had confided to him that if she could not become well enough to be a missionary, she wanted to go on to heaven. Thus, Jewel's faith in an eternal life ahead came through strongly when confronted with the end of her present life here.

Chapter 23: To Die is Gain

Following the colored line on the floor that would lead to the admission office, I appreciated the foresight of the person who had thought of such a helpful solution for directing strangers to needed locations at the Cleveland Clinic. Someone in the emergency department had instructed me to go take care of Jewel's admitting, but having to leave her alone in new surroundings while waiting to see a doctor made me uneasy. Consequently, I tried to hurry as fast as possible.

While my eyes scanned the floor ahead for the right color to proceed on, I continued to remember scripture verses as I frequently had done all morning in order to survive the stress that day moved with. Energy from breakfast calories had burned away hours earlier, and a clock on the wall indicated lunchtime already passed. Clinging to promises from God's Word served as my only lifeline for both emotional and physical strength.

I mentally repeated the words Jesus spoke to the ruler of the synagogue who faced a physically hopeless situation with his daughter: "Fear not, believe only, and she shall be made whole" (Luke 8:50). As I pondered those words, an experience that happened years before at Ganya flashed back. Still only a few weeks old, baby Joy had a high fever that was not responding to medication. And as I held her in my arms, pacing back and forth across the veranda of the mission house, I repeated those same words over and over. I remembered how the fever had eventually relented.

Therefore, a glimmer of hope flickered each time I thought of that scripture and others regarding our Lord's ability to heal any disease. I had the assurance that many people were praying for a miracle, and yet at no time when I sought the Lord Jesus did He give assurance that He planned to make Jewel well. Still, I realized I had to continue hoping in order to keep going.

When Harv arrived at the clinic, he had been directed to the admission office where he waited for me. When we returned to the emergency department, Jewel had not been seen by a doctor yet. A few hours passed before she was finally able to rest in a hospital bed that felt much more comfortable to her than the cot she had been on for so long in the busy emergency room. Her comfort became short-lived when a nurse came to place an ice pad under her body because of a continual high fever. Jewel smiled when she conceded the pad ranked slightly higher than the one used at Oberlin Memorial. She did not like the constant cold sensation though, and sweetly persuaded the staff to remove the pad at times.

Another plus for the clinic came with all drugs, including the pain medication, being administered intravenously rather than having so many shots. It did not take long for the staff to notice the congeniality of the new leukemia admission, who cooperated so fully, almost always with a smile. They realized she suffered, yet remained uncomplaining, alert, and interested in procedures as they worked on her. Jewel also pumped the student nurses with questions about their training as they took time to visit with her.

I noticed Jewel's eyes cloud with dread one afternoon when she saw the machine being pushed into her room for another bone marrow check. The technician asked me to step outside, and as I left the room, he said to Jewel, "Now you aren't going to cry for me this time, are you?" I knew for her to cry meant the procedure must have been very painful because she had endured so many unpleasant physical tests and exams during the past year with no tears.

The process involved having a long needle probed into either her chest or hip bone. One area hurt much more than the other, and I hoped she would be spared as much pain as possible. While praying for Jewel, I walked to the end of the corridor and sat down near the elevators where I could see her room and watch for the technician to leave.

In a few minutes, an elevator door opened and a man from housekeeping pushed a cart of cleaning supplies onto the floor. Then, as he dusted the waiting area, he began to whistle a familiar tune, and as he did, words to the music sang in my mind: "Precious Lord, take my hand. Lead me on, help me stand. I am tired, I am weak, I am worn. Through the storm, through the night. Lead me on to the light. Take my hand, Precious Lord, lead me home."

And as he whistled on, words from other verses came to my thoughts. "…Hear my cry, hear my call. Hold my hand, lest I fall. Take my hand, Precious Lord, lead me home." How consoling to be reminded the Savior spiritually held my hand, and I realized our tenderhearted Lord Jesus had placed the whistler in that spot, at that precise time, to minister to my heavy heart.

A smile broader than normal lighted Jewel's face the day some of her dorm friends from college surprised her with a visit. She always responded with a grateful smile each time flowers arrived, but seeing her friends walk into the room delighted her beyond words. When the girls left to go for lunch, one nurse involved with Jewel's care drew me aside and insisted I not let the visitors back in Jewel's room when they returned. The clinic did not have a sterilized room for leukemia patients at that time, and the nurse felt concerned the girls might infect Jewel with more germs. She reminded me that even a cold could be life-threatening to Jewel.

Even though I realized the possible danger, wisdom reassured me Jewel had received such a boost from being with her friends and looked forward to their return so greatly, I could not deprive her of that joy. Under the circumstances of her fast-deteriorating condition, I felt the comfort of having her friends with her took priority. Timing worked perfectly at noon and again in the afternoon that her allotted pain medication did not wear off until soon after the girls had left. Jewel expressed how glad she was they had not seen her in pain.

A couple from our church had brought Jewel a radio which furnished her with music from a Christian radio station in Cleveland. They also gave her a Polaroid camera for her to take pictures of visitors. The camera captured a visual memory of those cherished moments with her dorm friends, which she looked at time and time again after they were gone.

Lab tests on our immediate family determined Joy's blood best matched to be a donor of platelets for Jewel. The doctor working over Joy early one morning explained to us that only a few centrifuge machines existed in the United States as of then, and he reminded us to be glad the Cleveland Clinic possessed one. It did not take long for the doctor to realize he had a problem on his hands. Again and again, with no success, he attempted to find a vein to insert the needle that would attach Joy to the machine. All the while, I held a silent prayer vigil, knowing how deeply Joy disliked needles.

The Lord heard and came to the rescue, and Joy held up fine. The doctor, on the other hand, showed signs of becoming more and more frustrated. Finally, he walked over to the cupboard for another size needle, and on his way back to the bed, muttered, "With help from above!"

Gracious help from above did come, and soon, Joy's blood flowed through a clear plastic tube into the centrifuge for platelets to spin off, and then out into another plastic tube that deposited the blood back into her body. The process continued all morning as the instrument panel on the centrifuge monitored the white cells and platelets. The drug therapy used to kill leukemia cells had also destroyed Jewel's platelets, making a replacement necessary. It amazed me to learn our Great Creator has placed seven billion platelets in each ounce of human blood.

By noon, the amount of platelets on order had been reached and a mission accomplished atmosphere hovered in the room after a morning that had seemed so long. But the mood quickly changed when Harv appeared in the doorway with news that Jewel had started to hemorrhage internally. Hopeful enthusiasm of moments before immediately vanished. The shoulders of the doctor noticeably drooped and his movements slowed as he continued to disconnect Joy from the machine. It marked one of many times when I noticed sincere concern in a staff member at the clinic. At such a large hospital, I had not expected to see as much personal concern in fighting for a life, rather than considering a terminal patient as just another tragic number.

Because of Joy being tired and not having eaten yet that day, Harv took her for lunch and then home. Inside Jewel's room, I stopped at the bathroom to wash my hands. On the shelf above the sink, small glass jars containing urine samples stood in a row. Each jar showed an increase in the amount of blood over the previous one. Harv's words had warned me about internal bleeding, but seeing the reality in those glass containers brought shocking despair for a moment. I wondered if the platelets from Joy would stop the hemorrhaging or if they would only bleed out and be lost.

God promises strength to us in our weakness. Therefore, with His strength, I walked over to Jewel's bed and after greeting her, recounted the happenings of the morning. Even though nothing had seemed amusing at the time, we found some things to laugh about as I related incidentals from Joy's centrifuge experience. Grace from our Lord continued to work and brighten smiles on Jewel's face regardless of the circumstances and increasing weakness.

No improvement developed from receiving the platelets. Instead, a more powerful antibiotic started dripping through one IV after Harv signed permission to administer it. Being a new drug and still in experimental testing, I inwardly recoiled at the list of possible side effects that had been read to us. The doctors not only battled leukemia, but staph and two other major infections that had invaded Jewel's body. Bottles hung on both sides of her bed to send the many drugs through an IV in each arm. A visibly rapid pulse throbbed in Jewel's neck veins and we could only wonder how long her heart would endure such strain.

Soon after Jewel had been diagnosed with leukemia, I went to the county superintendent of schools where I worked with the intention of resigning my secretarial job, but he had encouraged me not to resign. Everyone at the school where Harv taught and my office had nothing but understanding support, as well as our neighbors and the congregation where Harv ministered.

Arrangements were made for me to leave the office early each afternoon. As soon as Harv arrived from his school, we drove to the hospital and remained with Jewel until late at night when she was ready to sleep. But as her condition worsened, I stayed with her all day and finally, around the clock. I found it extremely difficult to be away even long enough to go home to shower and change clothes.

Since the floor seemed understaffed, I did the small things the busy nurses did not have time for in keeping Jewel as comfortable as possible. Staying with her and helping made it easier for me to cope, and endurance from Father God also miraculously kept me going. One night, I stood by the bed sponging Jewel with alcohol water trying to prevent a very high fever from elevating any higher. Nagging thoughts of the possibility of Jewel starting convulsions prevailed in keeping me awake. Sometimes, during the night, Jewel opened her eyes and, with concern, said, "Can't you sit down for a while? You'll get too tired." Her thoughtfulness, even when she was ill, brought to me a misty-eyed smile after Jewel's eyes closed again.

Earlier, an experienced nurse had told me, "In all my years of nursing, I have never seen so many things go wrong with one patient." Not only did Jewel have the three vicious infections, but severe diarrhea from strong medications caused large, painful ulcers to develop. At one point, nagging hiccups persisted constantly for over thirty hours. Nothing alleviated the annoying condition, until they finally stopped.

Jewel also had to contend with itching from the rash of purple-red dots under her skin resulting from platelet failure. Even though the rash became extensive over her body, it never appeared on her face, for which we were thankful. When her hair began to fall out in her hairbrush, I quickly disposed of it without Jewel seeing. She had always taken care of her hair, brushing it diligently every night, resulting in long, glossy strands. Only a very small spot on her scalp became bald.

The doctor in charge of hematology at the Cleveland Clinic who had Jewel's case apologized to us for giving her so much pain medication, with an explanation that he wanted to ease her suffering as much as possible. Miraculously, though, Jewel remained alert in spite of the heavy drugs. Only once did I notice her slightly confused, and that happened when she awoke from a nap. Even then, her thoughts quickly cleared.

Late one afternoon, Jewel said, "I feel like hugging." So Harv and I took turns manipulating past the IV lines in both arms to hold her. She must have known that would be the last hugs on earth because the following morning, she slipped into a coma. No longer being able to talk with Jewel, the day moved slowly, and the night became even longer. With her body shutting down and starting to swell, the discoloration on her skin appeared all the more visible. Looking at Jewel, I thought as I had so many times during those weeks, *What is this terrible monster doing to you, my child?*

Once, during the night, when a nurse came to check vitals, she lifted an eyelid, focusing a light on Jewel's eye. Long lashes framed her beautiful, deep-set, brown eyes. It hurt to see her normally expressive eyes so dull and clouded with death. I quickly looked away.

Watching Jewel's breathing pattern enter a struggle to leave this earth, I thought of the night when, as a baby, she wrestled to enter the world during a long, breech birth. A few weeks earlier, when the doctor discovered the position of the baby, several X-rays had been taken of her head to assure a natural birth would be possible. Higher rates of leukemia were later found to be associated with unborn babies being exposed to X-ray radiation. Possibly it played a part in Jewel developing leukemia also.

This was not the first death watch that had invaded upon our family. Almost five years earlier, we had gathered in a hospital room at Wellington, where my Dad's frail body bent in a fetal position on the bed laboring for each breath, resulting from advanced cancer discovered five months before. Watching Mother bear her sadness so bravely, I had gripped the seat of the chair I sat on and repeated the message of Psalm 23 in my thoughts for courage to face this unwanted parting.

During those times, when death stalks, what a comfort to know the Great Shepherd will walk us through that shadowed valley just as He pledges to do in this beautiful psalm. And the promise likewise includes family members who belong to His fold. How faithful I found His care to be during those dark hours.

Only two weeks prior to his death, holding onto the pulpit desk for support while he gave his final sermon, Daddy ended with an announcement of resignation as pastor. Following that difficult service, Andy could not be found. We finally located him at our house under a bed. Andy's reaction to the realization that Grandpa would not be with us much longer had spurred him to run the few blocks home and find a place of refuge. It had been only a few weeks since the evening when they had cleaned and polished Grandpa's old shotgun that had been used in earlier years for small game hunting. Grandfather and grandson had known a quiet, fond relationship.

God's time had come, however. After Daddy stopped breathing that night, the peaceful expression on his face reassured evidence of victory in death. Another pilgrim who had been willing to walk the narrow way with his Savior Lord had entered the city of no death or tears—no pain or any other struggle encountered on earth. And above the sadness of having him gone hovered the dynamic certainty that someday, we would be together again.

Not long before Jewel became comatose, she had asked, "Did Grandpa suffer a lot before he died?" When I answered that he had, she said, "I still miss him." I knew it was her way of telling me she looked forward to seeing him. As I sat by her bedside through that final night, it seemed apparent that Grandpa Ford soon would have his "Toosie" join him in our eternal home.

Early the next morning, as someone repeatedly tried to locate a vein to draw blood from Jewel, part of me wanted to tell him to stop and not trouble her pathetic body any more. Yet something within clung to hope as I thought, *Perhaps the Lord has brought Jewel to death's entrance only to glorify Himself more. Maybe this blood work will show a dramatic improvement starting to happen.* I did not hold on for selfish purposes, for I realized that if Jewel should recover, she would eventually either return to Haiti or another country, since she felt so strongly for mission work.

On the other hand, it did not seem appropriate to demand from Father God my desires for Jewel to recover, rather than continue to pray, ask, and then trust His judgment as best. He is Almighty and well able to heal all diseases, as scriptures plainly teach. Nevertheless, if Jesus prayed during His time of anguish in the garden for the Father's will to be done, how can we, mere mortals of clay, do anything less than completely submit our hopes to the Great Potter, regardless of how much it hurts?

By the time the doctor came on morning rounds, blood had started to seep from Jewel's nostrils and mouth with each breath. The first day Harv and I had met with him, the doctor had warned that if Jewel's brain started to hemorrhage, there would be nothing they could do to correct it. He and the doctor with him quietly paused by the bedside for a few moments, looking down at the pitiful sight, knowing they had lost another battle—another patient. Being head of the hematology department at the clinic, I am certain Jewel's doctor had experienced the passing of many patients. Nevertheless, it seemed evident he had not become accustomed to those times. On his way to the door, the doctor stopped by my chair at the other side of the bed, placed a hand on my shoulder, and with a choked voice, said, "I'm sorry." That was all he uttered. And it was sufficient. I knew he sincerely felt our heartbreak.

The nurses who had cared for Jewel on that shift came in, one by one. I remember, in particular, one young nurse standing by Jewel for what seemed like several minutes with tears brimming and then overflowing. None of the nurses talked. I was grateful. Their presence spoke care louder that any words possibly could have.

My sister drove to Cleveland that morning, and she and Mother arrived at Jewel's room around noon. They had brought a sandwich for me. For several days, every bite of food had been difficult to swallow. But having them there with a home-made sandwich made eating slightly easier. Wilma sent me to the other side of the room, saying she would stay by Jewel.

I had eaten about half the sandwich when Wilma softly said, "Mother, come here." Jewel had stopped breathing. On February 19, 1973, her struggle ended, and she slipped from her disease-wracked body, taking her flight to see the person she had penned a note to in her college notebook: *"Jesus, I love you."*

The sandwich was never finished, but I valued the Lord's kind timing in arranging for me not to see Jewel's final breath. Within seconds, Harv returned to the room with a pastor we knew in Cleveland and we gathered near the bed while our pastor friend prayed. Soon after the prayer, I called my brother and asked him to notify the rest of the family. Thinking of how earnestly he and his family had been praying for Jewel's recovery, I wondered how best to tell him. Then when Joe came on the line, I said the first thing that came to mind: "We have lost, but Jewel has gained."

That thought from the Lord captured my attention as we collected Jewel's few possessions—the many cards and recent-ly sent flowers. Each time I looked at the appearance of her still body, I could only be grateful her spirit had been released and her suffering ended forever. She had died, but now lived "absent from the body…to be present with the Lord" (2 Corinthians 5:8). We later used those words for an inscription on the marker above Jewel's grave.

Many times during the seven weeks of Jewel's illness, I had sought a secluded place to release tears. But after her transfer, I could no longer cry. During the memorial service, the thought came to me that I should be crying. The row of college students and the people who filled the church might think I did not care enough. But Father God continued to restrain me from thinking of our loss—only of Jewel's wonderful gain. While she celebrated, my sad heart rejoiced with her and heaven seemed closer than ever before.

From the time we originally heard the leukemia diagnosis, and for many weeks following Jewel's death, when I first awoke each morning, the reality of it all swept waves of shock over my body. But as I read God's Word and prayed, peace from Christ Jesus faithfully quieted my disturbed nervous system, and in time, the wounds of trauma healed. Gratefully, our Lord taught me it was necessary, when thinking about Jewel, to concentrate on her blissful life above, rather than to permit flashbacks of her misery during those final weeks on earth.

We realized that life had to go on for Joy and Andy. It had been a rough time for them also. While Jewel was at the Cleveland Clinic, we could be with them only a short time in the mornings before going to work. Otherwise, they managed alone when they came home from school and during the evenings, except for when my mother or Harv's parents came.

Harv and I returned to our jobs the week following the funeral and tried to resume our regular family schedule. We found ourselves facing the adjustment of accepting the fact that the vacant place at the table and the empty bed no longer resulted from Jewel just being away at college. But through it all, a powerful assurance of mighty victory over death constantly surfaced. It reminded us to be all the more grateful for the cross our Lord Jesus Christ suffered on in order to conquer death for those who seek forgiveness and live for Him.

Chapter 24: The Better Land

After the Lord had so graciously kept our lives on hold in Wellington until the final high school graduation in our family, within weeks, another moving date appeared on our calendar. In August, we relocated to a parsonage in Geneva, a town in northeast Ohio near Lake Erie, where Harv accepted a minister position.

We had been in northeastern Ohio for a few years when Harv changed direction and returned to teaching full-time in a public school. Not only did he find satisfaction teaching in a classroom, it also released his summer months for overseas mission trips. And since my health had prevented us from ever continuing as career missionaries in Sierra Leone, I gladly gave my blessing to the summer projects that meant so much to Harv.

In the years that followed, Harv's journeys led to several countries, where he usually served as evangelist with mission groups that sponsored work/witness team projects for college and high school students. Even though rugged living conditions often went along with the package, Harv thrilled at the prospect of each upcoming assignment, arriving home with stories to tell!

Sooner or later, every family finds itself plunged into death separation experiences. Over and over, it happens as each generation passes on. But for those who know the Lord Jesus as Savior, departure of a Christian family member need not crush down with suffocating sorrow. With promises of eternal life from our Lord, we remember the interval of separation from those we love will only be temporary.

In the spring of 1988, my family and I drove down the extended lane leading to Rosewood Cemetery, headed for the lot where the bodies of Daddy and Jewel rest. Even though glad for Mother that she had been released from her suffering body and her spirit had taken flight to her eternal home, losing a mother presses hard—especially a praying mother.

The next-to-last time I had been with Mother, as I prepared to leave, she had held my and Wilma's hand and prayed for us. I knew her daily prayers that had supported me countless times through the years would be greatly missed. Also, I realized Mother's home would be emptied and sold, thus dropping a final curtain on tangible roots of the past.

Being a person who strongly believes that God's inspired Word speaks to us with the assurance, comfort, and vital direction needed for each trial we face, I have always been content simply to trust His promises. Father God, however, chose two means during that difficult time to remind me in a personal way that He understood and cared.

After Joe called me at work three days earlier to tell about Mother's death, I went home, packed, and started out on the four-hour drive. Harv would leave after school the next afternoon to join me at Rosewood. Nightfall had blackened the countryside as I drove, but as I turned a bend in the road, I saw a luminous, full moon positioned high in the sky in direct line above the straight highway ahead. For several miles, I watched in awe at what seemed a beautiful symbol of comfort the Master of Creation had arranged for me to view. My heart filled with serenity and peace as I realized a special nearness with the Spirit of the living God and His Son. It also served to remind me the Lord Jesus keeps His promises and would be with me always, down the remaining road of life.

During the music prior to Mother's memorial service, I received additional strength while listening to "How Great Thou

Art." The organist had played that same triumphant song at the close of Jewel's funeral. In the years that followed, it appeared many times as though the Comforter planned for me to hear the same piece prior to or during difficult situations. Each time, the words inspired reassurance with thoughts of the greatness of the Lord God, the sacrifice of His son on the cross, and the promise of living with Him forever.

The year after Mother's passing, four days after Christmas, we sat by the bedside of Harv's dad as one seizure after another gripped his frail body. Complications from injuries received in an automobile accident months earlier claimed his earthly life later that night. Again, we felt the solace of knowing another family member had exited a suffering body to enter the better land above.

One day in June, 1992, more than nineteen years from the time of Jewel's death, we again sat in a doctor's office at the Cleveland Clinic. Looking down from several floors up in an adjacent medical building, I watched as people entered and exited the main entrance to the hospital. Memories flashed as though it had been only a few weeks ago that we had entered those doors every day during the time of Jewel's hospitalization.

Diabetes had been discovered during a routine physical for Harv that spring. Further testing discovered prostate cancer, which suddenly darkened his health picture also. It had been diagnosed as advanced and aggressive, although still contained in the original site. An appointment had been made at the Cleveland Clinic for a second opinion on his prescribed treatment.

349

Regardless of diabetes, cancer, and strong medication, Harv remained determined to keep his scheduled plans for several weeks of evangelism in India that summer. With his urologist being from India, Harv received considerable support with his monthly injection given the day before he left, a supply of oral medication, and an appointment for an overdue shot the day after he returned from India.

Starting with a return visit to Sierra Leone in 1977, Harv had been out of the country on eleven summer mission trips. This tour in India marked the twelfth. When I met Harv at the airport, I immediately saw that the strenuous trip and living conditions had taken a toll. He always looked tired when returning from overseas, but that day, he appeared ten years older. Following a couple days of rest and proper diet, however, he bounced back and looked well again.

Harv began teaching that fall with intentions of retirement at the end of the school year. But that year, with too many days of not feeling well enough to cope with the stress that accompanies handling a classroom of students at times, Harv realized the time had come to stop teaching.

During the following summer of 1993, Harv traveled with a team to Bolivia. Except for breathing problems resulting from the high altitude that required emergency treatment at the hospital the night of their arrival, his health fared well during the rest of the time in Bolivia. Harv enjoyed the team members and the missionaries they worked with.

Following my retirement that fall, we relocated from Madison, Ohio to Marion, Indiana, close to where Joy and her family lived. For many years, Harv had dreamed and talked of someday visiting the Holy Land. Therefore, when I told him I wanted to cover his expenses for a tour to Israel with some of the benefit money I had received for early retirement, Harv grinned in speechless delight. After the trip, the excitement of the Holy Land tour remained just as fresh each time he viewed his slides and recounted the experiences. The trip to Israel took place in January, and in February, Harv left for another preaching journey in India. We realized we had not allowed an adequate amount of time for rest between the two trips, but his ministries in India had been scheduled months earlier and meant too much for him to give up.

Soon after the original confirmation of cancer, Harv and I decided he should keep the cancer in mind only to the extent of taking care of himself, but beyond that, try to live a normal life. At times, he did a much better job of living a normal live than taking care of himself. Each time I took him to the airport, I understood the reality that the mission trips, especially India, dealt a blow against him physically. But how can you suggest to a person with a terminal illness to give up something so meaningful?

As before, Harv returned from India exhausted, but with no second thoughts about having gone. So many results filled his memories that not even the strong Hindu opposition he and the national Christians had encountered when traveling and ministering dulled the joy of his weeks in India. Four months later, Harv flew with a team to Guatemala. There, they experienced the typical blessings of a mission trip, intertwined with the seemingly inevitable challenges of things not always going right. Seldom, if ever, could days be recorded as uneventful when working with a group of students in another country.

Refusing to let life becoming boring, Harv signed up for substitute teaching in the fall of 1994, knowing he had the option of turning down an assignment on days he did not feel well enough. Overall, it appeared to be good for him and he seemed happy to be back in the classroom environment. During the first week in November, Harv commuted to a church conference in Berne, Indiana where he met up with many friends he had not seen for years. He had looked forward to the conference and the week did not fail to bring the gratification he had expected.

But the evening before the final day, when he returned home exhausted and not feeling well, he decided not to go back the next day. During breakfast the following morning, however, after feeling a surge of energy while thinking about what he would be missing, Harv finished eating, dressed, and headed his car toward Berne.

Preparations for going with a work team to Kenya, Africa in January had been occupying Harv's thoughts and stimulating his dreams. But for the present, he anticipated accompanying Bill, an old friend from college, on a business trip to a southern state, leaving on Saturday following the conference in Berne. He spent Friday night with us in order to have an early start the next morning.

During dinner that evening, I noticed Harv had barely touched the food on his plate, but attributed the dull appetite to his being tired. Then, as Bill announced he had tickets for them to see a special football game the next afternoon on their way south, a broad grin brightened Harv's face and he seemed to perk up.

When Saturday morning dawned, however, Bill had to leave alone. Harv had spent a sleepless, miserable, and pain-filled night. As his pain persisted and even increased, around eight o'clock that morning, Harv said, "You'd better call Joy. I think I need to go to the hospital."

In a matter of hours, we heard the report from the emergency room doctor we had not wanted to hear for over two years. The cancer had metastasized to Harv's kidneys to the extent it was causing renal failure. It had also invaded his liver. From the start of his treatment, doctors had explained that the drug therapy Harv took should keep the cancer contained for some time, but if and when it spread to his bones or organs, there would be nothing more they could do. Almost six months earlier, tests had revealed that everything was clear except for the localized, original cancer site, and until that week, he had appeared to be doing well. Harv's next six-month exam would have been later in November.

Just a month before, Harv had sorted through an accumulation of papers, letters, mementos, and other things collected through the years. More than once during our married years, I silently accused him of being a "packrat" and smiled to myself when I saw him cleaning out his things. It did not occur to me at the time, but I later wondered if he may have realized time was running out.

By the time he was transferred from the emergency room cart onto a hospital bed, the medication had eased Harv's pain and continued to keep him fairly comfortable throughout Sunday. The urologist planned to scrape part of the cancer growth from the urinary tract on Monday morning to help relieve some pressure and pain.

Soon after that procedure began, the doctor came from surgery to tell Joy and me that he had found such extensive cancer growth that made the procedure impossible. He explained the possibility of trying to insert a shunt into Harv's kidney, which might prolong his life for perhaps three months or so. That procedure would be done in the X-ray department while Harv still remained under anesthetic. He somberly reminded us that even if a shunt could be placed through the dense growth, Harv would still have inevitable suffering with both his liver and kidneys now affected. He then left, giving us a few minutes to decide if they should attempt to insert a shunt.

Andy and Nancy had come from Ohio with their children Saturday evening and returned home Sunday evening, thinking the surgical work Monday morning would add more time. Joy and I immediately contacted Andy by phone and wrestled with the difficult decision together. The natural instinct for a family to cling to life finally dominated, as we agreed to have the doctor try to place a shunt.

As soon as we gave the doctor our decision, Harv was moved to X-ray. Soon after returning to the waiting area, Joy and I each began to experience second thoughts. Within minutes, Andy called and told me he was feeling doubts about the decision also. Harv's body had naturally entered a shutdown process. With his spiritual house set in order to face death, why shackle him to earth in a body with pain and morphine?

We immediately sent word to the doctor and found out the procedure had not been started. Harv's urologist and the doctor in X-ray each sympathetically expressed his agreement, considering the extent and rapid growth of the cancer— diagnosed in the beginning as aggressive, proving in the end to be just that. There had been rough spots, but overall, the Lord had extended to Harv two-and-a-half years of an amazingly active life following the original diagnosis.

After Harv awoke from the anesthetic, the doctor explained to him how the density of the cancer made it impossible for the intended procedure. He also told him about the possibility, but uncertainty, of trying to insert a shunt into the kidneys and asked Harv if he wanted them to attempt it. Even though Harv knew the cancer had spread, he had not fully grasped the shortness of his time until the doctor shook his head negatively when Harv asked, "Would a shunt make it possible for me to go to Kenya in January?" Once Harv realized the full spectrum of his situation, he said, "Leave things as they are."

During the second phone conversation with Andy, when we decided to reverse the first decision, Joy and I agreed with Andy when he said, "Knowing Dad, that's the way he would want it." And so it was. Sympathy for Harv stabbed at my heart during those tense moments of dialogue between him and the urologist. But God's marvelous grace supported Harv, Joy, and I so thoroughly. There were no tears or "whys." Peace ruled amidst the storm of sad reality. Our great and good Shepherd stood by us.

The doctor had told us that according to Harv's blood work, he would probably be in a coma by Tuesday night. Andy and his family returned Monday evening. During the next three days, Harv's alertness and appearance—except for some edema—made it difficult to comprehend that physical death loomed so close. It could not be denied, however. As well as the doctor keeping us updated, Andy and Joy, who were both in the medical field, followed the latest blood reports at the nursing desk.

By Tuesday evening, Harv was not yet in a coma as the doctor had predicted. Instead, in sharp awareness, he visited with college friends as they reminisced about happenings from years past. The recurrent laughter in Harv's hospital room seemed to strongly contrast the nearness of approaching death.

Naturally, the mood turned more somber when the time came for the men to leave. But Harv's reaction to his life being almost over did not allow for gloom to invade upon his friends, nor his family. The heavenly Shepherd walked with him through the valley of the shadow of death, just as promised in Psalm 23.

At least twice that week, we joined with a visitor in singing reassuring hymns of the faith. A very efficient senior nursing student assigned to Harv reported to her nursing instructor one afternoon, "This family is in real denial! They are even singing!" Immediately, the Christian instructor took advantage of the opportunity to explain why the patient and his family could sing in the face of death. As each day passed and we realized our time together was coming to an end, the heartening assurance that we would meet again in God's tomorrow helped buffer our farewells. On Friday, Harv slept often, and then slipped into unconsciousness.

Harv had a strong attraction for flying, and even took flying lessons when we lived in Illinois in hopes of someday using that ability on the mission field. Even though it could only be wishful dreaming to consider any type of small aircraft in Sierra Leone, it did provide an excuse for learning to fly. But then, shortly before noon on Sunday, November 13, 1994, at age sixty-six, Harv's soul departed earth on his greatest of all flights. Destination: City of God.

Thus, another soul, redeemed by the blood-offering at Calvary, gained entrance through the gate of heaven. I remember the comfort experienced from the words of "Amazing Grace," one hymn we sang in Harv's room that week:

Amazing grace, how sweet the sound,
That saved a wretch like me.
I once was lost, but now am found,
Was blind, but now I see.
And when this flesh and heart shall fail,
And mortal life shall cease;
I shall possess within the veil [Heaven],
A life of joy and peace.

Triumph over death surfaced in music and words during the memorial service, as is instinctive when a Christian has been drawn from this life to life above. Harv had gained many friends across the country through his years of travel. Their concerned encouragement via letters, phone calls, and prayers had helped him through his skirmish with cancer those two-and-a-half years. And so, from seven different states, some of those friends made their way to Marion in memory of their departed comrade in Christ. Much recounting of experiences they had shared with Harv here and in other countries took place that day. Most probably felt the same as one woman expressed: "He was so full of life. He just seemed like a person who never would die."

With little sleep during those final days, along with the emotional strain, my weary body sensed sustaining strength from the supporting prayers of God's people. And in the days and weeks that followed, one song used at the memorial service, with words penned by Frances R. Havegal many years ago, repeatedly sang to my heart in powerful reassurance:

Like a river, glorious, is God's perfect peace.

Over all victorious in its bright increase;

Perfect, yet it floweth, fuller every day.

Perfect, yet it groweth, deeper all the way.

Every joy or trial falleth from above,

Traced upon our dial by the Son of love.

We may trust Him fully—all for us to do.

They who trust Him wholly, find Him wholly true.

Stayed upon Jehovah, hearts are fully blest.

Finding as He promised, perfect peace and rest.

At first, Harv's mother found his death difficult to accept. More than once, I heard her express, "I don't know why he was taken instead of me. I've had my life." I understood. I remembered well the times I wished that I could bear the leukemia instead of Jewel suffering so severely. But I reminded Mammy Ache that life and death are not in our control. When many prayers do not bring the answer we seek, it becomes essential to submit the outcome to our sovereign, all-knowing Father God. This yielding ends the "why" questions, helps to prevent depression, and compensates in finding perfect peace and rest, just as our Lord promises.

We faced Thanksgiving less than two weeks after Harv's burial, and a few days later, his birthday. Then came the first Christmas without Harv in the family. And even though holidays tend to be difficult following a death, on each occasion, the healing balm of Christ Jesus applied comfort to our spirits, making us able to supply the five grandchildren with a naturally cheerful Christmas.

After Christmas, Mammy Ache seemed brighter and started making plans to return home. She had lived in Allentown all her life, and each time she came to see us, after a few weeks, she began to miss her friends, relatives, and her general routine back home.

As we prepared to leave for the airport on the morning she left, I reminded Mammy I wanted her to return for her usual visit in the spring. Even though she had reached the age of eighty-nine, her goal was to celebrate a century birthday. And with her health relatively fine for her many years, it did seem a possibility.

In June, however, complications followed knee replacement surgery. And six months following Harv's death—on the same day of the month, also a Sunday, and at the same hour—his mom left her earthly body to join the others in God's Celestial City.

Thus, as two decades slipped past, one by one, our family moved on to eternity. Though each death creates a vacant spot that leaves life never totally the same, because of the blessed hope of seeing them again, time eventually eases sadness. And with each departure, I found my faith renewed and strengthened in the reality that at death, those who have trusted in and lived for the Savior enter into His presence to be eternally safe in heaven's care.

With each departure, I found my faith renewed and strengthened in the reality that at death, the prepared soul will enter into the presence of the Lord. Having that assurance from God's Word brings total peace while watching the respiration rate of someone you love become slower, weaker, and finally stop.

Also, during the hours of each death-watch, realization dawned ever greater that death comprises what life on earth is about; we are born to die—born to prepare for eternity. Nothing at any stage in a human life, whether young, mid-life, or elderly, can be more vital than being prepared for that moment when the last breath exhales and we enter eternal realms.

Never will I forget the day Harv and I sat waiting to see his doctor for a report on recent tests. A patient and his wife emerged from the treatment area and paused by the desk to set up appointments at the hospital for further evaluation. As cursings laced each sentence tumbling from his mouth, it seemed apparent this man had not been prepared for the jolt that struck his life only minutes before when he heard a cancer diagnosis.

The option for each person to plan his or her eternal destiny has been delegated to us by a caring, heavenly Father. The decision involves only two selections as presented by the Lord Jesus: indescribable bliss in heaven with Him, or an eternity in hell, forever separated from the love of God.

Apparently, this patient had ignored his Maker and Savior throughout life. He had neglected to prepare for eternity.

He had failed to repent and accept the merciful salvation, peace, and love that Calvary provides. Now, facing death, he did not have strength and comfort from the Spirit of God. Instead, his only thought of Jesus Christ existed in continued, angry cursings as he walked from the office and the door closed behind him.

Stunned by the incident, I recalled the day Harv and I drove home after hearing his doctor confirm the diagnosis of cancer and firmly pronounce it to be an aggressive type. How different that scene had been compared to the event we just witnessed. Shaken, we had ridden in silence for a few miles. To be suddenly confronted with the fact that a life has had its time clock advanced to a terminal situation initially shocks the heart, even for Christians. Then, becoming conscious that Harv needed support, I reminded him that even cancer is not something too difficult for the Lord to heal and will not be fatal unless he permits. We talked about heaven and how much better to be there than here, just as the example of how the apostle Paul confronted the upcoming end of his life on earth: "Therefore, we are always confident, knowing that, whilst we are at home in the body, we are absent from the Lord: for we walk by faith, not by sight. We are confident, I say, and willing rather to be absent from the body, and to be present with the Lord" (2 Corinthians 5: 6–8).

Apprehension and fear cannot coexist in the mind alongside facts of heaven. They return when thoughts stray away from the Lord. How well Father God had helped me grow in that truth during Jewel's illness and death.

During one springtime, I watched a lone, blue wildflower in the field behind our house. It stood straight and looked as perfect as a picture. Each time I glanced out the window, I wished it could bloom for a long while. But in a matter of days, the blue flower began to wilt, droop over, and then die. Those days of enjoying the flower reminded me of Psalm 103:15–16: "As for man, his days are as grass, as the flower of the field so he flourisheth. For the wind passeth over it, and it is gone and the place thereof shall know it no more."

How quickly our life here on earth travels. For some, it lasts only a brief space. But for all who love the Lord God above everything else and diligently follow His Word, eternity will be a joyous, beautiful forever in the presence of Almighty God, living in the place our Great Shepherd has prepared for us. And we shall see our Redeemer reign as King of kings and Lord of lords.

Epilogue

While I was never able to return to Africa, Harv was not the only member of the family who served in further mission work. During her second year in college, Joy decided to change her major from education and enter the nursing profession. It thus happened on a day in March, 1983, that I walked from the Erie, Pennsylvania airport and stood by the fence to watch a plane taxi down the runway, take off, and disappear into the distant clouds. Joy had volunteered to help at a mission clinic in Sierra Leone for a few weeks and eagerly looked forward to visiting the land of her birth.

Joy's first letter from Freetown described progress in some areas of the city, while much poverty still remained in sections where it always had been. I realized our mission communications had also made an astounding upgrade since our years in Sierra Leone, as I read her account of radio call every morning at 7:30 between stations.

Joy wrote about the radio contact the first morning after she arrived. *"It was neat! They all welcomed me royally, and I got to talk with them. I have bad news, though. They are closing the Ganya station and I won't be able to go there. The Yalunkas and Fulas are fighting and burning villages, and it's too dangerous to visit.*

Bill and Ruth are there now to close the station and pack their things. Bill said on the radio this morning that the drums were warning of big trouble ahead. So far, Bill and Ruth

*have been safe, but they don't know how long it will last. I am
really disappointed not to see Ganya."*

The Harrigans had been able to return to Sierra Leone
about two years after we left. Eventually, other couples joined
them in ministering to the Yalunka people. And years later, Bill
and Ruth's youngest son Steve and his wife Sheila became a
part of the team. The Harrigan's other son Dan and his wife
Carole also served some years in Africa.

Even with additional missionaries, however, it had not
been a simple enterprise, as evil forces continued to battle for
control of Yalunka lives. But the vision Bill and Ruth carried
for that spot on earth remained strong despite all opposition.
However, with God's grace and power in action, they finished
their final term before retirement with many visible achievements from all the years of day-to-day, unrelenting labor for the
Master. Among the accomplishments, there stood
Yalunka churches with Bible trained pastors, believers in
Christ Jesus, schools, and much translation work completed.

Plans changed for Joy when the staff at Kamakwie
Wesleyan Hospital—the hospital where I had been treated—
heard about a registered nurse being in Sierra Leone for a visit.
Because they had a severe shortage of nurses at the time, one
doctor pleaded with our mission to loan Joy to the hospital for a
while. Consequently, with Joy being switched back and forth
between the two missions, her few weeks in Sierra Leone
extended into a four-month stay.

About midway through Joy's time in Africa, the disturbance in Yalunka territory had seemingly quieted. Bill and Ruth planned to return to Ganya to pick up their possessions and invited Joy to accompany them. Therefore, one day in May, Joy wrote, *"Don't get too sentimental now, but I am writing this letter to you from what I imagine is my old bedroom on the hill in the village of -- you guessed it-- GANYA! I finally made it*

here! (I had given up hope of getting here.) We got to Ganya around noon. On the way from Falaba, we had to cross bridges made from logs and sticks. Some were thirty to forty feet long with big drops, but they were all in good shape so I didn't have to close my eyes.

We stopped in the village briefly to let off a few riders. The people came running from everywhere to see Pa and Ma Harrigan—they really love them. Ganya hasn't grown at all— still essentially the same as it was in the fifties, with 2,000 people, according to Bill. It looks the same, except many houses now have pan roofing. I got my first glimpse of 'home' from the lower road with the sun reflecting off the metal roof. It was really an emotional experience climbing the famous hill; all I wanted to do was cry! I could just see Jewel and I running down it and getting carried back up.

There's a big, flamboyant tree in the yard that we planted as a bush. They keep cutting it back, but it grows like a weed and has pinkish-orange flowers." I smiled when I read that, as I remembered watering the young plant, using water from the pail filled with soaking diapers. Evidently, it had worked well as an organic fertilizer.

"They still have the same shower bucket we used. It's very effective! There's an old packing crate with shelves in it that was yours. Bill also uses a big, wooden box for tools that Grandpa Ford made; it even has the same lock and key. Bill showed me the spot where Dad fell down the attic stairs with a loaded gun and shot his hand and a beam in the ceiling.

The hole is still there.

Last Monday, Bill sent a radio message that if I could get to Kabala, he and Ruth were making their last trip to Ganya. At Kabala, I had a ride in the Red Jet! It's still going thirty years later! Jake pushes it down the hill and at the bottom, he jumps in and it starts—really putters away. A Lebanese Millionaire wants to buy the Jeep for a collector's item.

On the way to Ganya this morning, we stopped in Falaba to greet Bokari. He's the pastor there and also the D.S. [district superintendent of Yalunka churches]. He kept shaking my hand, grinning, and saying, 'So you are Joy-Joy.' At least he can say the letter J now. I was pretty young when he pushed me around in the stroller."

Naturally, Joy could not remember the stroller days, but we had pictures of Bokari giving her rides. Even though Joy's weeks in Africa abounded with interesting happenings, being able to visit Ganya and to see Bokari evidently became the highlight of her time in Sierra Leone.

In his young teen years, Bokari had set his heart on attending Bible school, and later, that dream became a reality. Then, through the years, other Yalunka youth likewise became inspired to enroll at the Bible school. Eventually, a second station was opened in another Yalunka town and overall, a brighter horizon seemed to loom for the ministry to that section of the country.

Unfortunately, mission work in Sierra Leone was interrupted when rebel forces tried to overthrow the government, making it necessary for missionaries to leave the country. In time, villagers in the interior also found themselves under the attack of merciless rebels. It seemed as though the very fury of hell released a storm of raids that left behind a heavy trail of blood, as helpless people were either killed or suffered mutilation.

When the time came that Bokari faced such an assault, God miraculously spared him when one rebel spoke to his accomplices, "Let the old man go." Then, along with other fleeing villagers, Bokari crossed the nearby border into Guinea, where he joined the Yalunka missionary team from Sierra Leone who had also entered the country to start a new ministry in Yalunka villages.

As often happens, intense suffering sparked a fire of deeper love and devotion to Christ among many believers in Sierra Leone. This seemed especially true among the Kuranko people. The flame grew, reaching out and engulfing additional villages with the Gospel of hope. As a result, many more Christians and churches exist today in parts of the interior of Sierra Leone than before the rebels stormed the land.

Following Joy's return from Africa, she continued to further her education in the field of nursing and eventually fulfilled her youthful dream of teaching, as well as being a nurse. In place of her original goal of teaching elementary students, she became a professor of nursing at Indiana Wesleyan University in Marion, Indiana. There she has had the opportunity of helping train nursing students, many of who went on to serve on foreign mission fields.

During college Andy spent two months in India, and after graduating from medical school and residency has practiced family medicine in a rural, under-served area in southern Ohio. In addition, four of my grandchildren have gone on multiple short-term mission trips, including several to Africa.

Final Note

Jane was very ill and became progressively frail her last four years of life. She suffered greatly from arthritis and had multiple other hospital admissions, including emergency surgery for a bowel obstruction and the removal of an eye due to melanoma. Joy and her family provided countless hours of support and care which allowed Jane to complete the book, but it still took her until August 23, 2013 to revise and complete it. The final part had to be dictated to Joy and her daughter-in-law Nancy, as she was too weak to write. She passed to heaven for a family reunion eleven days after finishing the manuscript, dying at home from metastatic melanoma.

Jane wanted all proceeds from her book sales to go to support world missions. However, we felt the book should be sold as close to cost as the publisher allows, thus allowing it to be accessible to more people. Instead of the family donating book profits, our hope is that each reader will be inspired to financially support and pray for world missions, therefore becoming an active partner with missionaries. If you are unclear about how to do this, we have some suggestions:

Prior to her death, Jane designated World Missionary Press as a favorite recipient of support. WMP is highly efficient. They print scripture booklets, Bible studies and New Testaments in 343 languages and provide them free to Christian workers, pastors and evangelists. You can contact them at this address:

World Missionary Press
PO Box 120, New Paris, IN 46553
www.wmpress.org

Please note "One Short Life" in the check memo.

There is another option we feel would please Jane. Joy's daughter and son-in-law, Jewel and Titus Romdenh, were accepted in 2015 as missionaries with World Gospel Mission. WGM is an inter-denominational organization that partners with individuals and churches worldwide to support missionaries in at least 21 countries. Jewel and Titus will be WGM's first full-time missionaries to Cambodia. Their web page details their biographies and family, future plans, blog and support information.

World Gospel Mission
PO Box 948 Marion IN 46952
www.wgm.org/romdenh

If you donate by check, please include a note designating your gift is for Jewel and Titus Romdenh, leaving the memo space blank.

Thank you,

Andy

Please visit us at www.oneshortlifebook.com.

You will be able to see most of the book photos in color, as well as additional photos. You will also find a link to purchase copies of One Short Life, contact information, and a comment section.

Made in the USA
Monee, IL
27 May 2021